MW01277840

150 LEADING CASES

Commercial Law

SECOND EDITION

ROLAND FLETCHER
LLM, LLB (Hons), PGCE, M Inst L Ex

OLD BAILEY PRESS

OLD BAILEY PRESS
at Holborn College, Woolwich Road,
Charlton, London, SE7 8LN

First published 2002
Second edition 2004

© Holborn College Ltd 2004

ISBN 1 85836 527 9

British Library Cataloguing-in-Publication

A catalogue record for this book is available from the British
Library.

Printed and bound in Great Britain

Contents

Acknowledgements

The publishers and author would like to thank the Incorporated Council of Law Reporting for England and Wales for kind permission to reproduce extracts from the Weekly Law Reports, and Butterworths for their kind permission to reproduce extracts from the All England Law Reports.

Preface

Old Bailey Press 150 Leading Cases are intended as companion volumes to the textbooks but they are also invaluable reference tools in themselves. Their aim is to supplement and enhance a student's understanding and interpretation of a particular area of law and provide essential background reading. Companion Revision WorkBooks and Cracknell's Statutes are also published.

This *Commercial Law 150 Leading Cases* is designed for use by any undergraduates who have commercial law within their syllabus. It will be equally useful for students who are taking the Graduate Diploma in Law and must study contract law as one of the 'foundational' subjects.

The purpose of the *150 Leading Cases* series is to provide an easy to use reference guide to key case law developments within the area of commercial law. The case law has been structured and presented within chapters, offering a broad selection of materials to focus on particular areas. This will allow students to isolate areas and develop an understanding of the law through recent important judgments. A selection of recent decisions from the House of Lords and Court of Appeal have been used to illustrate the application of the legal rules when dealing with commercial law. Among many of the decisions included are: *Shogun Finance Ltd* v *Hudson* (2003) (mistake and void or voidable contracts); *Jewson Ltd* v *Leanne Teresa Bayham as Personal Representative of the Estate of Thomas Michael Kelly* (2003) (implied terms; satisfactory quality and misrepresentation); *Chater* v *Mortgage Agency Services Number Two Ltd* (2004) (undue influence and misrepresentation); *Braymist Ltd* v *Wise Finance Co Ltd* (2002) (agency and pre-incorporation contracts); and *Clegg* v *Andersson (t/a Nordic Marine)* (2003) (implied terms and the right to reject goods).

The law is stated as of March 2004.

Table of Cases

Cases in bold type are the leading cases. Page numbers in bold indicate the main references to them.

Sale of Goods

1   Scope of the Sale of Goods Act

Barry* v *Davies [2000] 1 WLR 1962
Court of Appeal (Pill LJ and Sir
Murray Stuart-Smith)

* *Sale of goods – auction: without reserve – collateral contract and consideration*

Facts
This was an appeal by the third defendant (Heathcote Ball & Co (Commercial Auctions) Ltd), who acted in the sale of two Alan Smart engine analysers. The auction stated the sale was to be 'without reserve,' as instructed by the sellers. Mr Cross, the auctioneer, stated the engines were worth '£14,000 each' and were being sold on behalf of the VAT office. The respondent, Mr Davies, made a bid of £200 for each engine and no other bids were made. Mr Cross would not accept these bids and his explanation was:

> 'I could not see how I could sell for as little as this, even though it was without reserve. I think I am justified in not selling at an auction without reserve if I think I could get more in some other way later. I did not take up [the offer] £400. I thought they were worth more.' (p1964)

Mr Davies, at first instance, claimed damages on the basis that he was the highest bidder and a sale made by auction 'without reserve' entitles the highest bidder to claim the lot for which he bids. The judge at first instance, Charles Harris QC, agreed and also found there was a collateral contract between the auctioneer and highest bidder. This conclusion was based upon an operation of law. When a sale is made by auction using the wording 'without reserve', instead of the auctioneer inviting offers he is making an offer, which is accepted when the bid is made. The

auctioneers appealed against this decision on the basis that Judge Charles Harris QC was wrong in law and they were not bound to sell to the highest bidder when using the wording 'without reserve'. Also, they believed there was no collateral contract and there was no consideration to support such a contract.

Held
The Court of Appeal agreed with the court of first instance. Sir Murray Stuart-Smith confirmed the decision of Judge Charles Harris QC and in particular noted there was a collateral contract between the auctioneer and Mr Davies, and as regards consideration he stated:

> '… in my judgment there is consideration both in form of detriment to the bidder, since his bid can be accepted unless and until it is withdrawn, and benefit to the auctioneer as the bidding is driven up. Moreover, attendance at the sale is likely to be increased if it is known that there is no reserve.' (p1967)

Pill LJ was in total agreement with Sir Murray Stuart-Smith and stated:

> '… the auctioneer was under an obligation to sell to the highest bidder.'

Comment
This was an interesting case which dealt specifically with the issues and effect of a sale by auction expressed to be 'without reserve'. This case demonstrates the courts are prepared to reverse the rules in prescribed circumstances, which may result in an offer that cannot be refused and a collateral contract between the auctioneer and person making the highest bid.

Bowerman and Another v Association of British Travel Agents Limited [1996] CLC 451 Court of Appeal (Hirst, Waite and Hobhouse LJJ)

• *Offer and acceptance*

Facts

This case involved a skiing holiday for a party of school children. The first plaintiff was Emma Bowerman, a pupil at the school, and the second plaintiff was Stephen Wallace, a teacher at the school. The original holiday was booked with Adventurer Express, an ABTA tour operator, and was to commence on the 29 March 1991. However, prior to the commencement of the holiday Adventurer Express ceased trading. A refund was available under ABTA's scheme of protection in these circumstances and an alternative holiday was arranged within a week with another tour operator, Skibound Ltd. However, ABTA claimed the reimbursement did not extend to the insurance premium paid by each member of the original holiday and deducted £10 per head.

The appeal was directly related to a notice, which had to be displayed at every ABTA tour operator or travel agent's premises, which informed the public of ABTA's scheme of protection. The protection extended to the reimbursement of money paid for a holiday, where the holiday had not yet commenced. Mr Wallace saw the notice and claimed it constituted an offer to the public at large which formed part of the original contract with Adventurer Express. To support this argument Counsel for the appellants used the case of *Carlill v Carbolic Smoke Ball Company* [1893] 1 QB 256 (CA).

Held

ABTA had to reimburse the full cost of the holiday. The Court of Appeal found there was a contract between ABTA and the public who booked a holiday, having relied upon the scheme which was outlined in the notice.

Comment

The case demonstrates the Court is prepared to enforce a unilateral offer to the world, as enunciated in the case of *Carlill v Carbolic Smoke Ball Company*. This case also illustrates an intention to create legal relations, and would be assumed by an ordinary person when reading such a notice before entering into an agreement.

Esso Petroleum Ltd v Commissioners of Customs and Excise [1976] 1 WLR 1 House of Lords (Lord Wilberforce, Viscount Dilhorne, Lords Simon of Glaisdale, Fraser of Tullybelton and Russell of Killowen)

• *Offer of World Cup coins*

Facts

As a petrol sales promotion scheme, motorists were offered one coin bearing the likeness of a member of England's World Cup soccer team for every four gallons of petrol. Advertisements said, for example: 'One coin given with every four gallons of petrol.' The question arose as to whether, for tax purposes, the coins had been produced 'for general sale'.

Held (Lord Fraser of Tullybelton dissenting)

They had not.

Lord Simon of Glaisdale:

'Believing as I do that Esso envisaged a bargain of some sort between the garage proprietor and the motorist, I must try to analyse the transaction. The analysis that most appeals to me is ... a collateral contract of the sort described by Lord Moulton in *Heilbut, Symons & Co v Buckleton*:

" ... there may be a contract the consideration for which is the making of some other contract. 'If you will make such and such a contract I will give you one hundred pounds', is in every sense of the word a complete legal contract. It is collateral to the main contract ..."

So here. The law happily matches the reality. The garage proprietor is saying, "If you will buy four gallons of my petrol, I will give you one of these coins". None of the reasons which have caused the law to consider advertising or display material as an invitation to treat, rather than an offer, applies here. What the garage proprietor says by his placards is in fact and in law an offer of consideration to the motorist to enter into a contract of sale of petrol. Of course, not every motorist will notice the placard, but nor will every potential offeree of many offers be necessarily conscious that they have been made. However, the motorist who does notice the placard, and in reliance thereon drives in and orders the petrol, is in law doing two things at the same time. First, he is accepting the offer of a coin if he buys four gallons of petrol. Secondly, he is himself offering to buy four gallons of petrol: this offer is accepted by the filling of his tank ... Here the coins were not transferred for a money consideration. They were transferred in consideration of the motorist entering into a contract for the sale of petrol. The coins were therefore not produced for sale ... They are exempt from purchase tax.'

Helby v *Matthews* [1895] AC 471 House of Lords (Lords Herschell LC, Watson, Macnaghten, Shand and Morris)

- *Nature of hire purchase agreement*

Facts
The owner agreed to let a piano on hire to the debtor (hirer) on the terms that if the debtor paid all the instalments the piano would become his property but until that time, it remained the sole property of the owner. The debtor could terminate the hiring at any time by giving the piano back to the owner, together with any arrears outstanding. The debtor received the piano, paid a few instalments and then pledged it with a pawnbroker.

When the owner sought to recover the piano from the pawnbroker, the pawnbroker argued that he was protected by s9 Factors Act 1889 as the debtor was a person who had 'bought or agreed to buy' goods.

Held
The owner was entitled to succeed. The debtor had not 'agreed to buy' goods within the meaning of s9 Factors Act 1889 since he was under no legal obligation to buy the piano. He had a choice and could return it or become its owner by exercising his option to purchase under the contract.

Lord Herschell LC:

'I cannot think that an agreement to buy "if he does not change his mind" is any agreement to buy at all in the eye of the law. If it rests with me to do or not to do a certain thing at at a future time, according to the then state of my mind, I cannot be said to have contracted to do it. It appears to me that the contract in question was in reality a contract of hiring, and not in name or pretence only... I think it very likely that both parties thought it would probably end in a purchase, but this is far from showing that it was an agreement to buy.'

Rowland v *Divall*

See SALE OF GOODS, Chapter 4, below.

Wait, Re, The Trustee v *Humphries and Bobbett* [1927] 1 Ch 606 Court of Appeal (Lord Hanworth MR, Atkin and Sargant LJJ)

- *Specific or ascertained goods?*

Facts
Wait, a grain dealer, made a cif contract with a company for 1,000 tons of 'Western White' wheat to be shipped from North America to Bristol on MV 'Challenger'. Humphries and Bobbett made a cif contract with Wait to purchase 500 tons of the wheat. A bill of lading

was issued for 1,000 tons on the date the wheat was shipped which Wait received on 4 January. The bill was payable on 6 February. On 5 January he sent to Humphries and Bobbett a confirmatory invoice, and banked the payment received from them in a separate account. On 24 February Wait was adjudged bankrupt. The 'Challenger' arrived at Bristol with 1,000 tons of wheat bulk loaded on 28 February. Wait's trustee in bankruptcy refused either to return the money, or deliver the goods.

Held (Sargant LJ dissenting)

The appeal would be allowed as, inter alia, the agreement was not a 'contract to deliver specific or ascertained goods' within s52 of the Sale of Goods Act 1893.

Lord Hanworth MR:

'The problem to be solved comes back to the question: Were the 500 tons specific goods? They were never appropriated, and it is admitted that the legal property has not passed, for these were "future goods" within s5 of the Act in respect of which no property passed to the purchaser: see ss16, 17, and 18(5). There was no ascertainment or identification of the 500 tons out of the cargo in bulk of the motor vessel *Challenger*. The bankruptcy of the vendors does not, in my judgment, affect the question, though it may emphasise the hardship to the purchasers, for the question must be determined upon the rights of the parties under the contract upon the arrival of the wheat.

The argument for the buyers depends in no small measure upon the validity of the dictum of Lord Westbury in *Holroyd* v *Marshall* (1862) 10 HL Cas 191, which – if premature at the date of its utterance – is said now to be law by virtue of s52 of the Act. It was this passage from Lord Westbury's speech which Astbury J primarily relied upon [in the Divisional Court]. It is

not certain what were the words used by Lord Westbury in giving his illustration of the sale of a particular parcel of tea. The Law Journal report runs as follows (33 LJ Ch at p196):

"A contract for the sale of goods as, for example, of 500 chests of tea, was not a contract which would be specially performed, because it did not relate to any chests of tea in particular, but a contract to sell the 500 chests of a particular kind of tea, which 'are in my warehouse in Gloucester', was a contract relating to specific property, and which would be specifically performed."

These words appear to indicate clearly specific goods in a specific place, identified and ascertained as the subject matter of the contract ...

Considering the facts of the present case in the light of the authorities to which I have called attention, it is, in my judgment, not possible to hold that the 500 tons of wheat, ex motor vessel *Challenger*, were specific or ascertained goods, and thus specific performance would not be ordered as the remedy of the buyer under s52 of the Act. I do not read *Holroyd* v *Marshall* as conflicting with this view.'

Comment

For ss5, 16, 17, 18 and 52 of the 1893 Act, see now ss5, 16, 17, 18 and 52 of the Sale of Goods Act 1979 and the Law Commission Paper 215, *Sale of Goods Forming Part of a Bulk* (1993). The Commission's proposals have been implemented through the Sale of Goods (Amendment) Act 1995 by inserting two new sections, 20A and 20B, into the Sale of Goods Act 1979. The change in legislation now allows a person, meeting a specified criteria, who contracts to buy a specified quantity of goods from a designated bulk and who pays some or all of the price, to become a tenant in common of the bulk.

2 Formation of the Contract and Formalities

***Actionstrength Ltd (t/a Vital Resources)* v *International Glass Engineering IN.GL.EN SpA* [2002] 1 WLR 566 Court of Appeal (Simon Brown, Peter Gibson and Tuckey LJJ)**

- *Guarantee and enforceability under the Statute of Frauds 1677*

Facts

This was an appeal by the second defendant, Saint-Gobain Glass UK Ltd (SG), who believed the claimant, Actionstrength Ltd (AS) (trading as Vital Resources), did not have a genuine arguable defence and had applied for summary judgment, which had been refused. SG based the appeal on a point of law under s4 of the Statute of Frauds 1677.

The first defendant, International Glass Engineering IN.GL.EN SpA (IGE), contracted with the second defendant SG to build a float glass factory at Eggborough in Yorkshire. The first defendant IGE entered into an agreement with the claimant AS to provide the labour to build the float glass factory. The first defendant IGE was persistently late in making payment to the claimant, which resulted in a substantial sum outstanding.

The claimant AS complained to the second defendant SG and threatened to withdraw its labour unless the first defendant paid it the arrears. AS alleged that SG made a verbal agreement with AS stating that if AS did not withdraw its labour from the building site, SG would speak to the first defendant regarding the money owed to the claimant. Further, if the first defendant did not meet its obligations with the claimant, SG promised it would withhold payment to IGE and use this payment to pay the claimant the amount outstanding.

The claimant, in reliance on the second defendant's promise, agreed not to withdraw its labour and to proceed toward completion of the factory. However, by March 2000 the first defendant owed the claimant £1.3 million. It became apparent that IGE was unable to meet its obligation to the claimant and SG would have to make payment to the claimant. SG refused to make payment and the claimant withdrew its labour from the building site.

The claimant commenced proceedings against IGE and obtained default judgment on 12 June 2000. However, the judgment proved worthless as the first defendant has been put into liquidation in Italy. Therefore, the claimant pursued its claim against the second defendant SG and pleaded, at para 5, that the second defendant:

'Agreed that in consideration of the claimant not withdrawing its labour from the site as aforesaid – ie as it had told the second defendant it proposed to do – the second defendant would ensure that the claimant received any amount due to it from the first defendant under the supply contract if necessary by redirecting to the claimant payments due by the second defendant to the first defendant.'

SG had resisted the claim by denying any such agreement was ever entered into with the complainant and, also, if any such agreement had been entered into it would constitute a guarantee, which in the absence of being evidenced in writing is unenforceable by virtue of s4 of the Statute of Frauds 1677, which states:

'No action shall be brought ... whereby to

charge the defendant upon any special promise to answer for the debt, default or miscarriages of another person ... unless the agreement upon which such action shall be brought, or some memorandum or note thereof, shall be in writing, and signed by the party to be charged therewith, or some other person thereunto by him lawfully authorised.'

The claimant contended that the Statute of Frauds 1677 had no application to the agreement and the second defendant was estopped from relying upon the Statute.

Held

At first instance, Mitting J concluded that the second defendant undertook a primary obligation to pay the claimant and the facts should be examined at trial; he refused summary judgment. Mr Soole, who acted for the second defendant, challenged the decision of the court of first instance on appeal and this was discussed by Simon Brown LJ:

'... the question whether or not a guarantee is within the Statute of Frauds 1677 must be approached as a matter of substance rather than form. It is the essence of the second defendant's case that, however precisely one construes the terms of this agreement, in substance it imposed only a secondary liability upon the second defendant, a liability contingent upon the first defendant defaulting on its primary obligation under the subcontract with the claimant. Such liability, submits Mr Soole, falls foul of s4.'

Simon Brown LJ referred to the *Motemtronic Ltd* v *Autocar Equipment Ltd* judgment of 20 June 1996 (as yet unreported) and made reference to the following statement from that case:

'Mrs Ford. Where would money come from if M [the principal debtor] had to repay £1 million? Colin Searle (the second defendant, M's chairman). From wherever in the group the money was at the relevant time. I'll make sure it is there, I'm good for £1 million.'

The Court of Appeal, in that case, found

the wording merely constituted a statement of comfort and such a promise would fall within s4. Simon Brown LJ discussed the dictum of Lord Diplock in the case of *Moschi* v *Lep Air Services Ltd* [1973] AC 331:

'The reason for the need for such formality was set out by Lord Blackburn in *Stelle* v *M'Kinlay* (1880) 5 App Cas 754, 768: "It was thought by the English legislature that there was a danger of contracts of a particular kind being established by false evidence, or by evidence of loose talk, when it never was really meant to make such a contract; and there it was provided ..." and s4 is set out. The policy behind the Statute is to seek to introduce certainty in any case where a party accepts secondary liability for another's failure to meet his promise ... I have made it clear that in my judgment the mischief aimed at by s4 of the Statute of Frauds 1677 remains as valid as ever it did. It follows from this that in examining whether an oral contract is within or without the Statute, it is necessary to look at the substance rather than the form ... The first basis requirement of a contract of guarantee within s4 is that there must be someone other than the surety who is primarily liable ...'

Simon Brown LJ was of the opinion that the second defendant, as in the case of *Motemtronic Ltd* v *Autocar Equipment Ltd*, took on a secondary liability and was answerable for the debt of the defaulter (in the aforementioned case it was Autocar), in this instance the first defendant (IGE).

However, Mr McGhee, the claimant's representative, argued the contrary and cited *Andrews* v *Smith* (1835) 2 CM & R 627 using the dictum recorded at pp629–30:

'This is not a promise to answer for the debt or default of another, within the meaning of the Statute of Frauds. It is not a promise to be answerable out of the defendant's own funds, but to pay out of the funds of another, on receiving his direction for that purposes ... such a contract is direct, and not collateral, and therefore binding without being in writing.'

Simon Brown LJ, having heard the arguments, rejected the claimant's submission and found in favour of the second defendant. The promise made by the second defendant was unenforceable by virtue of s4 of the Statute of Frauds 1677. The appeal was allowed and the claim against the second defendant was struck out.

Comment

This case clearly demonstrates that the Statute of Frauds 1677 is still alive and enforceable when it comes to the formation of a contract. The facts of this case should send a clear message to those involved with secondary debtors: guarantees must be evidenced in writing.

Associated Japanese Bank (International) Ltd v *Credit du Nord SA* [1989] 1 WLR 255 High Court (Steyn J)

• *Guarantee – mistake as to subject matter*

Facts

Under a sale and leaseback transaction the plaintiffs (AJB) purchased four machines from a Mr Bennett and then leased them back to him. As a condition of the transaction, the defendants (CDN) guaranteed Bennett's obligations and at all material times both parties believed that the machines existed and were in Bennett's possession. After Bennett defaulted in payments under the lease it was discovered that the machines did not exist and that Bennett had perpetrated a fraud. When the plaintiffs sued on the guarantee, the defendants contended that it was void ab intio for common mistake.

Held

The plaintiffs' claim would be dismissed.

Steyn J:

'It might be useful if I now summarised what appears to me to be a satisfactory way of approaching this subject. Logically, before one can turn to the rules as to mistake, whether at common law or in equity, one must first determine whether the contract itself, by express or implied condition precedent or otherwise, provides who bears the risk of the relevant mistake. It is at this hurdle that many pleas of mistake will either fail or prove to have been unnecessary. Only if the contract is silent on the point is there scope for invoking mistake. That brings me to the relationship between common law mistake and mistake in equity. Where common law mistake has been pleaded, the court must first consider this plea. If the contract is held to be void, no question of mistake in equity arises. But, if the contract is held to be valid, a plea of mistake in equity may still have to be considered: see *Grist* v *Bailey* [1966] 2 All ER 875 ... Turning now to the approach to common law mistake, it seems to me that the following propositions are valid although not necessarily all entitled to be dignified as propositions of law.

The first imperative must be that the law ought to uphold rather than destroy apparent contracts. Second, the common law rules as to a mistake regarding the quality of the subject matter, like the common law rules regarding commercial frustration, are designed to cope with the impact of unexpected and wholly exceptional circumstances on apparent contracts. Third, such a mistake in order to attract legal consequences must substantially be shared by both parties, and must relate to facts as they existed at the time the contract was made. Fourth, and this is the point established by *Bell* v *Lever Bros Ltd* [1932] AC 161, the mistake must render the subject matter of the contract essentially and radically different from the subject matter which the parties believed to exist ... Fifth, there is a requirement which was not specifically discussed in *Bell* v *Lever Bros Ltd*. What happens if the party who is seeking to rely on the mistake had no reasonable grounds for his belief? An extreme example is that of the man who makes a contract with minimal knowledge of the facts to which the mistake relates but is content that it is a good speculative risk. In my judgment a party cannot be allowed to rely on a common mistake where the mistake consists of a belief which is entertained by him without any reasonable grounds for such relief: *McRae* v *Commonwealth Disposals Commission* (1951) 84 CLR 377 at 408. That is not because principles such as estoppel or negligence require it, but simply because policy and good sense dictate that the positive rules regarding common mistake should be so qualified ... a recognition of this qualification is consistent with the approach in equity where fault on the part of the party adversely affected by the mistake will generally preclude the granting of equitable relief: see *Solle* v *Butcher* [1949] 2 All ER 1107 at 1120.

Applying the law to the facts

It is clear, of course, that in this case both parties, the creditor and the guarantor, acted on the assumption that the lease related to existing machines. If they had been informed that the machines might not exist, neither AJB nor CDN would for one moment have contemplated entering into the transaction. That, by itself, I accept, is not enough to sustain the plea of common law mistake. I am also satisfied that CDN had reasonable grounds for believing that the machines existed. That belief was based on CDN's discussions with Mr Bennett, information supplied by ... a respectable firm of lease brokers, and the confidence created by the fact that AJB were the lessors.

The real question is whether the subject matter *of the guarantee* (as opposed to the sale and lease) was essentially different from what it was reasonably believed to be. The real security of the guarantor was the machines. The existence of the machines, being profit-earning chattels, made it more likely that the debtor would be able to service the debt. More importantly, if the debtor defaulted and the creditor repossessed the machines, the creditor had to give credit for 97.5 per cent of the value of the machines. If the creditor sued the guarantor first, and the guarantor paid, the guarantor was entitled to be subrogated to the creditor's rights in respect of recovery against the debtor ... No doubt the guarantor relied to some extent on the creditworthiness of Mr Bennett. But I find that the prime security to which the guarantor looked was the existence of the four machines as described to both parties. For both parties the guarantee of obligations under a lease with non-existent machines was essentially different from a guarantee of a lease with four machines which both parties at the time of the contract believed to exist. The guarantee is an accessory contract. The non-existence of the subject matter of the principal contract is therefore of fundamental importance. Indeed the analogy of the classic res extincta cases, so much discussed in the authorities, is fairly close. In my judgment, the stringent test of common law mistake is satisfied; the guarantee is void ab initio ...

Equitable mistake

Having concluded that the guarantee is void ab initio at common law, it is strictly unnecessary to examine the question of equitable mistake. Equity will give relief against common mistake in cases where the common law will not, and it provides more flexible remedies, including the power to set aside the contract on terms. It is not necessary to repeat my findings of fact save to record again the fundamental nature of the common mistake, and that CDN was not at fault in any way. If I had not decided in favour of CDN on construction and common law mistake, I would have held that the guarantee must be set aside on equitable principles.'

Comment

See also *Great Peace Shipping Ltd* v *Tsavliris Salvage (International) Ltd, The Great Peace* [2002] 4 All ER 689 where the Court of Appeal discussed contract and mutual mistake.

Atlas Express Ltd v *Kafco (Importers and Distributors) Ltd*
[1989] 3 WLR 389 High Court
(Tucker J)

• *Duress – commercial pressure*

Facts
The plaintiffs, a national road carrier, contracted with the defendants a small company, to deliver cartons of basketware to branches of Woolworth throughout the United Kingdom. Before entering into the contract, the plaintiffs' manager had inspected the cartons and estimated that each load would contain a minimum of 400 and possibly as many as 600 cartons: on that basis he agreed a charge of £1.10 per carton. In fact, the first load contained only 200 cartons, so the manager said they would not take any more unless the defendants agreed to pay a minimum of £440 per load. As they were heavily dependent on their Woolworth contract and could not at that time find an alternative carrier, the defendants agreed to the new terms but later refused to pay at the new rate.

Held
The defendants were not bound by the new terms: economic duress had vitiated the new agreement and, in any case, there was no consideration for it.

Tucker J:

'The issue which I have to determine is whether the defendants are bound by the [new] agreement signed on their behalf ... The defendants contend that they are not bound, for two reasons: first, because the agreement was signed under duress; second, because there was no consideration for it.

The first question raises an interesting point of law, ie whether economic duress is a concept known to English law.

Economic duress must be distinguished from commercial pressure, which on any view is not sufficient to vitiate consent. The borderline between the two may in some cases be indistinct. But ... authors ... appear to recognise that in appropriate cases economic duress may afford a defence, and in my judgment it does. It is clear to me that in a number of English cases judges have acknowledged the existence of this concept.

Thus, in *D & C Builders Ltd* v *Rees* [1965] 3 All ER 837 at 841 Lord Denning MR said: "No person can insist on a settlement procured by intimidation". And in *Occidental Worldwide Investment Corp* v *Skibs A/S Avanti, The Siboen and The Sibotre* [1976] 1 Lloyd's Rep 293 at 336 Kerr J appeared to accept that economic duress could operate in appropriate circumstances. A similar conclusion was reached by Mocatta J in *North Ocean Shipping Co Ltd* v *Hyundai Construction Co Ltd, The Atlantic Baron* [1978] 3 All ER 1170 at 1182.

In particular, there are passages in the judgment of Lord Scarman in *Pao On* v *Lau Yiu* [1979] 3 All ER 65 at 78-79 which clearly indicate recognition of the concept

...

A further case, which was not cited to me was *B & S Contracts and Design Ltd* v *Victor Green Publications Ltd* [1984] ICR 419 at 423, where Eveleigh LJ referred to the speech of Lord Diplock in another uncited case, *Universe Tankships Inc of Monrovia* v *International Transport Workers' Federation* [1982] 2 All ER 67 at 75-76:

"The rationale is that his apparent consent was induced by pressure exercised on him by that other party which the law does not regard as legitimate, with the consequence that the consent is treated in law as revocable unless approbated either expressly or by implication after the illegitimate pressure has ceased to operate on his mind."

In commenting on this Eveleigh LJ said of the word "legitimate" ([1984] ICR 419 at 423):

"For the purpose of this case it is sufficient to say that if the claimant has been influenced against his will to pay money under the threat of unlawful damage to his economic interest he will be entitled to claim that money back ..."

Reverting to the case before me, I find that the defendants' apparent consent to the agreement was induced by pressure which was illegitimate and I find that it was not approbated. In my judgment that pressure can properly be described as economic duress, which is a concept recognised by English law, and which in the circumstances of the present case vitiates the defendants' apparent consent to the agreement.

In any event, I find that there was no consideration for the new agreement. The plaintiffs were already obliged to deliver the defendants' goods at the rates agreed under the terms of the original agreement. There was no consideration for the increased minimum charge of £440 per trailer.'

Barton v County Natwest Ltd [1999] Lloyd's Rep Bank 408 Court of Appeal (Roch and Morritt LJJ, Lindsay J)

• *Fraudulent misrepresentation – personal guarantees*

Facts

This appeal involved the purchase of a leisure complex and a nightclub in Newquay, Cornwall. The appellants, Mr Barton and Mr and Mrs Amos, later became officers of a company called Regent Leisure Time Ltd (the company). The company borrowed just over £2 million from the bank to purchase the leisure complex and nightclub (the property). The loan was secured by the appellants acting as guarantors for the company. One of the conditions of the loan was that the bank required a forced sale valuation of the property in an amount of not less than £3.5 million. A forced sale valuation represents, to the bank, the open market value of the property if sold within six months of the valuation. The bank appointed the valuers to produce the report. However, the valuation produced was not a forced sale valuation, in accordance with the bank's definition, but a vacant possession valuation which reflected a value of £3.5

million. The valuer explained the difference, to the bank, between a forced sale valuation and a vacant possession valuation: the former valuation would be lower than £3.5 million. The appellants, prior to completion, asked the bank if they had obtained the forced sale valuation in accordance with the required amount and the bank said that it had.

The company was not successful in their business venture and the bank demanded repayment of the loan by the company and payment by each of the guarantors pursuant to their individual guarantees. The guarantors (appellants) failed to comply with this request and the bank commenced proceeding against them. The appellants counterclaimed on the basis of misrepresentation, in that they had relied upon the forced sale valuation, which was a condition precedent to the drawdown of the loan that such a valuation had been obtained and satisfied, and which had induced them to purchase the property.

Held

The bank were aware the valuation was a vacant possession valuation and not a forced sale valuation and, therefore, the valuation provided by the valuer was substantially below the required value of £3.5 million. The Court found the bank could not have genuinely believed a vacant possession valuation was the same as a forced sale valuation and on this basis found the bank's representation, to the appellants, had been fraudulent. The bank intended the appellants to rely upon this representation and it is a presumption in law that a reasonable person is likely to rely upon such a false statement unless the contrary is proved. Accordingly, such a presumption reversed the burden of proof and as the bank had failed to discharge this burden it was found that the appellants had been induced by the representation made by the bank. The appellants' claim against the bank for deceit was successful and they were entitled to rescind the guarantees and recover damages.

Comment

This decision confirms the principles laid down by the House of Lords' decision in *Derry* v *Peek* (1889) 14 App Cas 337 where it was demonstrated that for an action brought for the tort of deceit to be successful it is necessary to show fraud. In this context Lord Herschell defined such a false representation to have been made knowingly, or without belief in its truth, or recklessly, careless whether it be true or false. The facts of the present case firmly enunciate these principles.

Chater v *Mortgage Agency Services Number Two Ltd* [2004] 1 P & CR 4
Court of Appeal (Lord Phillips, Rix and Scott Baker LJJ)

* *Undue influence – misrepresentation*

Facts

The appellant (Mrs Chater, a lady in her 70s) appealed against the judgment of Warner J who granted an order for possession in favour of the respondent, Mortgage Agency Services Number Two Ltd (MA), and damages amounting to £63,501.18 against Mrs Chater (C) and her son Andrew Chater. In 1985, C purchased her council house for £7,000 with the aid of a small mortgage. In 1990, C entered into a joint mortgage with her son, using her property as security for the loan to raise money for her son's business. At the same time as the remortgage the property was transferred into the joint names of C and her son. C received a cheque, made out in joint names, for £24,000. However, C endorsed the cheque and the entire proceeds went to her son. Within a short period of time the mortgage fell into arrears and proceedings for possession were issued. C paid off the arrears and the property was re-transferred back into the sole name of C. However, fresh proceedings for possession were issued against C resulting in the judgment at first instance. The judge at first instance made his decision before the decision of the House of Lords in *Royal Bank*

of Scotland v *Etridge (No 2)* [2001] 4 All ER 449 and approached the facts of the case based upon the law as it was then understood to be. At first instance C's claim failed because MA was entitled to assume that the solicitor acting for C and her son would have considered whether there was a conflict of interest between mother and son, and whether C should have received independent advice to prevent undue influence taking place.

C based her appeal on the ground that her son had unduly influenced her and misrepresented the facts to her when she entered into a mortgage for a substantial sum, the purpose of which was to support her son financially in the purchase of a franchise in a laser printing business. C claimed MA had constructive notice that she may have been unduly influenced and/or a misrepresentation had taken place. C believed that MA had failed to take reasonable steps to investigate her circumstances, and any claim MA had against her was not enforceable.

Held

Scott LJ had to consider whether the lender had been placed in a position that suggested that it had constructive knowledge of the existence of either undue influence or misrepresentation, and whether the lender had failed to make relevant enquiries or take reasonable steps to verify the appellant's position. When a creditor becomes aware of certain risks and does not investigate the matter the creditor will be deemed to have constructive notice. In this instance it would have been either a misrepresentation or undue influence. Constructive notice will allow a court to set aside the transaction.

Scott LJ noted that Warner J at first instance had found C's evidence to be unsatisfactory and had remained unconvinced of her naïvety. However, he accepted Warner J's decision that C had reposed trust and confidence in her son, which may have resulted in a presumption of undue influence under Class 2B as defined in *Barclays Bank* v *O'Brien* [1994] AC 180 as a relationship where one party is able to demonstrate that he or she placed trust and confidence in the wrongdoer. However, this approach has now been overtaken by the decision in *Etridge (No 2)* where only certain types of relationship give rise to a presumption of undue influence. He also accepted that Andrew Chater had misrepresented the facts to his mother, and she had relied upon his misrepresentation. In addition to the misrepresentation Warner J had found that the loan application had suggested a number of scenarios and it was possible for MA to have considered the aspect of undue influence.

Scott LJ believed two questions needed to be answered in this appeal; first, had the appellant placed trust and confidence in her son in relation to the management of her financial affairs and, second, whether the transaction needed to be explained to the appellant? The judge at first instance did not ask these questions as the case pre-dated the decision of the House of Lords in *Etridge (No 2)*.

To address the first question, Scott LJ made reference to the dictum of Lord Nicholls in the case of *Etridge (No 2),* at para 8:

> 'Proof that the complainant placed trust and confidence in the other party in relation to the management of the complainant's financial affairs, coupled with a transaction which calls for explanation, will normally be sufficient, failing satisfactory evidence to the contrary, to discharge the burden of proof. On proof of these two matters the stage is set for the court to infer that, in the absence of a satisfactory explanation, the transaction can only have been procured by undue influence. In other words, proof of these two facts is prima facie evidence that the defendant abused the influence he acquired in the parties' relationship. He preferred his own interests. He did not behave fairly to the other. So the evidential burden shifts to him. It is for him to produce evidence to counter the inference which otherwise should be drawn.'

Scott LJ concurred with Warner J's finding that C did repose trust and confidence in her

son and did not disturb Warner J's decision. Mr Anderson (who acted on behalf of C) argued that this was a transaction, as between the parties, that cried out for questions to be asked. The appellant had gone from having a small mortgage on a property in her sole name, to granting a commercial mortgage over her property and only owning half of it. The son, Andrew Chater, chose the solicitor to carry out the transaction, and C signed the reverse of the cheque without any questions being asked. Mr Anderson believed these facts all pointed towards undue influence. However, Miss Sandells (who acted on behalf of the respondent) challenged this assertion. According to Miss Sandells, many parents give financial support to their children, which may also include support for business ventures. Miss Sandells believed that C knew the money was for a business venture and was not forced into the transaction; at the time she saw it as a reasonable risk. It is only with hindsight, once the business failed and the money lost, that one can see the true potential risk involved – but this does not constitute undue influence. Miss Sandells believed the real reason the appellant financially supported her son was because of her love and affection for him. Scott LJ acknowledged the force of this argument but was mindful that the very nature of undue influence is such that the victim will often not appreciate the significance of what is being done. Given the full facts of this case, this transaction called for an explanation; in the absence of a satisfactory explanation the allegation of undue influence would be accepted.

The misrepresentation related to two separate claims. First, the loan was to be insured, in the event that the son was unable to meet the repayments, and that the loan would not exceed £26,000. Neither of these statements turned out to be true. On the first claim Scott LJ examined the appellant's evidence, which was insufficient to justify a finding of misrepresentation. On the second claim, having re-examined the evidence, Scott LJ concluded that there was no misrepresentation: the appellant would have been aware of the amount of the loan when she signed the mortgage deed.

Having established there was no misrepresentation but there was evidence to demonstrate that the appellant was under undue influence, the Court of Appeal had to consider whether or not the respondent was, under the doctrine of notice, put on inquiry as to some equitable wrong.

Scott LJ approached this issue by first looking at the purpose of the loan as presented to the lender. The application stated the loan was for a 'purchase'. In fact this was not true, as C already owned the property, and the true purpose of the loan was to raise capital and use the property as security. The respondent knew a mother and son were making the application and the property was being transferred into joint names. The mere fact that the application was being made by a mother and son, and that it was the mother's house to be used as security for the loan, did not put the respondent on notice. Scott LJ came to this decision based upon the information that passed between the appellant and respondent. There was no information given to the respondent to indicate that the loan was to be used purely for the son's business venture; on the face of the application this was purely a domestic loan. The respondent was not under any obligation to discover what the loan was to be used for. As far as the respondent was aware, this was a loan to purchase a property and additional funds to be used for home improvements at the property. On this basis, Scott LJ could not find any reason why this transaction should have put the respondent on inquiry about undue influence.

Thus, the Court of Appeal did not allow the appellant's claim against the respondent but did confirm that C was indeed under the influence of her son when she entered into the mortgage agreement. However, the respondent was not put on inquiry as to any equitable wrong and was not obliged to take any further steps.

Comment

The equitable doctrine of undue influence has always been a controversial area as a result of the conflicting decisions that have arisen within the last 20 years. The volatile nature of the rules and judicial policy-making in this area is evidenced by the proliferation of appeals being heard. The decision of this case focused on undue influence by a third party, who benefited as a result of the influence. According to the Court of Appeal, even though undue influence was proven, the lender was not put on notice of an equitable wrong and therefore did not have to take reasonable steps to verify its position. It may be argued that this policy is self-protecting for financial institutions or, alternatively, that the decision will act as a deterrent and prevent abuse of the judicial system by those who only realise their mistakes after an unfortunate outcome has occurred.

Cundy v *Lindsay* (1878) 3 App Cas 459 House of Lords (Lord Cairns LC, Lords Hatherley, Penzance and Gordon)

• *Sale of goods induced by fraud*

Facts

Alfred Blenkarn hired a room at a corner house in Wood Street, Cheapside. The entrance was in Little Love Lane, but he described the premises as '37 Wood Street, Cheapside'. The respondents were linen manufacturers in Belfast. Blenkarn wrote to the plaintiffs concerning a purchase from them of their goods, describing his premises as comprising a warehouse and signing himself 'Blenkiron and Co'. Blenkiron and Co carried on business at number 132 Wood Street and were a highly respectable firm. The respondents, who knew of the firm but did not know their address, sent the goods to 'Blenkiron and Co' at 37 Wood Street. Blenkarn sold the goods to, inter alia, Messrs Cundy who were bona fide purchasers and who resold them in the course of their trade. Payment not being made, Blenkarn's fraud was discovered and criminal proceedings taken against him. Messrs Lindsay then sued Messrs Cundy for unlawful conversion.

Held

They were entitled to succeed.

Lord Cairns LC:

'... by the law of our country, the purchaser of a chattel takes the chattel, as a general rule, subject to what may turn out to be certain infirmities in the title. If he purchases the chattel in market overt, he obtains a title which is good against all the world, but if he does not ... and if it turns out that the chattel has been found by the person who professed to sell it, the purchaser will not obtain a title good against the real owner. If it turns out that the chattel has been stolen ... the purchaser will not obtain a title. If it turns out that the chattel has come into the hands of the person who professed to sell it by a de facto contract, that is to say, a contract which has purported to pass the property to him from the owner of the property, there the purchaser will obtain a good title, even although afterwards it would appear that there were circumstances connected with that contract which would enable the original owner of those goods to reduce it and set it aside, because these circumstances so enabling the original owner of the goods, or of the chattel, to reduce the contract and set it aside, will not be allowed to interfere with a title for valuable consideration obtained by some third party during the interval while the contract remains unreduced ... Blenkarn ... was acting here just in the same way as if he had forged the signature Blenkiron and Co ... and as if when, in return, the goods were forwarded and letters were sent accompanying them, he had intercepted the goods and intercepted the letters and had taken possession of the goods ... how is it possible to imagine that in that stage of things any contract could have arisen between the respondents and Blenkarn? Of him they knew nothing and

of him they never thought ... as, between him and them, there was no consensus of mind which could lead to any agreement or contract whatever ... My Lords, that being so, it is idle to talk of the property passing. The property remained ... the property of the respondents ...'

Comment

See also *Shogun Finance Ltd* v *Hudson* [2003] 3 WLR 1371 which applied the principle laid down in *Cundy* v *Lindsay*.

Downs v *Chappell and Stephenson Smart* [1997] 1 WLR 426 Court of Appeal (Butler-Sloss, Roch and Hobhouse LJJ)

• *Misrepresentation and damages*

Facts

The plaintiffs had purchased the first defendant's business, a bookshop. Before deciding on the purchase they asked to see the accounts to check trading profit and loss. They were given a one-page summary and they requested the accounts be verified by the first defendant's accountants, Stephensons Smart, the second defendant. The second defendant wrote a letter of verification, with the authority of Mr Chappell, knowing the figures to be false. The letter did not give a true reflection on profit and loss but represented a healthy business, with a growing turnover and substantial gross profit margin. This information led the plaintiffs to believe they would be able to cover their finances and have a reasonable income. The plaintiffs found, to their cost, the business was not viable. It did not generate the projected profits and income to live off.

The plaintiffs, Mr and Mrs Downs, brought an action against the first defendant, Kevin Chappell, for fraudulent misrepresentation and an action against the second defendant, Stephenson Smart a firm of accountants, for negligent misrepresentation. At first instance the defendants were found liable but it was held the plaintiffs had failed to prove any loss suffered as a result of the defendants' torts. The plaintiffs appealed on the latter issue, claiming consequential loss caused by the defendants' liability.

Held

Hobhouse J confirmed the first defendant had made a fraudulent misrepresentation, which induced the plaintiffs to enter the contract to their detriment and the second defendant was liable in negligent misrepresentation, as the plaintiffs were never told the truth. Hobhouse J was of the opinion that the plaintiffs had proved their case on causation, they only entered the contract due to the first and second defendant's representations and as a direct consequence found themselves 18 months later with an unviable business with limited marketability. The only remaining question was the loss suffered by the plaintiffs. The plaintiffs had since sold the shop, at a loss, but it was adduced that the plaintiffs had an opportunity to sell at a higher price in 1990, which the defendants claimed increased their loss.

Hobhouse J in his judgment applied similar cases that dealt with the torts of deceit and negligent misrepresentation and applied the cases of *Doyle* v *Olby* [1969] 2 QB 158, *Esso Petroleum* v *Marden* [1976] 1 QB 801 and *Hayes* v *Dodd* [1990] 2 All ER 815. Based upon these authorities and facts in question he allowed the plaintiffs' appeal and ordered the defendants to pay damages. He held the plaintiffs' loss to be assessed up to March 1990, when they had an opportunity to sell for £76,000, and awarded damages at £44,000.

Comment

This decision reinforces the legal rules on misrepresentation and demonstrates how the courts deal with consequential loss and calculate damages when dealing with fraudulent and negligent misrepresentation.

See also *Barton* v *County Natwest Ltd* [1999] Lloyd's Rep Bank 408, which examined the legal rules relating to fraudulent misrepresentation and personal guarantees.

Great Peace Shipping Ltd v *Tsavliris Salvage (International) Ltd, The Great Peace* [2002] 4 All ER 689 Court of Appeal (Lord Phillips MR, May and Laws LJJ)

* *Contract and mutual mistake*

Facts

The appeal concerned two vessels, the 'Cape Providence' (the appellant) and the 'Great Peace' (the respondent). The Cape Providence was carrying a cargo of iron ore from Brazil to China in September 1999, and during the voyage the vessel incurred serious structural damage in the middle of the South Indian Ocean. The respondent (Great Peace) offered their salvage services, which were accepted. The respondent was to obtain a tug and rendezvous with the Cape Providence. The purpose of the rendezvous was to escort her into safety and, if necessary, assist with the evacuation of her crew if she was in danger of sinking. The respondent contacted a firm of brokers, explained the situation and stressed the urgency in providing a tug to the Cape Providence. The brokers, a Mr Little and Mr Holder, informed the respondent that a vessel was available but would take an estimated five or six days to reach the Cape Providence. This information was received with consternation, as the vessel might have sunk resulting in the loss of lives. Captain Lambrides, the appellant's representative, instructed Mr Little to find an alternative tug. Mr Little contacted Ocean Routes, an organisation which provides reports about vessels at sea and weather forecasts. Mr Little received the names of four vessels within the vicinity of the Cape Providence. One of these vessels was the Great Peace and Mr Little was informed that this vessel was the nearest to the Cape Providence, with an estimated rendezvous time of 12 hours. However, the estimated position of the Cape Providence and the rendezvous time was incorrect. Mr Little contacted Great Peace's managers and spoke to Mr Lee. The circumstances were explained to

Mr Lee but at no time was the location of the vessels discussed. Mr Little further informed Mr Lee that he believed, from the information supplied by Ocean Routes, that the Great Peace was the closest vessel to the Cape Providence. Mr Lee informed Mr Little the Great Peace was currently under charter, transporting soya beans from New Orleans to China: he would first need to consult the charterers. Mr Lee requested the information by fax with the intention of informing Mr Little. Mr Little sent Mr Lee the following fax:

'Further to our [communication] at 22.22 hours BST 24 September, we are working on behalf of the owners of a cape size bulk carrier which has suffered serious structural damage in the Southern Indian Ocean … She is proceeding at five knots on course 050 degrees direction Sunda Strait. Owners have mobilised a tug from Singapore which should reach the casualty in the next five to six days. We understand from Ocean Routes that your vessel 'Great Peace' is in close proximity to the casualty and have been asked by hirers to check whether it would be possible to charter the 'Great Peace' on a daily hire basis to escort the casualty until arrival of the tug.

We would appreciate if you can check soonest with charters whether they can agree to the request, bearing in mind that the casualty is in serious danger.'

Mr Holder then took over from Mr Little. At approximately midnight, Mr Lee telephoned Mr Holder and offered the Great Peace for charter. The terms of the charter were discussed, which included a minimum hire of five days, and the purpose of the hire was to escort and stand-by the Cape Providence in case she sank. Mr Holder asked Mr Lee to confirm the position of the Great Peace and her speed. Mr Lee explained that he would obtain this information when he had discussed the matter further with the Master, when he was certain the appellants were interested in the terms of the offer.

At 06.40 Captain Lambrides instructed Mr Holder to fix the vessel at a gross rate of US$16,500 per day. Mr Holder contacted Mr

Lee and they confirmed the terms of the contract. Mr Holder then sent a fax to Mr Lee thanking him for his assistance and gave details of the Cape Providence's latest position, course and speed to ensure the vessels were able to meet as soon as possible. He ended his correspondence with the following sentence:

'Please instruct your Master to contact the Master of Cape Providence and alter course to rendezvous with the vessel as soon as possible.'

Mr Lee followed out these instructions and requested the Great Peace alter course and head for the Cape Providence. He sent a copy of his request to Mr Holder, which Mr Holder then passed to Captain Lambrides. Captain Lambrides then discovered, and informed Mr Holder, that the vessels were 410 miles apart from each other. These details were unknown to either Mr Holder or Mr Lee. Captain Lambrides then informed Mr Holder he intended to cancel the Great Peace but would first wait and see whether an alternative vessel would be available. By luck, a vessel called the Nordfarer was passing the Cape Providence and was able to give assistance to the Cape Providence.

The appellant informed Mr Holder it had contracted with the Nordfarer and instructed Mr Holder to cancel the agreement with the Great Peace. Mr Holder carried out these instructions by contacting Mr Lee and informing him the Great Peace was no longer needed, and discussed the cancellation fee. Mr Lee sent a fax to Mr Holder informing him he would attempt to negotiate a cancellation fee of two days hire with the Great Peace instead of the minimum five days due under the contract. Mr Holder discussed the contents of the fax with the appellant and was instructed to inform Mr Lee that it was not prepared to pay any cancellation fee. Mr Lee was informed of the appellant's refusal to pay a cancellation fee and informed the respondent, who issued proceedings.

The respondent claimed a sum of $82,500 under the terms of the contract or, alternatively, the same amount as would be payable as damages for wrongful repudiation of the contract. The appellant defended the action by claiming the contract had been concluded while both parties laboured under a fundamental mistake of fact. It claimed the contract was either void under common law or voidable in equity due to the mutual mistake that both parties believed the Great Peace was in close proximity to the Cape Providence when the contract was concluded, which was not in fact true. However, at first instance Toulson J rejected the appellant's defence and awarded the sum claimed by the respondent. The appellant appealed against this decision and reasserted its original defence based upon the vitiating factor of mistake.

Held

It is a common factor, in contract law, that the parties to the contract must have a consensus ad idem, a meeting of the minds, in order for an agreement to be formed. If this is not evident from the facts in question, the formation of the agreement will not be of the same mind, which will render the contract either void or voidable by operation of law. To find out whether or not a contract had been concluded the Court of Appeal had to carry out an objective appraisal to reveal whether an agreement had been formed.

Lord Phillips MR carried out an exposition of the cases of *Bell* v *Lever Bros Ltd* [1932] AC 161 and *Solle* v *Butcher* [1950] 1 KB 671 to review the existing legal principles that apply to common mistake. Through the use of these cases and others he was able to examine the common law rules that apply to mistake. In particular the legal principles that apply to mistake may be seen to be harsh, but to some extent the courts have supplemented the harshness of the common law with its equitable jurisdiction. For example, a contract may be void at common law but would be voidable in equity. This was the crux of this appeal: to review the difficulties between applying the common law and the equitable application of the legal rules developed by the courts.

It was alleged that there was no contract, as the parties did not have a meeting of the minds (agreement). This premise was based on the mistaken belief of both parties that the vessels were in close proximity to one another when, in fact, they were not. The appellant contended that this was a fundamental mistake and that no agreement was ever reached. Lord Phillips MR examined the application of *Bell* v *Lever Bros* to this case in order to decide whether the fulfilling of the contract would have produced an outcome that neither party contemplated. If this was in fact the case, the mistake would deprive the parties from achieving the purpose of the contract and the effect would be to render the contract void. However, should the Court consider the common jurisdiction should not apply to it, it may, in prescribed circumstances, apply the equitable principles of mistake, as held by Lord Denning in *Solle* v *Butcher*. The Court of Appeal's interpretation of *Solle* v *Butcher* was that a party who had entered into a contract who found the bargain to be bad should be allowed to avoid the contract, thus curing the injustice. The Court of Appeal were not prepared to follow this decision and found that *Solle* v *Butcher* was not good law.

The Court of Appeal then referred back to the facts in question: was the distance between the two vessels likely to render the purpose of the contract impossible to perform? It was found, at first instance, that the vessels would have met within 22 hours. The appellants did not immediately cancel the agreement and this suggested that the purpose of the contract could be achieved, otherwise they would have cancelled immediately. Thus, it was the conclusion of the Court of Appeal that the contract entered into by the parties could be achieved and was not impossible to perform. They found the parties had entered into a legally binding agreement for the hire of the Great Peace and the appellants were entitled to cancel the agreement subject to the cancellation fee of five days hire. When the appellants engaged the services of the Nordfarer this cancelled the agreement with the Great Peace, and the appellant became liable for the cancellation fee.

Comment

This appeal tested the common law and the equitable doctrine of mutual/common mistake. Lord Phillips used the cases of *Bell v Lever Bros* and *Solle v Butcher* to draw a comparison between the common law and the equitable rules. He believed the decision in *Solle v Butcher* was wrong. The decision has reviewed the area of common mistake and illustrated the problems produced through case law.

Lewis v Averay [1971] 3 WLR 603

Court of Appeal (Lord Denning MR, Phillimore and Megaw LJJ)

- *Contract – deception as to identity*

Facts

The plaintiff advertised his car for sale in a local newspaper for £450. A rogue calling himself Green, and claiming to be a well-known actor, saw the car and wrote a cheque for it. He asked to take the car there and then (without waiting for the cheque to be cleared) and gave as proof of identity a film studio pass in the name of Green and bearing his photograph.

While the cheque was going through the rogue sold the car to an innocent purchaser, Averay. Later Averay wanted to see if the seller had a manual for repairs and contacted Lewis, whose name and address were in the log-book. The rogue's cheque had by this time been returned. Lewis sued Averay in conversion, claiming the car was still his.

Held

The appeal would be allowed.

Lord Denning MR:

'The real question in the case is whether there was a contract of sale under which the property in the car passed from Mr Lewis to the rogue. If there was such a contract, then even though it was voidable for fraud, nevertheless Mr Averay would get a good title to the car. But if there was no contract of sale by Mr Lewis to the rogue – either because there was, on the face of it, no agreement between the parties, or because any apparent agreement was a nullity and void ab initio for mistake, then no property would pass from Mr Lewis to the rogue. Mr Averay would not get a good title because the rogue had no property to pass to him.

There is no doubt that Mr Lewis was mistaken as to the identity of the person who handed him the cheque. He thought that he was Richard Greene, a film actor of standing and worth; whereas, in fact he was a rogue whose identity is quite unknown. It was under the influence of that mistake that Mr Lewis let the rogue have the car. He would not have dreamed of letting him have it otherwise.

What is the effect of this mistake? There are two cases in our books which cannot, in my mind, be reconciled the one with the other. One of them is *Phillips v Brooks Ltd* [1919] 2 KB 243, where a jeweller had a ring for sale. The other is *Ingram v Little* [1960] 3 WLR 504, where two ladies had a car for sale. In each case the story is very similar to the present. A plausible rogue comes along. The rogue says he likes the ring, or the car, as the case may be. He asks the price. The sellers name it. The rogue says he is prepared to buy it at that price. He pulls out a cheque book. He writes, or prepares to write, a cheque for the price. The seller hesitates. He has never met this man before. He does not want to hand over the ring or the car not knowing whether the cheque will be met. The rogue notices the seller's hesitation. He is quick with his next move. He says to the jeweller in *Phillips v Brooks*: I am Sir George Bullough of 11 St James's Square'; or the ladies in *Ingram v Little*: 'I am P G M Hutchinson of Standstead House, Standstead Road, Caterham'; or to the post graduate student in the present case: 'I am Richard Greene, the film actor of the Robin Hood series'. Each seller checks up the information. The jeweller looks up the directory and finds there is a Sir George Bullough at 11 St James' Square. The ladies check up too. They look at the telephone directory and find there is a 'P G M Hutchinson of Standstead House, Standstead Road, Caterham'. The post graduate student checks up too. He examines the official pass of the Pinewood Studios and finds that it is a pass for 'Richard A Green' to the Pinewood Studios with this man's photograph on it. In each case the seller finds that this is sufficient confirmation of the man's identity. So he accepts the cheque signed by the rogue and lets him have the ring in the one case and the car and log book in the other two cases. The rogue goes off and sells the goods to a third person, who buys them in entire good faith and pays the price to the rogue. The rogue disappears. The original seller presents the cheque. It is dishonoured. Who is entitled to the goods? The original seller? Or the ultimate buyer?

It seems to me that the material facts in each case are quite indistinguishable the one from the other. In each case there was, to all outward appearance, a contract: but there was a mistake by the seller as to the identity of the buyer. This mistake was fundamental. In each case it led to the handing over of the goods. Without it, the seller would not have parted with them.

This case therefore, raises the question: What is the effect of a mistake by one party as to the identity of the other? It has sometimes been said that if a party makes a mistake as to the identity of the person with whom he is contracting, there is no contract, or if there is a contract, it is a nullity and void so that no property can pass under it.

For instance, in *Ingram* v *Little*, the majority of the court suggested that the difference between *Phillips* v *Brooks* and *Ingram* v *Little* was that in *Phillips* v *Brooks* the contract of sale was concluded (so as to pass the property to the rogue) before the rogue made the fraudulent misrepresentation ... whereas in *Ingram* v *Little*, the rogue made the fraudulent misrepresentation before the contract was concluded. My own view is that in each case, the property in the goods did not pass until the seller let the rogue have the goods.

Again it has been suggested that a mistake as to the identity of a person is one thing: and a mistake as to his attributes is another. A mistake as to identity, it is said, avoids a contract: whereas a mistake as to attributes does not. But this is a distinction without a difference. A man's very name is one of his attributes. It is also a key to his identity.

When two parties have come to a contract – or rather what appears, on the face of it, to be a contract – the fact that one party is mistaken as to the identity of the other does not mean that there is no contract or that the contract is a nullity and void from the beginning. It only means that the contract is voidable, that is, liable to be set aside at the instance of the mistaken person, so long as he does so before third parties have, in good faith, acquired rights under it.

Applied to the cases such as the present, this principle is in full accord with the presumption stated by Pearce LJ and also Devlin LJ in *Ingram* v *Little*. When a dealing is had between a seller like Mr Lewis and a person who is actually there present before him, then the presumption in law is that there is a contract, even though there is a fraudulent impersonation by the buyer representing himself as a different man than he is. There is a contract made with the very person there, who is present in person. It is liable, no doubt to be avoided for fraud, but it is still a good contract, under which title will pass unless and until it is avoided.

In this case, Mr Lewis made a contract of sale with the very man, the rogue, who came to the flat. I say that he 'made a contract' because, in this regard, we do not look into his intentions or into his mind to know what he was thinking, or into the mind of the rogue. We look to the outward appearances. On the face of the dealing, Mr Lewis made a contract under which he sold the car to the rogue, delivered the car and the log book to him and took a cheque in return. It was, of course, induced by fraud. The rogue made false representations as to his identity. But it was still a contract, though voidable for fraud. It was a contract under which this property passed to the rogue and, in due course, passed from the rogue to Mr Averay before the contract was voided.

Though I very much regret that either of these good and reliable gentlemen should suffer, in my judgment, it is Mr Lewis who should do so. I think the appeal should be allowed.'

Comment

Followed: *Phillips v Brooks Ltd* [1919] 2 KB 243. Distinguished and doubted: *Ingram v Little* [1960] 3 WLR 504. See also *Ingram v Little* [1960] 3 WLR 504 and *Car and Universal Finance Co Ltd v Caldwell* [1965] 1 QB 525 which discuss the significance of identity in the former case and voidable contracts in the latter.

Shogun Finance Ltd v Hudson

[2003] 3 WLR 1371 House of Lords (Lords Nicholls of Birkenhead, Hobhouse of Woodborough, Millett, Phillips of Worth Matravers and Walker of Gestingthorpe)

• *Fraud – sale of goods – contract – hire purchase – mistaken identity – Hire Purchase Act 1964 and the nemo dat rule – sale void or voidable?*

Facts

This was an appeal from the decision of Brooke, Sedley and Dyson LJJ. On 10 June 1996 a rogue (X), impersonating a Mr Patel, went to a motor dealer's premises, Chris Varieva Ltd (CV), and informed the manager, a Mr Bailey (B), he wanted to purchase a Mitsubishi Shogun that was on display. The price was agreed and method of payment (hire purchase) was arranged with Shogun Finance (SF). X drove the vehicle away and sold it to a Mr Hudson (H), the defendant, for £17,000.

H was not a car dealer but a private purchaser and had purchased the vehicle in good faith. When all the facts came to light SF claimed the value of the vehicle from H. SF claimed they did not contract with X but with

Mr Patel. SF claimed that the identity of the purchaser was fundamental to the contract and that they only ever intended to sell the car to a Mr Patel. However, H claimed he acquired title (ownership) of the vehicle under s27 of the Hire Purchase Act 1964, as amended, which provides:

'(1) This section applies where a motor vehicle has been bailed … under a hire purchase agreement … and, before the property in the vehicle has become vested in the debtor, he disposes of the vehicle to another person.
(2) Where the disposition referred to in subs(1) above is to a private purchaser, and he is a purchaser of the motor vehicle in good faith, without notice of the hire purchase … agreement … that disposition shall have effect as if the creditor's title to the vehicle had been vested in the debtor immediately before that disposition.'

These subsections entitle an innocent third party to obtain ownership of a vehicle that is subject to a hire purchase agreement.

The contention between SF and H was whether or not X had the vehicle on hire purchase or was merely a thief. If it was the latter X could never pass title to an innocent third party (see *Rowland v Divall* [1923] 2 KB 500). However, if the former was accepted X could pass good title to H under s27 of the Hire Purchase Act 1964.

On appeal, Dyson LJ dismissed the appeal and confirmed the decision of the court of first instance. He found X not to be the hirer named in the written hire purchase agreement and, therefore, was not the debtor. On this basis, H was not able to apply s27 of the 1964 Act to defend the action. He went on to consider whether or not the agreement was void for mistaken identity or voidable for fraudulent misrepresentation. If the latter were to be accepted, the common law would have allowed X to pass good title to H, as long as the agreement had not been avoided. This principle was based upon the cases of *Phillips v Brooks* [1919] 2 KB 243 and *Lewis v Averay* [1972] 1 QB 198. However, if the former were

accepted X could never pass title to an innocent purchaser, an assessment supported by
Cundy v *Lindsay* (1878) 3 App Cas 459 and
Ingram v *Little* [1961] 1 QB 31. More importantly, Dyson LJ examined the principle enunciated by Sir Nicholas Browne-Wilkinson V-
C in *Hector* v *Lyons* (1989) 58 P & CR 156
which distinguished between mistaken identity within a written agreement and an agreement made face-to-face. He was of the opinion
that when parties are identified within such a
written agreement then identity is fundamental
and the contract is void if one party turns out
to have been lying.

Dyson LJ went on to consider whether or
not CV, the car dealer, was acting as agent for
SF. If CV was an agent for SF then this would
be a face-to-face agreement and *Phillips* v
Brooks would apply, resulting in a voidable
contract. However, Dyson LJ was of the
opinion that the dealer was not the agent of
SF but had merely had various functions and
tasks delegated to him, which included ascertaining the identity of prospective hirers.
Dyson LJ followed this approach based upon
Mercantile Credit Co Ltd v *Hamblin* [1965] 2
QB 242, where Pearson LJ stated:

> 'In a typical hire purchase transaction the
> dealer is a party in his own right, selling his
> car to the finance company, and he is acting
> primarily on his own behalf and not as
> general agent for either of the two parties.
> There is no need to attribute to him an
> agency in order to account for his participa-
> tion in the transaction. Nevertheless the
> dealer is to some extent an intermediary
> between the customer and the finance
> company, and he may well have in a partic-
> ular case some ad-hoc agencies to do par-
> ticular things on behalf of one or other or it
> may be both of those two parties.'

Brooke LJ agreed with Dyson LJ's judgment
and also dismissed the appeal. However,
Sedley LJ dissented. H was given leave to
appeal to the House of Lords.

Held
Lord Phillips of Worth Matravers was of the
opinion that extrinsic evidence needed to be
sought to establish whether or not a contract
had been made and referred to Lord
Hatherly's dictum in *Cundy* v *Lindsay*:

> '... from beginning to end the respondents
> believed they were dealing with Blenkiron
> & Co, they made out their invoices to
> Blenkiron & Co, they supposed they sold to
> Blenkiron & Co, they never sold in any way
> to Alfred Blenkarn; and therefore Alfred
> Blenkarn cannot, by so obtaining the goods,
> have by possibility made a good title to a
> purchaser, as against the owners of the
> goods, who had never in any shape or way
> parted with the property nor with anything
> more than the possession of it.'

Thus, the intention was to deal with a specific
person who existed at the time and was known
to the offeree and not to contract with anyone
else. Lord Phillips contrasted this point with
the case of *Kings Norton Metal Co* v *Edridge*
(1897) 14 TLR 98. In this case a rogue
attempted to pass himself off as someone else.
He did this by having notepaper printed in the
name of Hallam & Co, and pretended to carry
on business in that name. The rogue ordered a
ton of brass rivet wire from the plaintiff manufacturers. The wire was delivered to the
rogue, on credit, and the rogue sold it on to
the defendant. In this instance the Court of
Appeal held that a contract had come into
being between the plaintiff and the rogue, who
had passed on title to the innocent third party
(the defendant) before the contract had been
avoided. The reason for the decision in this
case was based upon the fact that no such
company called Hallam & Co existed and did
not come within the decision of *Cundy* v
Lindsay. Therefore, if a person describes
himself by a false name it will not prevent the
conclusion of a contract. In *Kings Norton* the
plaintiff intended to deal with whoever was
using the name Hallam & Co. The plaintiff
was unable to demonstrate that he was intending to contract with anyone other than the
rogue.

Lord Phillips considered *Phillips* v *Brooks*
[1919] 2 KB 243 and *Lewis* v *Averay* [1972]

1 QB 198 but was not convinced, in this instance, that the ratio of those cases applied to this case. Instead, he concluded that a written document which ascertains the identity of a hirer, which turns out to be a fraud, is void based upon the application of *Cundy* v *Lindsay*. Therefore, the rogue never had a hire purchase contract with SF and was not able to pass title to Mr Hudson. Lord Hobhouse and Lord Walker concurred with the decision of Lord Phillips but Lord Nicholls and Lord Millett dissented.

Comment

Fraudulent misrepresentation and mistaken identity is governed to some extent by legis-lation, such as ss23 and 25 of the Sale of Goods Act 1979 and the Hire Purchase Act 1964. However, case law has developed this area and driven it to its final destination. This was a difficult case and an innocent party was going to lose out; in this instance it was H. This decision could have easily have gone the other way, since it was two to three in favour of SF. The question remains, nevertheless, as to whether this finding has clarified the law to any appreciable degree. On the contrary, it would generally appear the courts' decisions have produced a legal quagmire which needs to be resolved by Parliament. Until such time, *Shogun Finance* v *Hudson* must be followed.

3 Types of Obligations Created

Bissett v Wilkinson [1927] AC 177
Privy Council (Viscount Dunedin, Lords Atkinson, Phillimore, Carson and Merrivale)

- *Expression of opinion – number of sheep land would carry*

Facts
A vendor admitted that he had told prospective purchasers that certain land in New Zealand 'would carry 2,000 sheep' and that they bought the land in this belief. It turned out that the land did not have this capacity and, inter alia, the purchasers claimed rescission of the agreement.

Held
Their claim would fail.

Lord Merrivale:

'In an action for rescission, as in an action for specific performance of an executory contract, when misrepresentation is the alleged ground of relief of the party who repudiates the contract, it is, of course, essential to ascertain whether that which is relied on is a representation of a specific fact, or a statement of opinion, since an erroneous opinon stated by the party affirming the contract, though it may have been relied on and have induced the contract on the part of the party who seeks rescission, gives no title to relief unless fraud is established …

In the present case, as in those cited, the material facts of the transaction, the knowledge of the parties respectively, and their relative positions, the words of representation used, and the actual condition of the subject matter spoken of, are relevant to the two inquiries necessary to be made. What was the meaning of the representation? Was it true? …

As was said by Sim J [the trial judge]:

"In ordinary circumstances, any statement made by an owner who has been occupying his own farm as to its carrying capacity would be regarded as a statement of fact … This, however, is not such a case. The purchasers knew all about Hogan's block and knew also what sheep the farm was carrying when they inspected it. In these circumstances … the purchasers were not justified in regarding anything said by the vendor as to the carrying capacity as being anything more than an expression of his opinion on the subject."

In this view of the matter their Lordships concur.

Whether the vendor honestly and in fact held the opinion which he stated remained to be considered. This involved examination of the history and condition of the property. If a reasonable man with the vendor's knowledge could not have come to the conclusion he stated, the description of that conclusion as an opinion would not necessarily protect him against rescission for misrepresentation, but what was actually the capacity in competent hands of the land the purchasers purchased had never been, and never was, practically ascertained …

It is of dominant importance that Sim J negatived the purchasers' charge of fraud.

After attending to the close and very careful examination of the evidence which was made by learned counsel for each of the parties, their Lordships entirely concur in the view which was expressed by the learned judge who heard the case. The purchasers failed to prove that the farm, if properly managed, was not capable of carrying 2,000 sheep.'

Comment
See also *Attwood* v *Small* (1838) 5 Cl & Fin 232 which discusses the issues of a purchaser relying on information.

Derry **v** *Peek* (1889) 14 App Cas 337 House of Lords (Lord Halsbury LC, Lords Watson, Bramwell, FitzGerald and Herschell)

• *Misrepresentation – belief in truth in an action for deceit*

Facts
A special Act incorporating a tramway company provided that the carriages might be moved by animal power and, with the consent of the Board of Trade, by steam power. The directors issued a prospectus containing a statement that by this special Act the company had the right to use steam instead of horses. The plaintiff bought shares on the strength of this statment. The Board of Trade later refused to consent to the use of steam and the company was wound up. The plaintiff brought an action for deceit.

Held
1. In an action for deceit, it is not enough to establish misrepresentation alone; something more must be proved to cast liability on the defendant.
2. There is an essential difference between the case where the defendant honestly believes in the truth of a statement although he is careless, and where he is careless with no such honest belief.
3. A mere statement by the defendant that he believed something to be true is not conclusive proof that it was so. Fraud is established where it is proved that a false statement is made:
   a) knowingly;
   b) without belief in its truth;
   c) recklessly, careless as to whether it be true or false. There must, to prevent

fraud, always be an honest belief in its truth.

If fraud is proved, the motive of the person making the statement is irrelevant. It matters not that there was no intention to cheat or injure the person to whom the statement was made.

4. The defendants were not fraudulent in this case. They made a careless statement but they honestly believed in its truth.

Comment
See also *Edginton* v *Fitzmaurice* (1885) 29 Ch D 459 which discusses the issues of mis-statements and a material misrepresentation and *Barton* v *County Natwest Ltd* [1999] Lloyd's Rep Bank 408.

Esso Petroleum Co Ltd **v** *Mardon* [1976] 2 WLR 583 Court of Appeal (Lord Denning MR, Ormrod and Shaw LJJ)

• *Lease of petrol station – estimate of sales*

Facts
The plaintiffs acquired a busy main street site for a petrol station on the basis of calculations showing an estimated annual consumption of 200,000 gallons from the third year. The planning authority insisted on access only from side streets: this falsified the calculations but, through lack of care, the plaintiffs failed to revise their original estimate. During negotiations for a tenancy, the plaintiffs' representative, a person of 40 years' experience, told the defendant in good faith that throughput had been estimated at 200,000 gallons in the third year. This the defendant doubted, but in the light of the representative's greater expertise he took the tenancy. It turned out that the site was capable only of an annual throughput of some 70,000 gallons and, although he took a new tenancy at a reduced rent, the defendant lost heavily. In response to the plaintiffs' claim for possession and petrol supplied, the

defendant claimed damages for breach of warranty and negligent misrepresentation.

Held

He was entitled to succeed and the measure of damages was the loss he had suffered by having been induced to enter into a disastrous contract. By taking a new tenancy, he had acted reasonably in attempting to mitigate his losses.

Lord Denning MR:

'Counsel for Esso retaliated, however, by citing *Bisset* v *Wilkinson* where the Privy Council said that a statement by a New Zealand farmer that an area of land "would carry 2,000 sheep" was only an expression of opinion. He submitted that the forecast here of 200,000 gallons was an expression of opinion and not a statement of fact; and that it could not be interpreted as a warranty or promise.

Now, I would quite agree with counsel for Esso that it was not a warranty – in this sense – that it did not *guarantee* that the throughput *would be* 200,000 gallons. But, nevertheless, it was a forecast made by a party, Esso, who had special knowledge and skill. It was the yardstick ... by which they measured the worth of a filling station. They knew the facts. They knew the traffic in the town. They knew the throughput of comparable stations. They had much experience and expertise at their disposal. They were in a much better position than Mr Mardon to make a forecast. It seems to me that if such a person makes a forecast – intending that the other should act on it and he does act on it – it can well be interpreted as a warranty that the forecast is sound and reliable in this sense that they made it with reasonable care and skill. It is just as if Esso said to Mr Mardon. "Our forecast of throughput is 200,000 gallons. You can rely on it as being a sound forecast of what the service station should do. The rent is calculated on that footing." If the forecast turned out to be an unsound forecast, such as no person of skill or expierence should have made, there is a breach of warranty ... It is very different

from the New Zealand case where the land had never been used as sheep farm and both parties were equally able to form an opinion as to its carrying capacity.

In the present case it seems to me that there was a warranty that the forecast was sound, that is that Esso had made it with reasonable care and skill. That warranty was broken. Most negligently Esso made a "fatal error" in the forecast they stated to Mr Mardon, and on which he took the tenancy. For this they are liable in damages ...

It seems to me that *Hedley Byrne*, properly understood, covers this particular proposition: if a man, who has or professes to have special knowledge or skill, makes a representation by virtue thereof to another – be it advice, information or opinion – with the intention of inducing him to enter into a contract with him, he is under a duty to use reasonable care to see that the representation is correct, and that the advice, information or opinion is reliable. If he negligently gives unsound advice or misleading information or expresses an erroneous opinion, and thereby induces the other side into a contract with him, he is liable in damages ...

Applying this principle, it is plain that Esso professed to have – and did in fact have – special knowledge or skill in estimating the throughput of a filling station. They made the representation – they forecast a throughput of 200,000 gallons – intending to induce Mr Mardon to enter into a tenancy on the faith of it. They made it negligently. It was a "fatal error". And thereby induced Mr Mardon to enter into a contract of tenancy that was disastrous to him. For this misprepresentation they are liable in damages.'

Comment

See also *Solle* v *Butcher* [1950] 2 WLR 583 which discusses the distinction between mistake and misrepresentation and its application to set aside a lease. However, this case has since been criticised in *Great Peace Shipping Ltd* v *Tsavliris Salvage (International) Ltd* [2002] 4 All ER 689 where the Court of Appeal discussed contract and mutual mistake. See also *With* v *O'Flanagan* [1936] Ch 575 which deals with a continuing representation.

Hong Kong Fir Shipping Co Ltd v *Kawasaki Kisen Kaisha Ltd* [1962] 2 WLR 474 Court of Appeal (Sellers, Upjohn and Diplock LJJ)

• *Charter – vessel breakdowns*

Facts
The defendants chartered the vessel 'Hong Kong Fir' from the plaintiffs for 24 months; the charterparty provided 'she being fitted in every way for ordinary cargo service'. It transpired that the engine room staff were incompetent and the vessel spent less than nine weeks of the first seven months of the charter at sea because of breakdowns and consequent repairs required to make her seaworthy. The defendants repudiated the charterparty and claimed that the term as to seaworthiness was a condition of the contract, any breach of which entitled them so to do.

Held
The term was neither a condition nor a warranty and in determining whether the defendants could terminate the contract, it was necessary to look at the consequences of the breach to see if they deprived the innocent party of substantially the whole benefit he should have received under the contract. On the facts, this was not the case, because the charterparty still had a substantial time to run.

Diplock LJ:

'No doubt there are many simple contractual undertakings, sometimes express but more often, because of their very simplicity ("It goes without saying"), to be implied, of which it can be predicted that every breach of such an undertaking must give rise to an event which will deprive the party not in default of substantialy the whole benefit which it was intended that he should obtain from the contract. And such a stipulation, unless the parties have agreed that breach

of it shall not entitle the non-defaulting party to treat the contract as repudiated, is a "condition". So too, there may be other simple contractual undertakings of which it can be predicted that *no* breach can give rise to an event which will deprive the party not in default of substantially the whole benefit which it was intended that he should obtain from the contract; and such a stipulation, unless the parties have agreed that breach of it shall entitle the non-defaulting party to treat the contract as repudiated, is a "warranty".

There are, however, many contractual undertakings, of a more complex character which cannot be categorised as being "conditions" or "warranties" if the late nineteenth-century meaning adopted in the Sale of Goods Act 1893 and used by Bowen LJ in *Bentsen* v *Taylor Sons & Co* be given to those terms. Of such undertakings, all that can be predicted is that some breaches will, and others will not, give rise to an event which will deprive the party not in default of substantially the whole benefit which it was intended that he should obtain from the contract; and the legal consequences of a breach of such an undertaking, unless provided for expressly in the contract, depend upon the nature of the event to which the breach gives rise and do not follow automatically from a prior classification of the undertaking as a "condition" or a "warranty". For instance, to take Bramwell B's example in *Jackson* v *Union Marine Insurance Co Ltd* itself, breach of an undertaking by a shipowner to sail with all possible dispatch to a named port, does not necessarily relieve the charterer of further performance of his obligation under the charterparty, but if the breach is so prolonged that the contemplated voyage is frustrated, it does have this effect.

In 1874, when the doctrine of frustration was being foaled by "impossibility of performance" out of "condition precedent", it is not surprising that the explanation given by Bramwell B should give full credit to the dam by suggesting that, in addition to the express warranty to sail with all possible dispatch, there was an implied *condition precedent* that the ship should arrive at the named port in time for the voyage contemplated. In *Jackson* v *Union Marine Insurance Co Ltd* there was no breach of the express warranty; but if there had been, to engraft the implied condition upon the express warranty would have been merely a more complicated way of saying that a breach of a shipowner's undertaking to sail with all possible dispatch may, but will not necessarily, give rise to an event which will deprive the charterer of substantially the whole benefit which it was intended that he should obtain from the charter. Now that the doctrine of frustration has matured and flourished for nearly a century, and the old technicalities of pleading "conditions precedent" are more than a century out of date, it does not clarify but, on the contrary, obscures the modern principle of law where such an event *has* occurred as a result of a breach of an express stipulation in a contract, to continue to add the now unnecessary colophon "Therefore it was an implied *condition* of the contract that a particular 'kind of breach' of an express *warranty* should not occur". The common law evolves not merely by breeding new principles but also, when they are fully grown, by burying their progenitors.

As my brethren have already pointed out, the shipowner's undertaking to tender a seaworthy ship has, as a result of numerous decisions as to what can amount to "unseaworthiness", become one of the most complex of contractual undertakings. It embraces obligations with respect to every part of the hull and machinery, stores and equipment, and the crew itself. It can be broken by the presence of trivial defects easily and rapidly remediable, as well as by defects which must inevitably result in a total loss of the vessel.

Consequently, the problem in this case is, in my view, neither solved nor soluble by debating whether the shipowner's express or implied undertaking to tender a seaworthy ship is a "condition" or a "warranty". It is like so many other contractual terms; an undertaking, one breach of which may give rise to an event which relieves the charterer of further performance of his undertakings if he so elects, and another breach of which may not give rise to such an event but entitle him only to monetary compensation in the form of damages. It is, with all deference to Mr Ashton Roskill's skilful argument, by no means surprising that among the many hundreds of previous cases about the shipowner's undertaking to deliver a seaworthy ship, there is none where it was found profitable to discuss in the judgments the question whether that undertaking is a "condition" or a "warranty"; for the true answer, as I have already indicated, is that it is neither, but one of that large class of contractual undertakings, one breach of which may have the same effect as that ascribed to a breach of "condition" under the Sale of Goods Act 1893 and a different breach of which may have only the same effect as that ascribed to a breach of "warranty" under that Act. The cases referred to by Sellers LJ illustrate this and I would only add that in the dictum which he cites from *Kish* v *Taylor* it seems to me, from the sentence which immediately follows it, as from the actual decision in the case, and the whole tenor of Lord Atkinson's speech itself, that the word "will" was intended to be "may".'

Comment

The decision in *Hong Kong Fir* created uncertainty and was not applied in the case of *The Mihalis Angelos* [1970] 3 All ER 125: instead the classic approach of labelling a term either a warranty or a condition was applied. See also *Poussard* v *Spiers and Pond* (1876) 1 QB 410 and *Bettini* v *Gye* (1876) 1 QB 183 which demonstrate how the court will decide whether a term that has been broken is a warranty or a condition.

Jarvis v *Swan Tours Ltd* [1972] 3 WLR 954 Court of Appeal (Lord Denning MR, Edmund Davies and Stephenson LJJ)

• *Breach of contract – measure of damages*

Facts

The plaintiff booked a winter sports holiday with the defendants, on the strength of their brochure which promised a 'houseparty' with special entertainments. Many of the entertainments were lacking and the 'houseparty' consisted in the second week of the plaintiff alone.

Held

The plaintiff was entitled to recover not just the basic cost of the holiday, but compensation for disappointment and loss of entertainment he ought to have had.

Lord Denning MR:

'What is the legal position? I think that the statements in the brochure were representations or warranties. The breaches of them give Mr Jarvis a right to damages. It is not necessary to decide whether they were representations or warranties: because since the Misrepresentation Act 1967 there is a remedy in damages for misrepresentations as well as for breach of warranty.

The one question in the case is: what is the amount of damages? The judge seems to have taken the difference in value between what he paid for and what he got. He said that he intended to give "the difference between the two values and no other damages" under any other head. He thought that Mr Jarvis had got half of what he paid for. So the judge gave him half the amount which he had paid, namely £31.72. Mr Jarvis appeals to this court. He says that the damages ought to have been much more.

What is the right way of assessing damages? It has often been said that on a breach of contract, damages cannot be given for mental distress. I think that those limitations are out of date. In a proper case, damages for shock can be recovered in tort. One such case is a contract for a holiday, or any other contract to provide entertainment and enjoyment. If the contracting party breaks his contract, damages can be given for the disappointment, the distress, the upset and frustration caused by the breach. I know that it is difficult to assess in terms of

money, but it is no more difficult than the assessment which the courts have to make every day in personal injury cases for loss of amenities.

I think the judge was in error in taking the sum paid for the holiday, £63.45, and halving it. The right measure of damages is to compensate him for the loss of entertainment and enjoyment which he was promised and which he did not get.

Looking at the matter quite broadly, I think the damages in this case should be the sum of £125 ... I would allow the appeal accordingly.'

Leaf v International Galleries
[1950] 2 KB 86 Court of Appeal (Sir Raymond Evershed MR, Denning and Jenkins LJJ)

- *Misrepresentation – right to rescind*

Facts

The plaintiff bought from the defendants an oil painting of Salisbury Cathedral which was represented to him as a painting by Constable, a representation which was held to be one of the terms of the contract. Five years later he discovered that it was not a Constable and he sought rescission of the contract on the ground of innocent misrepresentation.

Held

He could not succeed.

Denning LJ:

'The question is whether the buyer is entitled to rescind the contract on that account. I emphasise that this a claim to rescind only. There is no claim in this action for damages for breach of condition or breach of warranty. The claim is simply one for rescission ... The only question is whether the buyer is entitled to rescind. The way in which the case is put by counsel for the buyer is this. He says this was an innocent misrepresentation and that in equity he is entitled to claim rescission even of an executed contract of sale on that account. He points out that the judge has found that it is quite possible to restore the parties to the same position that they were in originally, by the buyer simply handing back the picture to the sellers in return for the repayment of the purchase price.

In my opinion, this case is to be decided according to the well known principles applicable to the sale of goods. This was a contract for the sale of goods. There was a mistake about the quality of the subject matter, because both parties believed the picture to be a Constable, and that mistake was in one sense essential or fundamental. Such a mistake, however, does not avoid the contract. There was no mistake about the subject matter of the sale. It was a specific picture of "Salisbury Cathedral". The parties were agreed in the same terms on the same subject matter, and that is sufficient to make a contract: see *Solle* v *Butcher*. There was a term in the contract as to the quality of the subject matter, namely, as to the person by whom the picture was painted – that it was by Constable. That term of the contract was either a condition or a warranty. If it was a condition, the buyer could reject the picture for breach of the condition at any time before he accepted it or was to be deemed to have accepted it, whereas, if it was only a warranty, he could not reject it but was confined to a claim for damages.

I think it right to assume in the buyer's favour that this term was a condition, and that, if he had come in proper time, he could have rejected the picture, but the right to reject for breach of condition has always been limited by the rule that once the buyer has accepted, or is deemed to have accepted, the goods in performance of the contract, he cannot therefore reject, but is relegated to his claim for damages ... In this case this buyer took the picture into his house, and five years passed before he intimated any rejection. That, I need hardly say, is much more than a reasonable time. It is far too late for him at the end of five years to reject this picture for breach of any condition. His remedy after that length of time is for damages only, a claim which he has not brought before the court.'

Comment

Distinguished in *Peco Arts Inc* v *Hazlitt Gallery Ltd* [1983] 1 WLR 1315.

See also *Naughton* v *O'Callaghan* [1990] 3 All ER 191 and *Royscott Trust Ltd* v *Rogerson* [1991] 3 WLR 57 to demonstrate how the court awards damages for misrepresentation; *Harlingdon & Leinster Enterprises Ltd* v *Christopher Hull Fine Art Ltd* [1990] 3 WLR 13 which discusses ss13 and 14 of the Sale of Goods Act 1979 and *Drake* v *Agnew & Sons Limited* [2002] EWHC 294 which distinguishes between opinion and a representation and *Smith* v *Eric S Bush* [1990] 1 AC 831. The latter case discusses whether it is reasonable for a representee to make use of an opportunity to discover the truth of a representation: failure to exercise such an opportunity would defeat a claim in misrepresentation or, alternatively, raise a defence of contributory negligence.

With v *O'Flanagan* [1936] Ch 575 Court of Appeal (Lord Wright MR, Romer LJ and Clauson J)

- *Continuing representation – sale of medical practice*

Facts

Desiring to sell his medical practice, the defendant truthfully told the plaintiff that it brought in £2,000 pa and that he had a panel of 1,480 persons. During the four months of negotiations before the contract of sale was signed the defendant was ill: takings dwindled to practically nothing and the number of panel patients fell to 1,260. These facts were not disclosed to the plaintiff, but he discovered them immediately after completion and he sought rescission of the contract.

Held

He was entitled to succeed.

Romer LJ:

'The only principle invoked by the [plaintiff] in this case is as follows. If A, with a view to inducing B to enter into a contract makes a representation as to a material fact, then if at a later date and before the contract is actually entered into, owing to a change of circumstances, the representation then made would to the knowledge of A be untrue and B subsequently enters into the contract in ignorance of that change of circumstances and relying upon that representation, A cannot hold B to the bargain. There is ample authority for that statement and, indeed, I doubt myself whether any authority is necessary, it being, it seems to me, so obviously consistent with the plainest principles of equity.'

Comment

See also *Redgrave* v *Hurd* (1881) 20 Ch D 1 which discusses the opportunity to discover a misrepresentation, and *Smith* v *Eric S Bush* [1990] 1 AC 831 which discussed whether it was reasonable for a representee to make use of an opportunity to discover the truth of a representation: failure to exercise such an opportunity would affect a claim in misrepresentation or, alternatively, raise a defence of contributory negligence.

4 Duties of the Seller I: Title, Delivery and Quantity

Arcos Ltd v *E A Ronaasen & Son*
[1933] AC 470 House of Lords
(Lords Buckmaster, Blanesburgh,
Warrington, Atkin and Macmillan)

• *Purchase of goods – right to reject*

Facts
The appellants agreed to sell to the respondents redwood and whitewood staves of a thickness of half an inch. When they arrived, the respondents claimed to reject them on the ground that they did not correspond with the description in that they were more than half an inch thick.

Held
They were entitled to do so.

Lord Atkin:

'On the facts as stated by the umpire as of the time of inspection only about 5 per cent of the goods corresponded with the description, and the umpire finds it impossible to say what proportion conformed at the time of shipment. It was contended that in all commercial contracts the question was whether there was a "substantial" compliance with the contract; there always must be some margin, and it is for the tribunal of fact to determine whether the margin is exceeded or not. I cannot agree. If the written contract specifies conditions of weight, measurement, and the like, those conditions must be complied with. A ton does not mean about a ton, or a yard about a yard. Still less, when you descend to minute measurements, does 1/2 inch mean about 1/2 inch. If the seller wants a margin he must, and in my experience does, stipulate for it ...

No doubt, there may be microscopic deviations which business men, and, therefore, lawyers, will ignore. And in this respect it is necessary to remember that description and quantity are not necessarily the same, and that the legal rights in respect of them are regulated by different sections of the code, description by s13, quantity by s30 [of the Sale of Goods Act 1893]. It will be found that most of the cases that admit any deviation from the contract are cases where there has been an excess or deficiency in quantity which the court has considered negligible.

But, apart from this consideration, the right view is that the conditions of the contract must be strictly performed. If a condition is not performed, the buyer has a right to reject. I do not myself think that there is any difference between business men and lawyers on this matter. No doubt in business men often find it unnecessary or inexpedient to insist on their strict legal rights. In a normal market, if they get something substantially like the specified goods, they may take them with or without grumbling and claim for an allowance. But in a falling market I find that buyers are often as eager to insist on their legal rights as courts of law are ready to maintain them. No doubt at all times sellers are prepared to take a liberal view as to the rigidity of their own obligations and possibly buyers who in turn are sellers may also dislike too much precision. But buyers are not, as far as my experience goes, inclined to think that the rights defined in the code are in excess of business needs. It may be desirable to add that the result in this case is in no way affected by the umpire's finding that the goods were fit for the particular purpose for which they were required. The implied condition under s14(1), unless, of course, the contract provides otherwise, is additional to the condition under s13 [of the 1893 Act]. A man may require goods for a particular purpose and make it known to the seller so as to secure the implied condition of fitness for that purpose, but there is no reason why he should not abandon that purpose if he pleases and apply the goods to any purpose for which the description makes them suitable. If they do not correspond with the description there seems no business or legal reason why he should not reject them if he finds it convenient so to do.'

Comment

See *Jackson* v *Rotax Motor and Cycle Co* [1910] 2 KB 937 which also deals with the right to reject goods and also s15A of the Sale of Goods Act 1979. *Jewson Ltd* v *Leanne Teresa Bayham as Personal Representative of the Estate of Thomas Michael Kelly* [2003] EWCA Civ 1030 which deals with partial reliance and s14(3) of the Sale of Goods Act 1979 are also useful. Also refer to the Sale and Supply of Goods to Consumers Regulations, which came into force from the 31 March 2003, and provide additional protection for consumers, ie, people who are buying for purposes not related to their trade, business or profession.

Compagnie Commerciale Sucres et Denrées v *C Czarnikow Ltd, The Naxos* [1990] 1 WLR 1337 House of Lords (Lords Bridge of Harwich, Brandon of Oakbrook, Ackner, Oliver of Aylmerton and Jauncey of Tullichettle)

- *Breach of stipulation as to time*

Facts

A contract for the sale and purchase of 12,000 metric tons of sugar provided, inter alia, 'the Seller shall have the sugar ready to be delivered to the Buyer at any time within the con-

tract period' and that the buyer 'having given reasonable notice, shall be entitled to call for delivery of the sugar between the first and last working day inclusive of the period of delivery'. The contract also provided that delivery was to be made to 'one or more vessels presenting ready to load' during May/June 1986, and that the buyer was to give the seller 'not less than 14 days' notice of vessel(s) expected readiness to load'. On 15 May the buyers gave due notice to the sellers that their vessel would arrive at the agreed loading port to lift the full cargo between 29 and 31 May 1986. The vessel presented itself ready for loading on 29 May but, despite repeated calls by the buyers and a warning on 27 May that if loading did not commence on 29 May the buyers would hold the sellers in default, the sellers did not have the sugar ready to be delivered to the buyers. On 3 June the buyers telexed the sellers setting out those facts, holding them in default for not providing the cargo and informing them that the buyers were treating the contract as terminated and had purchased a replacement cargo. The buyers made a claim for the difference between the contract price of the cargo and the market price on 3 June represented by the cost of the replacement cargo and for loss of despatch which would have been earned had the vessel not remained idle while awaiting a cargo.

Held

The buyers' claim would be successful.

Lord Ackner:

'I agree ... that here "ready to be delivered" in its context means that the sugar must be available for loading without delay or interruption in the event that the vessel is able to start loading at once and to continue without interruption ...

Since the whole purpose of the buyers' call, which must be given on reasonable notice, was to enable the sellers to make arrangements for the sugar to be "ready to be delivered", counsel for the sellers submitted that it did not make sense to require the sellers to have such arrangements in place throughout the whole contractual period. But the requirements "*at any time within the contract period*" and not "*at all times*". The particular time is when the vessel duly nominated by the buyers presents herself ready to load ...

If I have thus correctly interpreted [the relevant clause] it can be restated in these terms: the seller shall have the sugar called forward available for loading without delay or interruption as soon as the vessel is ready to load the cargo in question ...

I [remind] myself of the statements of principle made in this House in *Bunge Corp v Tradax SA* [1981] 2 All ER 513 esp at 542 per Lord Wilberforce. Having stated that the courts should not be too ready to interpret contractual clauses as conditions, Lord Wilberforce said:

> "But I do not doubt that, in suitable cases, the courts should not be reluctant, if the intentions of the parties as shown by the contract so indicate, to hold that an obligation has the force of a condition, and that indeed they should usually do so in the case of time clauses in mercantile contracts."

Lord Wilberforce then accepted as being correct the statement of the law in 9 Halsbury's Laws (4th edn) paras 481-482 asserting:

> "(1) that the court will require precise compliance with stipulations as to time wherever the circumstances of the case indicate this would fulfil the intention of the parties, and (2) that broadly speaking time will be considered of the essence in 'mercantile' contracts ..."

This clearly was a mercantile contract and [the relevant clause] can properly be described as a "time clause". It imposes an obligation to have the goods called forward available for loading at a definite point of time: at the expiration of the notice given under [the contract] and as soon as the vessel presents herself ready to load within the contract period ...

[The relevant clause] was crucially important to the buyers since it removed the risk that the absence or insufficiency of cargo would be a cause of delay. Since it must be rare, if ever, for it to be in the sellers' interest to load a vessel very slowly, the rule ensures to a very large extent that loading will be promptly commenced and speedily carried out and thus enable the buyers punctually to perform their own obligations to their customers. The rule tends to provide certainty which is such an indispensable ingredient of mercantile contracts.'

Rickards (Charles) Ltd v Oppenheim
[1950] 1 KB 616 Court of Appeal (Bucknill, Singleton and Denning LJJ)

- *Waiver – condition as to time*

Facts

Wanting a new Rolls Royce, the defendant contracted with the plaintiffs to supply a chassis and to build a body on it within seven months, time being of the essence. As sub-contractors failed to complete the work within the stipulated time, the defendant waived the time condition by pressing for delivery on successive later dates. About three months after the original delivery date, the sub-contractor said the car would be ready in two weeks and, on the following day, the defendant gave the sub-contractor written notice that, unless he received the car within four weeks, he would be unable to accept delivery. The sub-contractors forwarded the notice to the plaintiffs after eight or nine days. The car was not delivered within the four weeks and, when it was, the defendant refused delivery.

Held

The defendant could rescind the contract. After waiving the initial stipulation as to time, he had been entitled to give reasonable notice again making time the essence and this he had done.

Denning LJ:

> 'If the defendant, as he did, led the plaintiffs to believe that he would not insist on

the stipulation as to time, and that, if they carried out the work, he would accept it, and they did it, he could not afterwards set up the stipulation in regard to time against them. Whether it be called waiver or for-bearance on his part, or an agreed variation or substituted performance, does not matter. It is a kind of estoppel. By his conduct he made a promise not to insist on his strict legal rights. That promise was intended to be binding, intended to be acted on, and was, in fact, acted on. He cannot afterwards go back on it. That, I think, … was … antic-ipated in *Bruner v Moore*. It is a particular application of the principle which I endeav-oured to state in *Central London Property Trust Ltd v High Trees House Ltd*.

Therefore, if the matter stopped there, the plaintiffs could have said that, notwithstand-ing that more than seven months had elapsed, the defendant was bound to accept, but the matter does not stop there, because delivery was not given in compliance with the requests of the defendant. Time and time again the defendant pressed for delivery, time and time again he was assured that he would have early delivery, but he never got satisfaction, and eventually at the end of June he gave notice saying that, unless the car was delivered by 25 July, he would not accept it. The question thus arises whether he was entitled to give such a notice, making time of the essence … In my judgment, he was entitled to give a reasonable notice making time of the essence of the matter. Adequate protection to the suppliers is given by the requirement that the notice should be reasonable.'

Rowland v *Divall* [1923] 2 KB 500
Court of Appeal (Bankes, Scrutton and Atkin LJJ)

• *No right to sell goods – recovery of price paid*

Facts
In May 1922 the plaintiff dealer bought a car from the defendant. He sold it in July, but in September the police took possession of the vehicle on the ground that it was a stolen car and that the person who had sold it to the defendant had no title to sell it. The plaintiff sued to recover the price which he had paid the defendant for the car.

Held
He was entitled to succeed as the defendant had been in breach of the condition implied by statute that he had the right to sell the car.

Scrutton LJ:

'It certainly seems to me that in a case of rescission for the breach of a condition that the seller has a right to sell the goods, it cannot be that the purchaser is deprived of his right to get back the purchase money because he cannot restore the goods which, from the nature of the transaction, are not the goods of the seller at all, and which the seller has, therefore, no right to in any cir-cumstances. For these reasons it seems to me, with deference to the learned judge below, that he came to a wrong conclusion and that the plaintiff is entitled to recover the whole of the purchase money, as and for the total failure of the consideration, inas-much as the seller did not give that which he contracted to give, namely, the legal own-ership of the car and the legal right to pos-session of it.'

Comment
Applied in *Butterworth v Kingsway Motors Ltd* [1954] 1 WLR 1286. See also *Central Newbury Car Auctions Ltd v Unity Finance Ltd* [1957] 1 QB 371 which discusses the transfer of title by a non-owner and estoppel and *Du Jardin v Beadman Bros Ltd* [1952] 2 QB 712 which deals with possession of goods obtained through trickery and title. See, too, the case of *National Employers Mutual General Insurance Association Ltd v Jones* [1988] 2 WLR 952 and *Butterworth v Kingsway Motors* [1954] 1 WLR 1286 which discuss the implications of a total failure of consideration and the rights to rescind the con-tract.

5 Duties of the Seller II: Quality

Arcos Ltd v E A Ronaasen & Son

See SALE OF GOODS, Chapter 4, above.

Ashington Piggeries Ltd v Christopher Hill Ltd [1971] 2 WLR 1051 House of Lords (Viscount Dilhorne, Lords Hodson, Guest, Wilberforce and Diplock)

• *Sale of goods implied conditions*

Facts

In 1960, on behalf of the appellants one Udall, a mink expert, approached the appellant animal feeding stuff compounders with a view to the latter preparing a mink food – 'King Size' – in accordance with Udall's formula which included herring meal. It was made clear to the respondents that the food was required for mink, an area in which the respondents had no previous experience. The ingredients were to be supplied by the respondents and were to be of the best quality available. At first, there were no problems, but then the respondents began using Norwegian herring meal and heavy losses began to occur as, in certain quantities, this meal contained a substance which was highly toxic to mink. The meal was part of a consignment purchased from the Norwegian third party and, at the time, nobody knew of the harmful effects which arose from a chemical reaction with a preservative. Herring meal had not been used for mink in the United Kingdom prior to 1960, but it had been so used in other counties, including Norway. The respondents sued for the price of King Size sold and delivered and the appellants counterclaimed for damages arising from mink losses. The respondents in turn sued the third party for an indemnity.

Held

The respondents were liable for breach of the condition implied by s14(1) of the Sale of Goods Act 1893 and (Lord Hodson and Lord Diplock dissenting) s14(2) of the 1983 Act. The third party were liable (Lord Diplock dissenting) as being in breach of the conditions implied by s14(1) but not (Viscount Dilhorne dissenting) for breach of the condition implied by s13 of the Act of 1893.

Lord Wilberforce:

'We are only concerned with the appellants' rights under their contract of sale and under the Sale of Goods Act 1893 and consequentially with the respondents' rights against third parties from whom in turn the respondents acquired the meal. It is not, and cannot be, contended that because the presence of this chemical in the meal was unsuspected, and latent, at the date of the contract, and for some time after, that of itself affords a defence (other than a special defence under the fair average quality provisions) either to the intermediate sellers or to the manufacturers ...

1. *Section 13 of the Act.* The question is whether the compound mink food sold by the respondents (under the name "King Size") corresponded with the description ... I think that buyers and sellers and arbitrators in the market, asked what this was, could only have said that the relevant ingredient was herring meal and, therefore, that there was no failure to correspond with description. In my opinion, the appellants do not succeed under s13.

2. *Section 14(1) of the Act.* I do not think it is disputed, or in any case disputable, that a particular purpose was made known by the buyers so as to show that they relied on the sellers' skill and judgment. The particular purpose for which "King Size" was required

was as food for mink. Equally I think it is clear (as both courts have found) that there was reliance on the respondents' skill and judgment ...

In my opinion, the appellants made good their case. They proved the cause of their losses to lie in the inclusion of a generally (ie non-specific as regards mink) toxic ingredient in the good. It was not for them to show that this same food killed, or poisoned, other species. So to require would place far too high a burden on a buyer. The buyer may have no means of ascertaining what the effect on other species may be. The whole of the contaminated consignment may have been fed to the buyer's animals. Is the buyer to fail because he cannot show that this particular consignment killed, or at least injured, other animals? He must, I think, carry his proof to the point of showing that the guilty ingredient has some generally (as opposed to specifically) toxic quality. But once he has done this, has he not shown, at least with strong prima facie force, that a feeding stuff which contained it was unsuitable?

Is he not entitled to throw on to the seller the burden of showing, if he can, that the damage to the buyer's animals was due to some factor within the field of responsibility reserved to the buyer? I would answer yes to these questions. In the end, it is for the judge to decide whether, on the evidence, the buyers have proved their case...

So much for the facts, but there remains one legal argument on this part of the case. Section 14(1) contains the words "and the goods are of a description which it is in the course of the seller's business to supply". The respondents relied on these words and persuaded the Court of Appeal to decide that the requirement was not satisfied because, briefly, the respondents were not dealers in mink food. A similar argument was put forward on the words in s14(2) "where goods are bought by description from a seller who deals in goods of that description" ...

I do not accept that, taken in its most linguistic strictness, either subsection bears the meaning contended for. I would hold that

(as to subs(1)) it is in the course of the seller's business to supply goods if he agrees, either generally, or in a particular case, to supply the goods when ordered, and (as to subs(2)) that a seller deals in goods of that description if his business is such that he is willing to accept orders for them. I cannot comprehend the rationale of holding that the subsections do not apply if the seller is dealing in the particular goods for the first time or the sense of distinguishing between the first and the second order for the goods or for goods of the description. The Court of Appeal offered the analogy of a doctor sending a novel prescription to a pharmacist, which turns out to be deleterious. But as often happens to arguments of this kind, the analogy is faulty; if the prescription is wrong, of course the doctor is responsible. The fitness of the prescription is within his field of responsibility. The relevant question is whether the pharmacist is responsible for the purity of his ingredients and one does not see why not. But, moreover, consideration of the preceding common law shows that what the Act had in mind was something quite simple and rational: to limit the implied conditions of fitness or quality to persons in the way of business, as distinct from private persons. Whether this should be the law was a problem which had emerged, and been resolved, well before 1893 ...

One asks, therefore, what difference the insertion in the Sale of Goods Act 1893 of the word "description" made to these well accepted rules. It seems at least clear that the words now appearing in s14(1) "and the goods are of a description which it is ... the seller's business to supply" cannot mean more than " the goods of a kind ..." "Description" here cannot be used in the sense in which the word is used when the Act speaks of "sales by description", for s14(1) is not dealing with sales by description at all. If this is so, I find no obstacle against reading "goods of that description" in a similar way in s14(2). In both cases the word means "goods of that kind" and nothing more. Moreover, even if this is wrong, and "description" is to be understood in a technical sense, I would have no difficulty in holding that a seller deals in goods "of that description" if he accepts orders to supply them in the way of business; and this whether or not he has previously accepted orders for goods of that description. So, all other elements being present as I have tried to show, I would hold that s14(1) applies to the present case. I would agree with the judge that s14(2) equally applies and disagree with the reasons (based on the "description" argument) which led the Court of Appeal to a contrary opinion. That the goods were unmerchantable was conceded in both courts, in my opinion, rightly so. Goods may quite well be unmerchantable even if "purpose built". Lord Wright made this quite clear in the *Cammell Laird* case; so equally with "King Size" mink food ...

The appeal of ... the respondents against ... the third party raises different, and in one respect at least, more difficult issues. The goods supplied were in this case Norwegian herring meal and they were supplied under the terms of a commodity market contract in writing. A number of points arise under it. On the following I express my concurrence with others of your Lordships, and do not think it necessary to add reasons of my own. (1) The respondents were not in breach of a term in the contract implied by virtue of s13 of the Sale of Goods Act 1893. The goods supplied were, in my opinion, Norwegian herring meal. The words "fair average quality of the season" were not in this contract part of the description. I do not find it necessary to consider whether, if they were, there was a breach of any implied condition that the goods should correspond with this description. They were not relied on as themselves importing a warranty; but if the contention is open I am in agreement with my noble and learned friend, Lord Diplock, for the reasons which he gives, that they do not cover the particular defect which existed. (2) The exemption clause contained in general condition 3 does not exclude a claim for breach of any warranty implied under s14(1) of the Act.

This leaves the substantial question

whether a term as to reasonable fitness ought to be implied under s14(1) of the Act. There was also raised a question as to remoteness of damage but, in the view which I take, this depends on the same considerations as those necessary for determination of liability under s14(1). I now consider this question ... What is necessary to determine is whether any particular purpose for which the goods were required was made known by the buyers to the sellers so as to show that the buyers relied on the sellers' skill and judgment; what the particular purpose was; finally, whether the particular purpose included feeding to mink. The particular purpose relied on by the respondents was that the meal was required for inclusion in animal feeding stuffs to be compounded by them. They do not contend that feeding to mink was explicitly stated as a purpose; but they say that feeding to mink was known to both parties as a normal user for herring meal, and that it was sold without any reservation or restriction as to the use to which it might be put ... it is clear that this House in *Kendall* v *Lillico* accepted that the "making known" so as to show reliance which the section requires is easily deduced from the nature and circumstances of the sale, and that the word "particular" means little more than "stated" or "defined". As Lord Pearce said in *Kendall* v *Lillico*, there is no need for a buyer formally to "make known" that which is already known: and here there is no doubt that the third party, through its selling agents ... , and also directly, knew what the herring meal was required for, ie for inclusion in animal feeding stuffs to be compounded by the appellants and no special purpose in relation to mink was relied on... I observe indeed, that my noble and learned friend, Lord Guest, who felt difficulty in *Kendall* v *Lillico* as to the application of s14(1) against persons who were dealers in the market, said that he could well understand, where the sale is by a manufacturer to a customer, that the inference (ie of reliance) can easily be drawn. I agree ... that it ought to be drawn in this case.

Then was the purpose, to be used for

inclusion in animal feeding stuffs to be com-pounded by the buyers, a particular purpose? In my opinion, certainly yes. It is true that the purpose was wide, wider even that the purpose accepted as particular in *Kendall* v *Lillico* (for compounding into food for cattle and poultry) and, if one leaves aside a possible alternative use as fer-tiliser, on which there was some indefinite evidence, the purpose so made known covers a large part of the area which would be within s14(2). But I do not think, as the law has developed, that this can be regarded as an objection or that in accepting a purpose so defined, as a "a particular purpose", the court is crossing any forbid-den line. There remains a distinction between a statement (express or implied) of a particular purpose, though a wide one, with the implied condition (or warranty) which this attracts, and a purchase by description with no purpose stated and the different condition (or warranty) which that attracts. Moreover, width of the purpose is compensated, from the seller's point of view, by the dilution of his responsibility; and to hold him liable under an implied war-ranty of fitness for the purpose of which he has been made aware, wide though this may be, appears as fair as to leave him exposed to the vaguer and less defined standard of merchantability. After all, the seller's lia-bility is, if I may borrow the expression of my noble and learned friend, Lord Morris of Borth-y-Gest, no more than to meet the requirement of a buyer who is saying to him "that is what I want it for, but I only want to buy if you sell me something that will do". I think that well expresses the situation here.

The next point is whether, when the meal turned out to be unsuitable for feeding to mink, this was a matter to be treated as within the respondents' responsibility. There are two distinct points here: the first is whether feeding to mink was a normal use, within the general purpose of inclusion in animal feeding stuffs; the second is whether, assuming that the respondents' implied war-ranty did not extend beyond that of general suitability for animals, including possibly

mink, the buyers were able to show a breach of that warranty. The first point involves an issue of fact which received lengthy exami-nation in the courts below. The decision on it depended to a great extent on the view taken of two Norwegian witnesses called by the third party, who were the assistant direc-tor of the third party and the chief executive of a Norwegian herring oil factory at the rel-evant time. These witnesses were called to show that the third party did not know in 1961 that herring meal might be fed to mink. Unfortunately the courts below reached dif-ferent conclusions. Milmo J did not accept the disclaimer of the Norwegian witnesses. He found that both were aware in or before 1961 that herring meal was being fed to mink in Norway and that herring meal was a normal and well-known ingredient of the diet of mink kept in captivity in Norway and (he added) in other countries. On this basis he found that [the third party] knew of the practice of feeding herring meal to mink ...

On this issue the careful re-examination of the evidence which took place in this House, convinced me that the Court of Appeal was not justified in reversing in this matter the findings of fact of the trial judge ...

If I am right so far on the question of suit-ability and reliance, similar considerations arise on the question whether the consign-ment was in fact unsuitable, so as to involve a breach of warranty, to those already dis-cussed as between the appellants and the respondents, and for the same reasons the conclusion follows in my opinion, that a breach of warranty under s14(1) was proved. The respondents did not, in this part of the appeal, pursue a claim under s14(2). Finally, any question as to remoteness of damages is disposed of by the finding that feeding to mink was a normal user and con-templated as such by both parties to the con-tract.'

Comment

Followed: *Cammell Laird & Co Ltd* v *Manganese Bronze and Brass Co Ltd* [1934] AC 402 and *Kendall (Henry) & Sons* v

William Lillico & Sons Ltd [1968] 3 WLR 110. See also *Wilson v Rickett, Cockerell & Co Ltd* [1954] 1 QB 598 which demonstrates the principles of merchantable (satisfactory) quality and fitness for purpose.

Aswan Engineering Establishment Co v Lupdine Ltd [1987] 1 WLR 1 Court of Appeal (Fox, Lloyd and Nicholls LJJ)

- *Implied terms – quality of goods*

Facts

The buyers bought a quantity of waterproofing compound which was supplied in plastic pails. These were packed into containers and shipped to Kuwait, where they were left on the quayside. Due to the heat on the quay the pails melted and the waterproofing compound was lost. The buyers claimed against the sellers who, in turn, sued the company which supplied them. The buyers succeeded against the sellers but they failed in their claim against the original suppliers. The essence of the sellers' claim was that, in order to be merchantable, the pails should have been fit for use to store goods under any conditions in which they might be stored in the normal course of business.

Held

Goods do not have to be fit for every conceivable use to which they may be put in order to be merchantable. Section 14(2) of the Sale of Goods Act 1979 is designed to give the buyer a remedy where the goods bought do not meet the minimum acceptable standard, namely that they should be fit for at least one of the normal uses to which they might be put. Section 14(3), on the other hand, is designed to give the buyer a remedy where the goods are not fit for his particular purpose even if they are of the minimum standard which any buyer should expect. The onus is on the buyer to make known his particular purpose, otherwise he cannot complain if he gets goods of the minimum standard acceptable to the law.

Lloyd LJ examined the case law prior to 1973 and said that the statutory definition of merchantable quality which was introduced in that year (and which is now s14(6) of the 1979 Act) did not revolutionise the law. He summarised the position prior to 1973 and then the position today:

'I will now attempt to summarise the position as it was in my own words. To bring s14(2) into operation, a buyer had to show that the goods had been bought by description from a seller dealing in goods of that description. If so, then, subject to a proviso which is immaterial for present purposes, the goods were required to be of merchantable quality. In order to comply with that requirement, the goods did not have to be suitable for every purpose within a range of purposes for which goods were normally bought under that description. It was sufficient that they were suitable for one or more such purposes without abatement of price since, if they were, they were commercially saleable under that description.

It has been submitted that the direction in which the law has developed over the last century and a half ... has been radically changed by s14(6) of the 1979 Act ... The reason why parliament did not [state in s14(6) either that the goods should be fit for all purposes for which they are commonly bought or for only one of those purposes] is, I think, to be found in the speech of Lord Reid in *Henry Kendall & Sons v William Lillico & Sons Ltd* ... Lord Reid points out that goods of any one kind may be sold under more than one description, corresponding to different qualities.

To take the facts of the present case, heavy duty pails are no doubt of higher quality than ordinary pails, and for that reason no doubt command a higher price. Pails which are suitable for the lower quality purpose may not be suitable for the higher quality purpose. It would obviously be wrong that pails sold under the description appropriate to the higher quality should be held to be merchantable because they are fit for a purpose for which pails are sold under the description appropriate to the lower quality. Since the definition [in s14(6)] presupposes that goods of any one kind may be sold under more than one description, it follows that the definition had, of necessity, to refer to more than one purpose. In my opinion, this is the true and sufficient explanation for the reference to "purposes" in the plural. The reference to the purpose in the singular was required in order to cover one-purpose goods ... It would be wrong to infer from the use of the phrase "purpose or purposes" that Parliament intended any far-reaching change in the law ... On the contrary, the definition is as accurate a reproduction of Lord Reid's speech in *Henry Kendall & Sons v William Lillico & Sons Ltd* as it is possible to compress into a single sentence ...

The definition has not revolutionised the law ... I can well understand an argument that goods should be regarded as unmerchantable if they contain a hidden defect which, while leaving the goods suitable for some purposes, renders them unsuitable for others. If the buyer does not know, and cannot find out, for what purposes the goods are unsuitable, they are no more than a trap. That was the argument which appealed to Lord Pearce in *Henry Kendall & Sons v William Lillico & Sons Ltd*, and was one of the two reasons why he dissented on the point. But the majority took the opposite view. One must assume that the hypothetical buyer knows not only that the goods on offer are defective but also what the nature of the particular defect is.'

Comment

See also *Brown (BS) & Son Ltd v Craiks Ltd* [1970] 1 WLR 752 which discusses the interpretation of s14(2) under the Sale of Goods Act 1979. See, too, *Kendall (Henry) & Sons v William Lillico & Sons Ltd; Hardwick Game Farm v Suffolk Horticultural Poultry Producers Association Ltd (SAPPA)* [1969] 2 AC 31.

Also consider damage caused by a defective product under the law of negligence and strict liability through the Consumer

Protection Act 1987. In *Aswan* there was no liability for breach of contract but there was a potential claim if the product, plastic pails, had damaged other property, ie, the contents in the pails. Normally there is no liability for the product, but if it can be demonstrated that the product has caused damage to other property there may be a claim in either negligence or under the 1987 Act.

Clegg v Andersson (t/a Nordic Marine) [2003] 2 Lloyd's Rep 32 Court of Appeal (Civil Division) (Sir Andrew Morritt V-C, Hale and Dyson LJJ)

* *Implied terms – the right to reject goods*

Facts

The appellant, Clegg, entered into an agreement in December 1999 to buy a yacht costing £236,000 from the respondent, Andersson. The yacht was delivered to Andersson on 25 July 2000 and by him to Clegg on 12 August 2000. Upon delivery Clegg found the keel to be substantially heavier than the manufacturer's specification. This resulted in a succession of correspondence between Clegg and Andersson from 28 August 2000 to 1 March 2001 in which, amongst other issues, the overweight keel, its consequences and possible remedies to it were discussed. On 6 March 2001, Clegg's solicitor wrote to Andersson and rejected the yacht, claiming there had been breach of a condition under ss13(1) and/or 14(2) of the Sale of Goods Act (SGA) 1979. It was claimed, in other words, that the yacht did not adequately correspond to its description, nor was it of satisfactory quality. Andersson rejected this claim and Clegg commenced legal proceedings for the return of the purchase money and damages for breach of contract.

At first instance Seymour J concluded neither ss13(1) nor 14(2) SGA 1979 had been breached. In addition to this finding, he also believed that if there had been a breach of condition, Clegg had lost the right to reject the yacht before 6 March 2001, pursuant to s35 of the 1979 Act and the decision in *Bernstein v Pamson Motors (Golders Green) Ltd* [1987] 2 All ER 220. The claimant was granted leave to appeal.

Held

Hale LJ considered the evidence that had been presented at first instance, the interpretation of the Sale of Goods Act 1979 and its application to the facts in question. She outlined the purpose of the Act and affirmed that, by operation of law, there is an implied term that goods sold in the course of a business must be of satisfactory quality. Section 14(2) states:

'Where the seller sells goods in the course of a business, there is an implied term that the goods supplied under the contract are of satisfactory quality.'

Section 14(2A) goes on to state:

'For the purposes of this Act, goods are of satisfactory quality if they meet the standard that a reasonable person would regard as satisfactory, taking account of any description of the goods, the price (if relevant) and all the other relevant circumstances.'

This section is then qualified by s14(2B):

'For the purposes of this Act, the quality of goods includes their state and condition and the following (among others) are in appropriate cases aspects of the quality of goods –
(a) fitness for the purposes for which goods of the kind in question are commonly supplied,
(b) appearance and finish,
(c) freedom from minor defects,
(d) safety, and
(e) durability.'

Hale LJ did not agree with Seymour J's decision at first instance, and reversed the decision by finding that the yacht was not of satisfactory quality. She based her decision on the interpretation of the test: '[whether] a reasonable person would regard [the goods] as satisfactory' and made reference to external material, namely the Joint Report of the Law

Commission and the Scottish Law Commission (*Sale and Supply of Goods* (1987) Law Com No 160). This states that the test is 'not whether the reasonable person would find the goods acceptable; it is an objective comparison of the state of the goods with the standard which a reasonable person would find acceptable'. This statement, in conjunction with the amendments brought by the Sale and Supply of Goods Act 1994, makes it clear that fitness for purpose and satisfactory quality are two distinct concepts. A customer would be entitled to expect a high quality product, priced accordingly, to be free from even minor defects.

Hale LJ then considered whether the appellant had lost the right to reject the yacht, as it had been argued that acceptance had taken place in accordance with s11(4) SGA 1979, which states:

'Subject to s35A [Sale of Goods Act 1979] below where a contract of sale is not severable and the buyer has accepted the goods or part of them, the breach of a condition to be fulfilled by the seller can only be treated as a breach of warranty, and not as a ground for rejecting the goods and treating the contract as repudiated, unless there is an express or implied term of the contract to that effect.'

This was the moot point of the appeal. If acceptance had taken place then a condition was converted, by operation of law, into a warranty if breached. Hale LJ was mindful of the facts and examined s35(1) of the Act, which states:

'The buyer is deemed to have accepted the goods subject to subs(2) below –
(a) when he intimates to the seller that he has accepted them, or
(b) when the goods have been delivered to him and he does an act in relation to them which is inconsistent with the ownership of the seller.'

Hale LJ considered the implications of this section. The buyer would lose the right to reject if he had informed the seller he had accepted the goods or if he adopted the transaction (for example, by using the goods or selling them on to a third party) by acting inconsistently with the seller's reversionary interest in the goods. Further, there was the issue of the time lapse between delivery of the goods and rejection which had to be considered, as s35(4) stipulates:

'The buyer is also deemed to have accepted the goods when after the lapse of a reasonable time he retains the goods without intimating to the seller that he has rejected them.'

The appellant had informed the respondent in writing, on several occasions, about the defects in the goods. He had sought additional information from the seller to make a properly informed choice between acceptance, rejection or cure. Hale LJ found that the appellant had not lost his right to reject the goods, and that since the implementation of the Sale and Supply of Goods Act 1994 the decision of *Bernstein* v *Pamson Motors (Golders Green) Ltd* no longer represented the law. The appeal was allowed.

Comment
This decision is significant for two reasons. First, it firmly establishes that the decision in *Bernstein* v *Pamson Motors (Golders Green) Ltd* is no longer a true reflection of the law when dealing with acceptance, and also acknowledges the intention of the Law Commission through the implementation of the Sale and Supply of Goods Act 1994. Second, the right to reject goods for a breach of a condition is not automatically lost under s11(4) SGA 1979.

Davies v *Sumner* [1984] 1 WLR 1301 House of Lords (Lords Keith of Kinkel, Elwyn-Jones, Bridge of Harwich, Brandon of Oakbrook and Templeman)

• *Car traded 'in course of a trade or business'?*

Facts
Mr Davies was a self-employed courier. He needed a new car and traded in his old car in part-exchange. The milometer read 18,100 miles. In fact the car had travelled 181,100 miles, but because there were only five digits on the meter this fact did not show. He was given a part-exchange allowance of £3,800 for the old car. Mr Davies was prosecuted for having applied a false trade description to the car. He was convicted in the magistrates' court but had his appeal allowed by the Divisional Court on the ground that he did not dispose of the vehicle in the course of a trade or business. The prosecutor appealed.

Held
The appeal would be dismissed

Lord Keith of Kinkel:

'Section 1(1) of the Act of 1968 provides:

"Any person who, in the course of a trade or business –
(a) applies a false trade description to any goods; or
(b) supplies or offers to supply any goods to which a false trade description is applied;
shall, subject to the provisions of this Act, be guilty of an offence."

There can be no doubt that the respondent, when he traded in his car, applied a false trade description to it, in respect that he represented that it had travelled 18,100 miles when the true mileage was 118,100 miles. "Trade description" is defined by s2(1) of the Act as being an indication, "direct or indirect, and by whatever means given" of any of various matters with respect to any goods including: "(j) other history, including previous ownership or use". The question is whether the respondent applied the trade description to the car "in the course of a trade or business ..."

In *Havering London Borough Council* v *Stevenson* [1970] 1 WLR 1375, the defendant, who carried on a car hire business, had a usual practice of selling the cars employed in it every two years. He sold them at the current trade price and paid the proceeds into the business for the purpose of buying new cars. In relation to one such sale he falsely represented to the purchaser of the car that the mileage it had travelled was substantially less than was actually the case. A charge against him under s1(1)(b) was dismissed by magistrates, but an appeal by the prosecutor by way of case stated was allowed by the Divisional Court ... This decision, the correctness of which was not challenged by Mr Somerset Jones for the respondent, vouches the proposition that in certain circumstances the sale of certain goods may, within the meaning of the Act, be in the course of a trade or business, notwithstanding that the trade or business of the defendant does not consist in dealing for profit in goods of that, or indeed any other, description. Any disposal of a chattel held for the purposes of a business may, in a certain sense, be said to have been in the course of that business irrespective of whether the chattel was acquired with a view to resale or for consumption or as a capital asset. But in my opinion s1(1) of the Act is not intended to cast such a wide net as this. The expression "in the course of a trade or business" in the context of an Act having consumer protection as its primary purpose conveys the concept of some degree of regularity, and it is to be observed that the long title to the Act refers to "misdescriptions of goods, services, accommodation and facilities provided in the course of trade". Lord Parker CJ in the *Havering* case [1970] 1 WLR 1375 clearly considered that the expression was not used in the broadest sense. The reason why the transaction there in issue was caught was that in his view it was "an integral part of the business carried on as a car hire firm". That would not cover the sporadic selling off of pieces of equipment which were no longer required for the purpose of a business. The vital feature of the *Havering* case appears to have been, in Lord Parker's view, that the defendant's business *as part of its normal practice* bought and disposed of cars. The need for some degree of regularity does not, however, involve that a one-off adventure in

the nature of trade, carried through with a view to profit, would not fall within s1(1) because such a transaction would itself consistute a trade ...

Where a person carried on the business of hiring out some description of goods to the public and has a practice of selling off those that are no longer in good enough condition, clearly the latter goods are offered or supplied in the course of his business within the meaning of s1(1). But the occasional sale of some worn out piece of shop equipment would not fall within the enactment.'

Grant v *Australian Knitting Mills Ltd* [1936] AC 85 Privy Council (Lord Hailsham LC, Lords Blanesburgh, Macmillan and Wright, Sir Lancelot Sanderson)

• *Dangerous underwear – liability*

Facts

The appellant contracted dermatitis by reason of the defective condition (resulting from the presence of an irritating chemical, free sulphite) of woollen underwear which retailers had sold to him at their shop and the manufacturers had put forth for retail and indiscriminate sale.

Held

The retailers and the manufacturers were liable in contract and tort respectively.

Lord Wright:

'So far as concerns the retailers, counsel for the respondents conceded that, if it were held that the garments contained improper chemicals and caused the disease, the retailers were liable for breach of implied warranty, or rather condition, under s14 of the South Australia Sale of Goods Act 1895, which is identical with s14 of the English Sale of Goods Act 1893 ...

He limited his admission to liability under exception (2), but their Lordships are of opinion that liability is made out under both exception (1) and exception (2) to s14 and feel that they should so state out of deference to the views expressed in the court below.

Section 14 begins by a general enunciation of the old rule of caveat emptor, and proceeds to state by way of exception the two implied conditions by which it has been said the old rule has been changed to the rule of caveat vendor: the change has been rendered necessary by the conditions of modern commerce and trade ... There are numerous cases on the section, but as these were cited below it is not necessary to detail them again. The first exception, if its terms are satisfied, entitles the buyer to the benefit of an implied condition that the goods are reasonably fit for the purpose for which the goods are supplied, but only if that purpose is made known to the seller "so as to show that the buyer relies on the seller's skill or judgment." It is clear that the reliance must be brought home to the mind of the seller, expressly or by implication. The reliance will seldom be express; it will usually arise by implication from the circumstances; thus to take a case like that in question of a purchase from a retailer the reliance will be in general inferred from the fact that a buyer goes to the shop in the confidence that the tradesman has selected his stock with skill and judgment; the retailer need know nothing about the process of manufacture; it is immaterial whether he be manufacturer or not; the main inducement to deal with a good retail shop is the expectation that the tradesman will have bought the right goods of a good make; the goods sold must be, as they were in the present case, goods of a description which it is in the course of the seller's business to supply; there is no need to specify in terms the particular purpose for which the buyer requires the goods; which is none the less the particular purpose within the meaning of the section because it is the only purpose for which anyone would ordinarily want the goods. In this case the garments were naturally intended and only intended to be worn next to the skin ... their Lordships think that the requirements of exception (1) were complied with. The conversation at the shop in which the appellant discussed questions of price and of the dif-

ferent makes did not affect the fact that he was substantially relying on the retailers to supply him with a correct article.

The second exception in a case like this in truth overlaps in its application the first exception; whatever else "merchantable" may mean, it does mean that the article sold, if only meant for one particular use in the ordinary course, is fit for that use. "Merchantable" does not mean that the thing is saleable in the market simply because it looks all right; it is not merchantable in that event if it has defects unfitting it for its only proper use but not apparent on ordinary examination; that is clear from the proviso, which shows that the implied condition only applies to defects not reasonably discoverable to the buyer on such examination as he made or could make. The appellant was satisfied by the appearance of the underpants; he could not detect and had no reason to suspect the hidden presence of the sulphites; the garments were saleable in the sense that the appellant or anyone similarly situated and who did not know of their defect, would readily buy them; buy they were not merchantable in the statutory sense because their defect rendered them unfit to be worn next the skin. It may be that after sufficient washing that defect would have disappeared; but the statute requires the goods to be merchantable in the state in which they were sold and delivered; in this connection a defect which could easily be cured is as serious as a defect that would not yield to treatment. The proviso to exception (2) does not apply where, as in this case, no examination that the buyer could or would normally have made would have revealed the defect. In effect, the implied condition of being fit for the particular purpose for which they are required and the implied condition of being merchantable produce in cases of this type the same result. It may also be pointed out that there is a sale by description even though the buyer is buying something displayed before him on the counter; a thing is sold by description, though it is specific, so long as it is sold not merely as the specific thing but as a thing corresponding to a description, eg woollen under-garments, a hot water bottle, a secondhand reaping machine, to select a few obvious illustrations.'

Comment
See also *Beale* v *Taylor* [1967] 1 WLR 1193 and *Godley* v *Perry* [1960] 1 WLR 9. See also *Griffiths* v *Peter Conway Ltd* [1939] 1 All ER 685 which discusses the implied term fit for its purpose and the plaintiff's abnormal circumstances, which were not made known to the seller.

Jewson Ltd v *Leanne Teresa Boyham as Personal Representative of the Estate of Thomas Michael Kelly* [2003] EWCA Civ 1030 Court of Appeal (Clarke and Sedley LJJ, Cresswell J)

• *Implied terms – satisfactory quality – misrepresentation*

Facts
The appellant, Jewson Ltd (J), appealed against the decision of David Foskett QC who found the appellant at first instance to be in breach of a term implied by ss14(2) and 14(3) of the Sale of Goods Act 1979. This case involved the sale and purchase of 12 electric boilers to the respondent, Mr Kelly (K). Unfortunately, since the first trial Mr Kelly has died, but by agreement and order of the Court the respondent is replaced by the personal representative of his estate. J, a building merchant, sold and delivered 12 Amptec electric boilers to K, which were to be installed within a building that was being converted from a former convent school into a number of self-contained flats. The respondent decided to install these electric boilers, which had been manufactured by a company known as Amptec Heating Technology Ltd (Amptec) and purchased the boilers from J for approximately £7,500 exclusive of VAT, each boiler costing about £625 plus VAT. K also pur-

chased other materials which, according to the appellant, he did not pay for, and J claimed the sum of £53,322.43. The respondent raised the issue of the suitability of these boilers and counterclaimed for breach of contract, consequential losses and sought to set off his claim against the outstanding sum owed to J.

The appellant's standard terms and conditions applied to the sale and were relied upon to resist the respondent's claim at first instance. Clause 8.7 of these conditions stated:

'The customer is deemed to be fully conversant with the nature and performance of the goods including any harmful or hazardous effects resulting from their usage and shall not be reliant in any way upon the advice, skill or judgment of the company. The company's employees or agents are not authorised to make any representations concerning the goods other than those confirmed by the company in writing.'

Whilst cl 8.10 stated:

'The company shall not be liable for any consequential loss or indirect loss suffered by the customer or any third party in relation to this contract (except personal injury directly attributable to the negligence of the company) and the customer shall hold the company fully and effectively indemnified against such losses whether arising from breach of a duty in contract or loss in any way including losses arising from the company's negligence.'

At first instance the court accepted that these clauses were deemed reasonable, given the relationship between the parties and the nature of the circumstances. However, J was aware of the particular purpose for which the boilers were intended and had informed K during their negotiations that the boilers were suitable for his requirements. K alleged the boilers had an unsatisfactory Standard Assessment Procedure (SAP) rating for the individual properties in question. The SAP refers specifically to the energy efficiency of the heating system for an individual residential property. The building regulations in force at the time required a 'new build' dwelling to be in the region of 80–85, which varied depending on the floor size. However, there was no statutory minimum when dealing with a conversion (as was the case here), and thus there was no ground for refusing to accept the boilers under the building regulations based upon an unsatisfactory SAP. However, a potential lender and their surveyor, when carrying out a valuation on the property, will consider the SAP calculations. K claimed that the unsatisfactorily low SAP readings led to the loss of potential purchasers and further claimed that J was in breach of contract under the Sale of Goods Act 1979 (as amended by the Sale and Supply of Goods Act 1994), s14(2) of which states:

'Where the seller sells goods in the course of a business, there is an implied term that the goods supplied under the contract are of satisfactory quality.
(2A) For the purposes of this Act, goods are of satisfactory quality if they meet the standard that a reasonable person would regard as satisfactory, taking into account any description of the goods, the price (if relevant) and all other relevant circumstances.'

The SAP rating for these boilers should have been in the region of between 55 and 100. However, expert opinion was given that these boilers scored a rating of between 44, 30, ten and below. The literature, supplied by the manufacture (Amptec), that accompanied the boilers made various claims, for example:

'The Amptec boiler processes very low volumes of water at very high speeds making it 99.6 per cent heat efficient and impressively cheap to run. Because it's so compact, the Amptec boiler is particularly suitable for houses, flats, small shops and mobile homes. Because it's electric, it's ideal when there's no gas main; for new housing, properties in rural areas and renovations.'

Similar claims were made throughout the literature, which emphasised the unobtrusive nature of the boiler, its safety, efficiency, ease of installation and cheap running costs. These claims were not in dispute. Several of the 13 flats had been purchased for the anticipated

price and in certain cases the price had been exceeded. There was no direct evidence that the Amptec boilers were not working satisfactorily.

At first instance Foskett J found in favour of the respondent. He was of the opinion that the appellant was aware that the boilers were to be installed in the flats and to be sold for a profit. However, due to the low SAP rating the boilers, in this instance, were not fit for their purpose and not of satisfactory quality. Thus, it was alleged that the appellant was in breach of contract. Therefore, the respondent claimed the use of the Amptec boilers had resulted in the sale of the flats being abandoned or delayed and a financial loss occurred as a result. This argument was accepted and it was found that the respondent had relied upon the claimant's skill and judgment: the boilers were not fit for their purpose. Regarding cl 8.10 of the appellant's standard conditions of sale which referred to the exclusion of 'consequential ... or indirect' losses, in this instance it was found that the breach of contract had resulted in losses 'directly and naturally' arising from the breach. Thus, the losses fell within the first rule laid down in *Hadley* v *Baxendale* (1854) 9 Ex 341 and could not be excluded. J sought leave to appeal, which was granted.

Held

Clarke LJ believed that little or no attention was given to the possibility that there may have been only a partial reliance on the seller's skill and judgment. He discussed the judgment given by Lord Wilberforce in *Ashington Piggeries Ltd* v *Christopher Hill Ltd* [1971] 1 All ER 847:

'Equally I think it is clear (as both courts have found) that there was reliance on the respondents' skill and judgment. Although the Act [s14(1) of the Sale of Goods Act 1893] makes no reference to partial reliance, it was settled, well before the *Cammell Laird* case [[1934] AC 402] was decided in this House, that there may be cases where the buyer relies on his own skill or judgment for some purposes and on that of the seller for others. This House gave that principle emphatic endorsement.'

In the same case Lord Diplock also made reference to partial reliance:

'The key to both subsections is reliance – the reasonable reliance of the buyer upon the seller's ability to make or select goods which are reasonably fit for the buyer's purpose coupled with the seller's acceptance of responsibility to do so. The seller has a choice whether or not to accept that responsibility.'

He then went on to say:

'I turn next to "partial reliance". The actual words of subs(1) appear to contemplate two classes of contracts only; one, where the buyer does not rely at all upon the skill or judgment of the seller to see to it that the goods supplied are reasonably fit for a particular purpose; the other where the buyer does so rely and the other requirements of the subsection are satisfied. As a matter of linguistics it is possible to construe the expression "so as to show that the buyer relies" as referring to a reliance which was only partial, in that sense that the reliance was not the only or even the determining factor which induced the buyer to enter into the contract.'

Given the principles enunciated by Lord Diplock, they must be considered in light of the provisions of s14(3): the burden of proof is placed on the seller to demonstrate that the buyer did not rely upon his skill and judgment. The above facts, at first instance, illustrate that K made it clear to J why he wished to purchase the boilers. However, he did not give any information on the nature of the building being converted. Thus, it is arguable that without such information the appellant was not in a position to formulate an opinion on the SAP ratings. Based upon this premise Mr de Garr Robinson, who acted on behalf of the appellant, submitted an argument for partial reliance, namely that the Amptec boilers were fit only for their purpose as boilers. Clarke LJ accepted this submission based upon the find-ings that the SAP ratings were within the respondent's expertise as a developer. The role of J was to give information relating to the characteristics of the boilers, and it was for K and his advisers to formulate an opinion by using such information in conjunction with the characteristics of the building and flats. Therefore, Clarke LJ found this was indeed a case of partial reliance, which K relied upon to the effect that the boilers were reasonably fit for their purpose, that is, they were fit for their purpose as boilers. This decision was supported by the dictum of Lord Steyn in *Slater and Others* v *Finning Ltd* [1997] AC 473:

'After all, if the buyer's purpose is insufficiently communicated, the buyer cannot reasonably rely on the seller's skill and judgment to ensure that the goods answer that purpose.'

Given Clarke LJ's analysis, this also overruled the decision of David Foskett QC on the implied term. Clarke LJ found there was no breach of s14(2) of the 1979 Act. He came to this conclusion with reference to the dictum of Tomlinson J in the case of *Britvic Soft Drinks Ltd* v *Messer UK Ltd* [2002] 1 Lloyd's Rep 20. Once it had been found that K did not rely upon the skill or judgment of J in relation to the boilers' SAP ratings, it was equally clear that a reasonable man would conclude that the boilers were of satisfactory quality as boilers. Therefore, he declared that J was neither in breach of s14(2) nor s14(3) of the 1979 Act.

Comment

This was an important decision, given the interpretation and decision at first instance. The defence of partial reliance put forward by J will certainly cause a ripple effect within this area of the law. However, this clearly demonstrates a number of factors to be taken into account when attempting to interpret and apply the Sale of Goods Act 1979 (as amended) when dealing with issues of satisfactory quality and fitness for purpose. However, the Sale and Supply of Goods to Consumers Regulations 2002 introduce a set of consumer rights, when dealing with faulty goods in EU countries, and regulate transactions between businesses and consumers. It will be interesting to see how future decisions relying on this case will be made and how the Regulations will be applied within a consumer context.

Marimpex Mineralöl Handelsgesellschaft mbH v Louis Dreyfus et Cie Mineralöl GmbH
[1995] 1 Lloyd's Rep 167 Queen's Bench Division (Commercial Court) (Clark J)

• *Sale of goods by description – quality of goods rendered unfit by reason of bacterial contamination – damages*

Facts
The plaintiffs agreed to sell a quantity of Russian gasoil to the defendants. The sale was by description. The oil was described as 'normal Russian gasoil'. After the vessel carrying the oil arrived at the port of delivery, a dispute arose as to whether the gasoil was of merchantable quality. The defendants argued that because the oil was so heavily contaminated with bacteria it was unmerchantable. Without treatment, or substantial discounting, it would be impossible for the oil to be re-sold; which had been the defendants' intention. The defendants deducted a substantial amount from the price due to the plaintiffs.

Held
The defendants took all reasonable steps to mitigate their loss, but there was no doubt that the market generally viewed such contaminated oil as being considerably below the value of uncontaminated Russian gasoil. The contamination of the whole cargo was such that it was not marketable, either without some sort of remedial treatment, or at a sizable discount. Since more than 10 per cent of the cargo was involved it was not fit for purpose under s14(b) Sale of Goods Act 1979 and the plaintiffs were in breach of the condition as

to merchantable quality. The measure of damages was the difference between contaminated and uncontaminated values, together with consequential loss.

Clarke J:

'In my view the gasoil was neither normal Russian gasoil, nor of merchantable quality … it was not saleable for any purpose without either treatment or a discount.'

'In my judgment Dreyfus took all reasonable steps to minimise the consequences of the contamination. They had originally intended to sell the gasoil to their German customers for ultimate use as heating or diesel oil. They decided that in the light of the Saybolt analysis they were not, as they put it in a fax dated August 13, "prepared to risk supplying unmerchantable gasoil". In my judgment that was a reasonable conclusion in the light of the information available to them at that time. At each stage they informed Marimpex of the options which they were considering and invited their comments.'

Comment
See also *Heil* v *Hedges* [1951] 1 TLR 512 which discusses merchantable (satisfactory) quality when goods are purchased.

Oscar Chess Ltd v Williams [1957] 1 WLR 370 Court of Appeal (Denning, Hodson and Morris LJJ)

• *Age of car – condition or representation?*

Facts
In May 1955, the defendant acquired a new car from the plaintiffs, who were motor car dealers and who took the defendant's Morris in part exchange. The defendant said it was a 1948 model, as per the registration document, and the plaintiffs made him an allowance of £290. The registration book had been altered by an unknown third party and the car was, in reality, a 1939 model worth £175. The county court judge held that it was a condition of the contract that the car was a 1948 model.

Held (Morris LJ dissenting)

The defendant's statement as to the age of the car was a mere representation, not a term of the contract. He had no special knowledge as to its age and the plaintiffs knew that he was relying on the date in the registration book. Therefore the defendant was not liable.

Denning LJ:

'I entirely agree with the judge that both parties assumed that the Morris was a 1948 model and that this assumption was fundamental to the contract. But this does not prove that the representation was a term of the contract. The assumption was based by both of them on the date given in the registration book as the date of first registration. They both believed it was a 1948 model when it was only a 1939 one. They were both mistaken and their mistake was of fundamental importance.

The effect of such a mistake is this: It does not make the contract a nullity from the beginning, but it does, in some circumstances, enable the contract to be set aside in equity. If the buyer had come promptly, he might have succeeded in getting the whole transaction set aside in equity on the ground of this mistake: see *Solle* v *Butcher*; but he did not do so and it is too late for him to do it: see *Leaf* v *International Galleries*. His only remedy is in damages and, to recover these, he must prove a warranty.

In saying that he must prove a warranty, I used the word "warranty" in its ordinary English meaning to denote a binding promise. Everyone knows what a man means when he says "I guarantee it" or "I warrant it" or "I give you my word on it". He means that he binds himself to it. That is the meaning it has borne in English Law for 300 years, from the leading case of *Chandelor* v *Lopus* (1603) Cro Jac 4 onwards. During the last 50 years, however, some lawyers have come to use the word "warranty" in another sense. They use it to denote a subsidiary term in contract, as distinct from a vital term, which they call a "condition". In so doing, they depart from the ordinary meaning, not only of the word "warranty" but also of the word "condition". There is no harm in their doing this, so long as they confine this technical use to its proper sphere, namely to distinguish between a vital term, the breach of which gives the right to treat the contract as at an end, and a subsidiary term which does not. But the trouble comes when one person uses the word "warranty" in its ordinary meaning and another uses it in its technical meaning. When Holt CJ in *Crosse* v *Gardner* (1689) Carth 90 (as glossed by Buller J in *Pasley* v *Freeman* (1789) 3 Term Rep 51, 57) and *Medina* v *Stoughton* (1700) 1 Salk 210 made his famous ruling that an affirmation at the time of a sale is a warranty, provided it appears on evidence to be so intended, he used the word "warranty" in its ordinary English meaning of a binding promise: and when Lord Haldane LC and Lord Moulton in 1913 in *Heilbut, Symons & Co* v *Buckleton* adopted his ruling, they used it likewise in its ordinary meaning. These different uses of the word seem to have been the source of confusion in the present case. The judge did not ask himself, "Was the representation (that it was a 1948 Morris) intended to be a warranty?" He asked himself "Was it fundamental to the contract?" He answered it by saying that it was fundamental; and therefore it was a condition and not a warranty. By concentrating on whether it was fundamental, he seems to me to have missed the crucial point in the case, which is whether it was a term of the contract at all. The crucial question is: was it a binding promise or only an innocent misrepresentation? The technical distinction between a "condition" and a "warranty" is quite immaterial in this case, because it is far too late for the buyer to reject the car. He can, at best, only claim damages. The material distinction here is between a statement which is a term of the contract and a statement which is only an innocent misrepresentation. This distinction is best expressed by the ruling of Lord Holt: Was it intended as a warranty or not? Using the word "warranty" there in its ordinary English meaning: because it gives the exact shade of meaning that is required. It is something to which a man must be taken to bind himself.

In applying Lord Holt's test, however, some misunderstanding has arisen by the use of the word "intended". It is sometimes supposed that the tribunal must look into the minds of the parties to see what they themselves intended. That is a mistake. Lord Moulton made it quite clear that "the intention of the parties can only be deduced from the totality of the evidence". The question whether a warranty was intended depends on the conduct of the parties, on their words and behaviour, rather than on their thoughts. If an intelligent bystander would reasonably infer that a warranty was intended, that will suffice. And this, when the facts are not in dispute, is a question of law. That is shown by *Heilbut, Symons & Co* v *Buckleton* itself, where the House of Lords upset the finding by a jury of a warranty.

It is instructive to take some recent instances to show how the courts have approached this question. When the seller states a fact which is or should be within his own knowledge and of which the buyer is ignorant, intending that the buyer should act on it and he does so, it is easy to infer a warranty: see *Couchman* v *Hill*, where the farmer stated that the heifer was served, and *Harling* v *Eddy*, where he stated that there was nothing wrong with her. So also, if he makes a promise about something which is or should be within his own control: see *Birch* v *Paramount Estates Ltd* [1958] 167 EG 396, decided on 2 October 1956, in this court, where the seller stated that the house would be as good as the show house. But if the seller, when he states a fact, makes it clear that he has no knowledge of his own, but has got his information elsewhere and is merely passing it on, it is not so easy to imply a warranty. Such a case was *Routledge* v *McKay* [1954] 1 WLR 615, 636, where the seller "stated that it was a 1942 model and pointed to the corroboration found in the book", and it was held that there was no warranty.

Turning now to the present case; much depends on the precise words that were used. If the seller says "I believe it is a 1948

Morris, here is the registration book to prove it", there is clearly no warranty. It is a statement of belief, not a contractual promise. But if the seller says "I guarantee that is a 1948 Morris. This is borne out by the registration book, but you need not rely solely on that. I give you my own guarantee that it is ", there is clearly a warranty. The seller is making himself contractually responsible, even though the registration book is wrong.

In this case, much reliance was placed by the judge on the fact that the buyer looked up *Glass's Guide* and paid £290 on the footing that it was a 1948 model: but that fact seems to me to be neutral. Both sides believed the car to have been made in 1948 and, in that belief, the buyer paid £290. That belief can be just as firmly based on the buyer's own inspection of the log book as on a contractual warranty by the seller.

Once that fact is put on one side, I ask myself: What is the proper inference from the known facts? It must have been obvious to both that the seller had himself no personal knowledge of the year when the car was made. He only became owner after a great number of changes. He must have been relying on the registration book. It is unlikely that such a person would warrant the year of manufacture. The most he could do would be to state his belief and then produce the registration book in verification of it. In these circumstances, the intelligent bystander would, I suggest, say that the seller did not intend to bind himself so as to warrant that it was a 1948 model. If the seller was asked to pledge himself to it, he would at once have said "I cannot do that. I have only the log book to go by, the same as you."

The judge seems to have thought that there was a difference between written contracts and oral contracts. He thought that the reason why the buyer failed in *Heilbut, Symons & Co* v *Buckleton* and *Routledge* v *McKay* was because the sales were afterwards recorded in writing and the written contracts contained no reference to the representation. I agree that that was an important factor in those cases. If an oral representation is afterwards recorded in writing, it is good evidence that it was intended as a warranty. If it is not put into writing, it is evidence against a warranty being intended. But it is by no means decisive. There have been many cases where the courts have found an oral warranty collateral to a written contract, such as *Birch* v *Paramount Estates*. But when the purchase is not recorded in writing at all, it must not be supposed that every representation made in the course of the dealing is to be treated as a warranty. The question then is still: Was it intended as a warranty? In the leading case of *Chandelor* v *Lopus* in 1603 a man, by word of mouth, sold a precious stone for £100 affirming it to be a bezar stone, whereas it was not. The declaration averred that the seller affirmed it to be a bezar stone, but did not aver that he warranted it to be so. The declaration was held to be ill because "the bare affirmation that it was a bezar stone, without warranting it to be so, is no cause of action". That has been the law from that day to this and it was emphatically reaffirmed by the House of Lords in *Heilbut, Symons & Co* v *Buckleton*.

One final word: it seems to me clear that the motor dealers who bought the car relied on the year stated in the log book. If they had wished to make sure of it, they could have checked it then and there by taking the engine number and chassis number and writing to the makers. They did not do so at the time, but only eight months later. They are experts and, not having made that check at the time, I do not think they should now be allowed to recover against the innocent seller, who produced to them all the evidence he had, namely the registration book. I agree that it is hard on the dealers to have paid more than the car is worth: but it would be equally hard on the seller to make him pay the difference. He would never have bought the Hillman at all unless he had got the allowance of £290 from the Morris. The best course in all these cases would be to "shunt" the difference down the train of innocent sellers until one reaches the rogue who perpetrated the fraud: but he can rarely be traced or, if he can, he rarely has the

money to pay the damages. So one is left to decide between a number of innocent people who is to bear the loss. That can only be done by applying the law about representations and warranties as we know it: and that is what I have tried to do. If the rogue can be traced, he can be sued by whomsoever has suffered the loss: but if he cannot be traced, the loss must lie where it falls. It should not be inflicted on innocent sellers, who sold the car many months, perhaps many years, before and have forgotten all about it and have conducted their affairs on the basis that the transaction was concluded. Such a seller would not be able to recollect, after all this length of time, the exact words he used, such as whether he said "I believe it is a 1948 model", or "I warrant it is a 1948 model". The right course is to let the buyer set aside the transaction if he finds out the mistake quickly and comes promptly, before other interests have irretrievably intervened; otherwise the loss must lie where it falls: and that is, I think, the course prescribed by law. I would allow this appeal accordingly.'

Comment
See *Beale* v *Taylor* [1967] 1 WLR 1193 which held that a representation was a term of the contract.

Priest v Last [1903] 2 KB 148 Court of Appeal (Sir Richard Henn Collins MR and Stirling LJ)

- *Hot water bottle – fitness for purpose*

Facts
The plaintiff went into a chemist's shop to buy a hot water bottle. It was in the ordinary course of his business for the chemist to sell hot water bottles and the plaintiff asked him if the india rubber bottle which he was offering to him would stand boiling water. He was told that it would stand hot water but not boiling water. The plaintiff bought the hot water bottle and on the fifth time it was used it burst, scalding the plaintiff's wife. The plaintiff had purchased the hot water bottle

for use by his wife in order to relieve her cramp. It was shown in evidence that the bottle was not fit for use as a hot water bottle. The plaintiff claimed under s14(1) of the Sale of Goods Act 1893.

Held

The plaintiff's claim would be successful. Although some goods can be used for many purposes, others (including hot water bottles) have only one particular purpose. The mere fact of asking for such goods is an implied notification of the purpose for which they are required.

Sir Richard Henn Collins MR:

'This was an action by the purchaser of a hot-water bottle against the vendor for damages for the breach of an implied warranty under s14, that the article sold was fit for the purpose for which it was sold. It was found as a fact that the hot-water bottle was not fit for the purpose and that this was the cause of it bursting and injuring the buyer's wife.

It was contended under s14 that the requirement that the particular purpose for which the article is bought be made known to the seller can only be done by something beyond what is contained in the recognised description of the article itself ... I do not think it is a sound contention that something which is bought for its ordinary purpose cannot without more come within the section because the particular purpose must be made known.

The object with which the words were introduced into legislation is clear. There are many goods which have in themselves no special or peculiar efficacy for any one particular purpose, but are capable of general use for a multitude of purposes. In that sort of case it must be shown that it was sold with reference to a particular purpose for a warranty to arise. But where the description of the goods points to one particular purpose only it seems to me the first requirement of the subsection is satisfied, namely that the particular purpose is made known to the seller. The learned judge drew

(by invitation of the parties) inferences of fact which necessarily arose in this case from the nature of the transaction itself.

A draper, unskilled in the matter of hot water bottles, goes to the shop of a person who makes it part of his business to supply such bottles and asks for one which is supplied to him as such. It seems to me that the transaction amounts to a contract to supply him with an article reasonably fit for use as a hot water bottle under any circumstances in which such bottles are usually applicable, including the purpose of applying heat to any part of the human body. The inference is one of fact which must depend on all the circumstances of the case. It cannot be excluded by the fact that the article was generally known and was sold by a name which indicated that the purpose for which it was required.'

Comment

See also *Godley* v *Perry* [1960] 1 WLR 9 which further discusses the implied terms fitness for purpose.

R & B Customs Brokers Co Ltd v United Dominions Trust Ltd [1988] 1 All ER 847 Court of Appeal (Dillon and Neill LJJ)

• *Exclusion clause – 'dealing as consumer'*

Facts

The plaintiffs bought from the defendant finance company a Colt Shogun ('the car'), the car having been supplied by the third party motor dealer who took the plaintiffs' Volvo in part exchange. The plaintiffs took the car on 21 September but, for some unknown reason, the defendants did not sign the conditional sale agreement ('the agreement') until 3 November and this was accepted to be the date of the contracts between the dealer and the defendants and the defendants and the plaintiffs respectively. Between these dates, the plaintiffs discovered that the car's roof leaked and the dealer took it in for repair on 5 November. The leak was not cured then or subsequently and in the following February the plaintiffs rejected the car and claimed their money back. The car was the second or third vehicle which the plaintiffs had acquired on credit terms and the agreement provided, inter alia, that any implied conditions as to the condition or quality of the car or its fitness for any particular purpose in relation to business transactions were excluded.

Held

Unless excluded by the agreement's express terms, the sale was subject to an implied condition as to fitness under s14(3) of the Sale of Goods Act 1979. On the facts, this was a consumer transaction (as opposed to a business transaction) and the implied condition was not excluded. It followed that the plaintiffs were entitled to judgment.

Dillon LJ:

> '... I have no doubt that the requisite degree of regularity is not made out on the facts. [The plaintiff's] evidence that the car was the second or third vehicle acquired on credit terms was in my judgment and in the context of this case not enough. Accordingly, I agree with the judge that, in entering into the conditional sale agreement with the defendants, the company was "dealing as consumer". The defendants' [agreement] is thus inapplicable and the defendants are not absolved from liability under s14(3).'

Slater and Others v *Finning Ltd*
[1997] AC 473 House of Lords
(Lords Keith of Kinkel, Griffiths, Jauncey of Tullichettle, Slynn of Hadley and Steyn)

• *Implied term – fitness for purpose*

Facts

The appellants owned a fishing vessel, Aquarius II, which they purchased in 1981. In

1985 the appellants decided to uprate the power of the engine from 750 to 850 horse-power. The respondents' engineer carried out some work on the Aquarius II and replaced various parts. Further work was needed and the respondents investigated the problems and found the crankshaft needed to be replaced and also advised the camshaft to be replaced at the same time. The appellants agreed and the respondents arranged for a new camshaft to be delivered. However, a number of faults appeared and the appellants insisted a new engine was the only solution, which was supplied and fitted by the respondents.

The appellants claimed payment of £662,500 damages, which resulted from a breach of the implied condition under s14(3) of the Sale of Goods Act 1979. The respondents counter-claimed for £63,700, plus interest, for the supply of goods and services.

Held

Lord Keith of Kinkel examined the facts of this case and made reference to the construction of s14(3) of the Sale of Goods Act 1979, which states:

> 'Where the seller sells goods in the course of a business and the buyer, expressly or by implication, makes known –
> (a) to the seller, or
> (b) where the purchase price or part of it is payable by instalments and the goods were previously sold by a credit-broker to the seller,
> any particular purpose for which the goods are being bought, there is an implied condition that the goods supplied under the contract are reasonably fit for that purpose, whether or not that is a purpose for which goods are commonly supplied, except where the circumstances show that the buyer does not rely or that it is unreasonable for him to rely, on the skill or judgment of the seller or credit-broker.'

The respondents were aware the camshaft was to be installed in the Aquarius II. However, the vessel had a peculiar characteristic, which gave rise to excessive torsional resonance in the engine camshaft. Therefore, due to the idiosyncratic nature of the Aquarius II the camshaft was not fit for its purpose. Given these facts, Lord Keith stated '[the] cause of the trouble did not lie in the camshafts themselves but in some external feature peculiar to Aquarius II' (p481). He applied the case of *Griffiths* v *Peter Conway Ltd* [1939] 1 All ER 685 where a plaintiff had purchased a tweed coat and contracted dermatitis, due to her sensitive skin. She had not informed the seller of her sensitive skin and the coat would not affect the skin of a normal person. As the defendants were not made aware of the plaintiff's abnormal sensitivity to tweed the action was dismissed and affirmed by the Court of Appeal. Based upon this finding Lord Keith was of the opinion that:

'The particular purpose for which the camshafts were required was that of being fitted in the engine of a vessel which suffered from a particular abnormality or idiosyncrasy, namely a tendency to create excessive torsional resonance in camshafts. The respondents, not being aware of that tendency, were not in a position to exercise skill and judgment for the purpose of dealing with it.' (p482)

Having found the Aquarius II to have an idiosyncrasy, which was not made known to the respondents, Lord Keith reinforced this point using the case of *Christopher Hill Ltd* v *Ashington Piggeries Ltd* [1972] AC 441. This case concerned mink breeders who had purchased animal feed. The animal feed caused the mink to die due to a particular ingredient, namely herring meal which contained a toxic agent called DMNA. This was dangerous to a variety of animals, not only mink. However, mink were more sensitive to the toxin than other animals. Lord Wilberforce's dictum, at p490, was used by Lord Keith to illustrate an idiosyncrasy and whether or not the seller was aware and had used his skill and judgment:

'If Mink possessed an idiosyncrasy, which made the food as supplied unsuitable for them though it was perfectly suitable for

other animals, this would be the buyers' responsibility, unless, as is not the case here, they had made this idiosyncrasy known to the sellers so as to show reliance on them to provide for it.' (p482)

Given the comparison between these two cases and their application to the question Lord Keith came to the following conclusion:

'... where a buyer purchases goods from a seller who deals in goods of that description there is no breach of the implied condition of fitness where failure of the goods to meet the intended purpose arises from an abnormal feature or idiosyncrasy, not made known to the seller by the buyer. ... In these circumstances it would be totally unreasonable that the seller should be liable for breach of s14(3) ... for these reasons I would dismiss this appeal.'

Lord Steyn agreed with Lord Keith and gave this analogy to the current case:

'... a firm specialising in the supply of motor car tyres. A customer walks in and asks for a tyre suitable for his car, which is parked, on the forecourt. The firm supplies a tyre. The car breaks down due to the collapse of the tyre. There was nothing wrong with the tyre. But a defect in the steering mechanism caused the problem. Is the supplier, who was ignorant of the steering problem, liable to the customer because the tyre was unfit for the particular vehicle? If the answer is in the affirmative, such a supplier (if he is unable to disclaim liability) may be forced to resort to time-consuming and expensive investigations of cars to which tyres are to be fitted. Such a view of the law would therefore tend to complicate commonplace transactions.' (p485)

Comment
This case reinforces the principles laid down in *Griffiths* v *Peter Conway* and *Christopher Hill Ltd* v *Ashington Piggeries Ltd*. A purchaser is not able to rely upon the seller's expertise and skill if the goods are not fit for their purpose under s14(3) due to an idiosyncrasy or abnormality not made known at the

time of the contract. See also *Rogers* v *Parish (Scarborough) Ltd* [1987] 2 WLR 353.

Stevenson v *Rogers* [1999] 1 All ER 613 Court of Appeal (Butler-Sloss and Potter LJJ, Sir Patrick Russell)

• *Sale of goods – implied condition when dealing within the course of a business*

Facts
This was an appeal by the purchaser of a vessel sold to him in 1988 by the respondent, who carried on business as a fisherman, and was selling the vessel in order to replace it with a new one. Whether or not there was an implied term that the vessel was of satisfactory condition depended on whether the vessel was sold in the course of a business or the sale was a private transaction.

The appellant contested the finding that the contract of sale contained no implied term claiming the vessel should have been of satisfactory quality under s14(2) of the Sale of Goods Act 1979 (as amended) because the contract had been made 'in the course of a business'. Throughout the appeal an analogy was drawn between the Trade Descriptions Act (TDA) 1968, which implies criminal liability when offering or applying false trade descriptions in the 'course of a business', and the Unfair Contract Terms Act (UCTA) 1977, which distinguishes between consumers and traders. The cases of *Davies* v *Sumner* [1984] 1 WLR 1301 (TDA 1968) and *R & B Customs Brokers Co Ltd* v *United Dominions Trust Ltd* [1988] 1 WLR 321 (UCTA 1977) were used to test the interpretation of such concepts as 'regularity', 'incidental sales', and 'integral parts of the business'.

Held
The Court of Appeal found the sale of the vessel was made in the course of a business within the meaning of s14(2) of the Sale of Goods Act 1979 and the contract did indeed include the implied term relating to satisfactory quality.

Comment
This case is a turning point in the law in relation to earlier decisions made, which distinguished between contracts made in the course of a business, and has extended liability in a commercial transaction.

Varley v *Whipp* [1900] 1 QB 513 High Court (Channell and Bucknill JJ)

• *Sale by description – reaping machine*

Facts
The parties contracted to buy and sell a reaping machine which the defendant had never seen and which the plaintiff stated to have been 'new the previous year' and to have been used to cut only 50 or 60 acres. The machine was delivered and shortly afterwards the defendant wrote complaining that it did not correspond with the plaintiff's statements. The defendant returned the machine; the plaintiff sued for the price. The county court judge held that the contract was for a sale by description and that the defendant could only treat the misdescription as a breach of warranty, but not as a ground for rejecting the machine, and gave judgment for the plaintiff for the amount claimed. The defendant appealed.

Held
The appeal would be allowed.

Channell J:

'The point in issue is whether the words used by the seller with regard to the machine were part of the description or merely amounted to a collateral warranty. If property passed before the defendant wrote to the plaintiff complaining, nothing the defendant could do afterwards would divest it. The reaping machine was not even the property of the seller at the time. It was described as "being at Upton, as being a self-binder, as being nearly new, and as having been used to cut only about 50 or 60 acres". All these statements were made with regard to the machine and we have to consider how much of these statements was identification of the machine, and how much was mere collateral warranty.

... The term "sale of goods by description" must apply to all cases where the purchaser has not seen the goods, but is relying on the description alone, as here where the buyer has bought by the description. Here the condition of correspondence with description is a different thing than a warranty. The usual application is to be the case of unascertained goods, but I think it must also be applied to this case where there is no identification otherwise than by description. Section 17 of the Sale of Goods Act states that property passes when buyer and seller intend it to pass and this intuition is to be gleaned from terms, conduct and circumstances ... The earliest date when property could be said to pass would be when the machine was accepted by the purchaser. It never was accepted. Therefore the defendant was entitled to reject.'

6   Duties of the Buyer

British and Commonwealth Holdings plc v Quadrex Holdings Inc [1989] 3 WLR 723 Court of Appeal (Sir Nicolas Browne-Wilkinson VC, Woolf and Staughton LJJ)

- *Time 'of the essence'?*

Facts
The plaintiff and defendant companies, both wishing to acquire control of a third company, entered into a written agreement whereby the defendant would withdraw its bid, leaving the way clear for the plaintiff to acquire the company and the plaintiff would then sell the company's wholesale broking division to the defendant. The defendant had trouble finding the purchase money for the broking division and on 25 January 1985 the plaintiff served on it a notice fixing 28 February as the final date to complete the contract. The defendant failed to complete and the plaintiff started proceedings claiming damages for the defendant's repudiation of the contract. The defendant denied time was of the essence and further claimed that the plaintiff company was itself in breach and the cause of the delay. At first instance the plaintiff successfully obtained summary judgment with damages to be assessed and an interim order for £75 million. The defendant appealed.

Held
1. Although the contract specified completion to take place as soon as reasonably practicable after certain preliminaries had been fulfilled, no date had been fixed or was capable of being fixed at the time of the contract and therefore time was not, originally, 'of the essence'. However the commercial nature of the contract was such that if a date had been specified, it would have been 'of the essence'. If an innocent party, the plaintiff would have been entitled to serve notice making time 'of the essence'; but
2. the plaintiff's status was not that of an innocent party and therefore their ability to issue such a notice was in doubt.

The appeal was therefore allowed, leave given to defend the summary judgment order and the interim order reduced to £5 million.

Sir Nicolas Browne-Wilkinson VC:

'The phrase "time is of the essence of the contract" is capable of causing confusion since the question in each case is whether time is of the essence of the particular contractual term which has been breached ...

In equity, time is not normally of the essence of a contractual term. The rules of equity now prevail over the old common law rule: see the Law of Property Act 1925 s41. However, in three types of cases time is of the essence in equity: first, where the contract expressly so stipulates; second, where the circumstances of the case or the subject matter of the contract indicate that the time for completion is of the essence; third, where a valid notice to complete has been given. In the present case there was no express stipulation that time was of the essence. The subject matter of the sale (shares in unquoted private companies trading in a very volatile sector) is such that if a date for completion had been specified, in my judgment time would undoubtedly have been of the essence of completion ... For the reasons I have given, time could not be of the essence of completion on a date which was neither specified nor capable of exact determination by the parties. The only question is whether time was made of the essence by the service of a valid notice to complete.

In the ordinary case, three requirements have to be satisfied if time for completion is to be made of the essence by the service of a notice, viz (1) the giver of the notice (the innocent party) has to be ready, willing and able to complete, (2) the other party (the guilty party) has to have been guilty of unreasonable delay before a notice to complete can be served and (3) the notice when served must limit a reasonable period within which completion is to take place.'

Comment

Section 41 of the Law of Property Act 1925, which Sir Nicolas Browne-Wilkinson refers to, has in effect fused the rules of common law and equity. Thus, the rule is that time is not initially of the essence but will become of the essence if reasonable notice is given and the innocent party is able, willing and ready to complete their side of the bargain. See also *United Scientific Holdings Ltd* v *Burnley Borough Council* [1978] AC 904; *Bunge Corporation* v *Tradax SA* [1981] 2 All ER 513; *Rickards (Charles) Ltd* v *Oppenheim* [1950] 1 All ER 420; *Behzadi* v *Shaftesbury Hotels Ltd* [1991] 2 All ER 477 and *Union Eagle Ltd* v *Golden Achievement Ltd* [1997] 2 All ER 215. Also see Reg 19 of the Consumer Protection (Distance Selling) Regulations 2000 which discusses time and performance in relation to a consumer contract that has been made through the medium of distance selling, as defined under the Regulations.

7 Exclusion of Liability

Chapelton v *Barry Urban District Council* [1940] 1 KB 532 Court of Appeal (Slesser, MacKinnon and Goddard LJJ)

- *Hire of deck chair – conditions*

Facts
Beside deck chairs stacked on a beach was a notice: 'Barry Urban District Council ... Hire of chairs, 2d per session of 3 hours ...' The plaintiff took two of the chairs and he received from the attendant two tickets which he put in his pocket without reading the statement printed on the back that 'The Council will not be liable for any accident or damage arising from hire of chair'. The canvas of the plaintiff's chair gave way and he suffered injury.

Held
He was entitled to damages.

MacKinnon LJ:

> 'If a man does an act which constitutes the making of a contract, such as taking a railway ticket, or depositing his bag in a cloakroom, he will be bound by the terms of the documents handed to him by the servant of the carriers or bailees, as the case may be. If, however, he merely pays money for something, and receives a receipt for it, or does something which may clearly only amount to that, he cannot be deemed to have entered into a contract in the terms of the words which his creditor has chosen to print on the back of the receipt, unless, of course, the creditor has taken reasonable steps to bring the terms of the proposed contract to the mind of the man. In this case there is no evidence at all upon which the county court judge could find that the defendants had taken any steps at all to bring the terms of

their proposed contract to the mind of the plaintiff. In those circumstances, I am satisfied that the defendants could not rely upon the words on the back of the ticket issued to the plaintiff, and, having admittedly been negligent in regard to the condition of the chair, they had no defence to the plaintiff's cause of action.'

Comment
Parker v *South Eastern Railway Co* (1877) 2 CPD 416 which discusses reasonable notice concerning clauses on the back of tickets. See, too, *Curtis* v *Chemical Cleaning & Dyeing Co Ltd* [1951] 1 KB 805 which involved a receipt containing an exclusion clause and an innocent misrepresentation.

Director General of Fair Trading v *First National Bank* [2002] 1 All ER 97 House of Lords (Lords Bingham of Cornhill, Steyn, Hope of Craighead, Millett and Rodger of Earlsferry)

- *Unfair terms under the Unfair Terms in Consumer Contract Regulations 1994 (now replaced by the 1999 Regulations)*

Facts
This was the first case to deal with unfair terms under the Unfair Terms in Consumer Contract Regulations 1994 (now replaced by the 1999 Regulations). The Regulations' raison d'être is to regulate standard form contracts and protect weaker parties from abuse by stronger contracting parties. The Regulations may apply to all types of contractual terms, not just exclusion clauses.

    The Director General of Fair Trading

(DGFT) applied for an injunction to prevent First National Bank (FNB) from using a clause in one of their standard term contracts that was a used as a regulated agreement under the Consumer Credit Act 1974.

FNB is licensed to carry on consumer credit business and lends money to customers which are regulated by the Consumer Credit Act 1974. Agreements made between customers and FNB are made on standard term contracts.

Under the Unfair Terms in Consumer Contract Regulations (UTCC) consumers have been given increased protection when they enter into standard form contracts. For example, reg 4(1) of the 1994 provisions provided:

'In these Regulations, subject to paragraphs (2) and (3)… "unfair terms" means any term which is contrary to the requirement of good faith [which] causes a significant imbalance in the parties' rights and obligations under the contract to the detriment of the consumer.'

This is now contained in reg 5 of the 1999 Regulations. Regulation 5 has a two-pronged test, based on good faith and an imbalance in rights resulting in a detriment. The concept of 'good faith' is from the continental system and not the British system, which denotes fairness.

There does not appear to be any universal concept of fairness or good faith within any member state and the Unfair Terms in Consumer Contract Directive (93/13/EEC) which introduced the Regulations does not purport to state the law of any single member state, only guidance to what may equate to unfairness or good faith. Schedule 3 of the 1994 Regulations sets out various examples of terms which may be regarded as unfair and contrary to good faith, now contained in Schedule 2 of the 1999 Regulations. To determine whether or not the clause is unfair and not in good faith the court will look at the contract as a whole, and not just the clause in question.

The DGFT exercised his powers under reg 8 to obtain an injunction and attempted to prevent First National Bank from using a term contained within a consumer credit agreement, regulated under the Consumer Credit Act 1974. The term allowed the bank to claim post-judgment interest at the contract rate. The DGFT claimed the inclusion of such a term in a regulated agreement, was unfair within the meaning of reg 4, and he also claimed the clause was unlikely to be noticed by the average borrower at the time the contract was made.

The term in question was Condition 8 which stated:

'Time is of the essence for making all repayments to FNB as they fall due. If any repayment instalment is unpaid for more than seven days after it became due, FNB may serve a notice on the Customer requiring payment before a specified date not less than seven days later. If the repayment instalment is not paid in full by that date, FNB will be entitled to demand payment of the balance on the Customer's account and interest then claimed or incurred by FNB in trying to obtain the repayment of the unpaid instalment of such balance and interest. *Interest on the amount which becomes payable shall be charged in accordance with Condition 4, at the rate stated in paragraph D overleaf (subject to variation) until payment after as well as before any judgement (such obligation to be independent of and not to merge with the judgement).*'

Emphasis was added to the last sentence, as it is this sentence the DGFT claimed to be unfair, and for the sake of brevity shall be referred to as 'the term'. The DGFT alleged 'the term', known as a simple rate agreement, ensured the bank would be entitled to interest at the contract rate on the principal, plus accrued interest at the date of judgment until *the judgment is discharged*.

Held

At first instance (*Director General of Fair Trading* v *First National Bank plc* [2000] 1 All ER 240) Evans-Lombe J explained the common law position when dealing with a judgment being entered against the defendant and any future interest on that judgment:

'... once judgment is entered, the principal is owing on the judgment, not under the contract. The contract merges in the judgment. If the contract contains a provision making interest payable on any principal sum due under it, then, in the absence of express provision to the contrary, the covenant to pay interest will be regarded as ancillary to the covenant to pay the principal with the result that, if judgment is obtained for the principal, the covenant to pay interest will merge in the judgment. Accordingly, unless the contract contains a provision excluding the operation of merger in respect of the covenant to pay interest, the entitlement of the judgment creditor to claim interest on the judgment will be governed by statute. It is open to the parties to a contract expressly to agree that a covenant to pay interest shall not merge in any judgement for the principal sum due. Where they so agree, interest may be charged under the contract on the principal sum due, even after judgment for that sum.' (p243)

Clause 8 ('the term') prevented the operation of merger and this allowed FNB to recover not only the outstanding principal but any interest accruing on that sum after judgment, as well as before judgment. If FNB had not included such a clause they would not have automatically been entitled to interest after judgment.

At first instance, Evans-Lombe J did not regard the term as unfair:

'I have ... come to the conclusion that cl 8 is not, by its effect, inherently unfair. It seems to me that a term not inherently unfair can still constitute a breach of the requirement of good faith if it unfairly deprives consumers of a benefit or advantage which they may reasonably expect to receive. ... The only "substantive" advantage of which cl 8 deprives borrowers is their exemption from having to pay interest on the amount of any judgment obtained against them consequent on their default in making payments pur-

suant to their loan agreements with the bank.' (pp251–52)

However, the Court of Appeal ([2000] 2 WLR 1353) did not agree with this conclusion. Peter Gibson LJ was of the opinion that:

'... the relevant term is unfair within the meaning of the Regulations of 1994 to the extent that it enables the bank to obtain judgment against a debtor under a regulated agreement ... The bank, with its strong bargaining position as against the relatively weak position of the consumer, has not adequately considered the consumer's interests in this respect. In our view the relevant term in that respect does create unfair surprise and so does not satisfy the test of good faith; it does cause a significant imbalance in the right and obligations of the parties ...' (p1366)

To complete the cycle, Lord Bingham of Cornhill, in the House of Lords' judgment, gave his interpretation and application of the Regulations:

'I do not think that the term can be stigmatised as unfair on that ground that it violates or undermines a statutory regime enacted for the protection of consumers. It is of course foreseeable that a borrower, no matter how honourable and realistic his intentions when entering into a credit agreement, may fall on hard times and find himself unable to honour his obligations. The bank's standard conditions recognise that possibility by providing for the contingency of default ... When the contract is made, default is a foreseeable contingency, not an expected outcome ... On balance, I do not consider that the term can properly be said to cause a significant imbalance in the parties' rights and obligations under the contract to the detriment of the consumer in a manner or to an extent which is contrary to the requirement of good faith.' (paras 22–24)

Thus, the House of Lords confirmed the decision of Evans-Lombe J, at first instance, finding the clause not to be unfair in this instance.

Comment

The interpretation of 'good faith' under the continental system appears to have caused some confusion for the judiciary. However, given the arguments put forward from first instance to House of Lords it is apparent there is a universal definition of 'good faith' but its application will be governed by the nature and circumstances prevailing and, more importantly, judicial interpretation.

Expo Fabrics (UK) Ltd v Martin
[2003] EWCA Civ 1165 Court of Appeal (Lord Phillips of Worth Matravers MR, Waller and Carnwath LJJ)

• *Satisfactory quality – standard terms – reasonableness test and Unfair Contract Terms Act 1977*

Facts

The appellant, Mr Martin (M), appealed against the decision of Knight J who gave judgment, at first instance, to the respondents, Expo Fabrics Ltd (E) in the sum of £73,946.95 which represented the price of cloth sold to the appellant. The issue arose when M claimed that one of the batches of cloth was not of satisfactory quality. However, E defended the claim on the basis of a time limitation clause in the contract (at cl 6(a)), which stated:

'Any claim by the buyer which is based on any defect in the quality or condition of the goods or their failure to correspond with specification shall (whether or not delivery is refused by the Buyer) be notified in writing to the Seller within 20 days from the date of delivery, if the buyer does not notify the Seller accordingly the Seller shall have no liability for such defects or failure and the Buyer shall be bound to pay the price as if the goods had been delivered in accordance with the contract.'

Clause 6(b) then went on to state:

'Where any valid claim in respect of any of the goods which is based on any defect in

the quality or condition of the goods or their failure to meet specifications is notified to the Seller in accordance with these conditions the Seller shall be entitled to replace the goods (or the part in question) free of charge, or at the Seller's sole discretion refund to the Buyer the price of the goods (or a proportion of part of the price) but the Seller shall have no further liability to the Buyer.'

In addition to the above, cl 7 of the contract explained the position if the goods (raw materials) were used by the purchaser to manufacture goods and then the material was found not to be of satisfactory quality:

'No liability whatever is or can be accepted for any goods which have been subjected to the Buyer or the Buyer's servants or agents to any process and/or cut or made up, and in any event, the seller shall be under no obligation to accept the return of the goods unless the Seller has agreed to do so.'

At first instance Knight J found that the batch complained of was unsatisfactory. However, the above terms had been incorporated into the contract and excluded E from incurring liability. Furthermore, he found the terms to be reasonable and not void pursuant to the Unfair Contract Terms Act 1977 and a claim for loss of profit by M was unsustainable.

M appealed on three grounds: first, the terms had not been incorporated into the contract; second, if they had been incorporated they were void pursuant to the Unfair Contract Terms Act 1977; and third, M believed Knight J was wrong to conclude the claim for loss of profit was unsustainable. Permission to appeal on the first and third ground was not granted but on the second ground permission was given to argue the question of reasonableness under the Unfair Contract Terms Act 1977.

Held

Waller LJ considered the ground of appeal in relation to the facts and the application of the Unfair Contract Terms Act 1977, and made reference to s3 of that Act:

'(1) This section applies as between contracting parties where one of them deals as consumer or on the other's written standard terms of business.

(2) As against that party, the other cannot be reference to any contract term –

(a) when himself in breach of contract, exclude or restrict any liability of his in respect of the breach; or

(b) claim to be entitled –

(i) to render a contractual performance substantially different from that which was reasonably expected of him, or

(ii) in respect of the whole or any part of his contractual obligations, to render no performance at all,

except in so far as (in any of the cases mentioned above in this subsection) the contract term satisfies the requirements of reasonableness.'

In addition to the above, reference was made by Mr Colbey, who acted on behalf of the appellants, to s6(3):

'As against a person dealing otherwise than a consumer, the liability specified in subs(2) above can be excluded or restricted by reference to a contract term, but only in so far as the term satisfies the requirement of reasonableness.'

Waller LJ considered the interpretation of reasonableness with reference to s11(1) and (2) of the 1977 Act and sought guidance from Sch 2, which gives information on the reasonableness test. Waller LJ considered the position of the parties when they entered into the agreement, the time limit imposed under cl 6 and the implementation of cl 7. He also referred to Sch 2 and evidence given by Mr Ellis, an expert in relation to the use of such terms within the trade, who stated:

'Such a clause [cl 6] is very common and is usual in conditions of sale of textile fabric. The length of period between delivery and notification of complaints varies, but is more often between seven and 14 days of receipt of goods by the buyer. This means that these terms are more generous than usual.'

He then discussed cl 7 and in his opinion:

'This term is invariably included in any textile fabric manufacturer's conditions of sale. The reason for this being that once the fabric has been cut, it is impossible to reprocess it if there is any complaint. It is thus incumbent upon the garment manufacturer to ensure that the fabric is correct before the garments are cut. The only exception, which is normally understood between buyer and seller of textile fabric, is when the fault is a latent one, which cannot reasonably be discovered until after the fabric has been cut. Pile shedding [which is the complaint in this case] is not a latent fault and I am of the opinion that shedding could have been very easily determined before the fabric was cut.'

Waller LJ considered the strength of this evidence and whether these clauses were fair and reasonable by reference to the dictum of Lord Bridge in *George Mitchell (Chesterhall) Ltd v Finney Lock Seeds* [1983] 2 AC 803, at paras 815F–816B:

'This is the first time your Lordships' House has had to consider a modern statutory provision giving the court power to override contractual terms excluding or restricting liability, which depends on the court's view of what is "fair and reasonable". The particular provision of the modified s55 of the Act of 1979 which applies in the instant case is of limited and diminishing importance. But the several provisions of the Unfair Contract Terms Act 1977 which depend on "the requirement of reasonableness" defined by s11 by reference to what is "fair and reasonable", albeit in a different context, are likely to come before the courts with increasing frequency. It may, therefore, be appropriate to consider how an original decision as to what is "fair and reasonable" made in the application of any of these provisions should be approached by an appellate court. It would not be accurate to describe such a decision as an exercise of discretion ... the court must entertain a whole range of considerations, put them in the scales on one side or the other, and decide at the end of the day on which side the balance comes down. There will sometimes be room for a legitimate difference of judicial opinion as to what the answer should be, where it will be impossible to say that one view is demonstrably wrong and the other demonstrably right. It must follow, in my view, that, when asked to review a decision on appeal, the appellate court should treat the original decision with the utmost respect and refrain from interference with it unless satisfied that it proceeds upon some erroneous principle or was plainly and obviously wrong.'

Waller LJ then reviewed the original decision given by Knight J by considering the application of s11 to the facts in question. He found the time limit of 20 days to be reasonable. As regards cls 6(b) and 7 it was no longer necessary to consider them, having found cl 6(a) to be reasonable, and he dismissed the appeal. Carnwath LJ and Lord Phillips MR agreed with the decision of Waller LJ and appeal to the House of Lords was refused.

Comment

This case gave an interesting interpretation and application of the statutory guidelines laid down in Sch 2 of the Unfair Contract Terms Act 1977. The case confirmed the approach taken by the appellate courts when dealing with exclusion clauses and confirmed what is deemed to be reasonable by considering the individual facts in question. This was a commercial contract: the decision reflected the bargaining position and experience of the parties involved in addition to whether the clause was fair and reasonable.

George Mitchell (Chesterhall) Ltd v *Finney Lock Seeds Ltd* [1983] 2 AC 803 House of Lords (Lords Diplock, Scarman, Roskill, Bridge of Harwich and Brightman)

• *Clause limiting liability – fundamental breach*

Facts

The appellant seed merchant agreed to supply the respondent farmers with 30 lbs of Dutch winter cabbage seed for £201.60. The parties had dealt with each other over a number of years and the contract was covered by a clause purporting to limit liability on the part of the suppliers, to replacing the seed supplied or refunding the purchase price and further purporting to 'exclude all liability for any loss or damage arising from the use of any seeds or plants supplied by us and for any consequential loss or damage arising out of such use ... or for any other loss or damage whatever'. The appellants supplied a different seed to the one contracted for and as a result the respondents' crop was ruined. The respondents brought an action for damages claiming £61,513 for breach of contract.

Held

1. A limitation clause is to be construed contra proferentem and has to be clearly expressed but is not subject to the strict rules of construction applicable to exclusion clauses. Accordingly on its true construction the clause here was effective to limit the appellants' liability to replacement of the seeds or a refund of the price paid.

2. However, s55 of the Sale of Goods Act 1979 (as set out in para 11 of Sch 1) applied here and accordingly it was not fair or reasonable to permit the appellants to rely on the clause because: (a) they had not relied on it in the past but had negotiated a settlement; (b) the supply of the seed was due to the negligence of the appellants' associate company; (c) the appellants could have insured against the risk encountered.

Lord Bridge of Harwich:

'The relevant condition, read as a whole, unambiguously limits the appellants' liability to replacement of the seeds or refund of the price. It is only possible to read an ambiguity into it by the process of strained construction which was deprecated by Lord Diplock in the *Photo Production* case and by Lord Wilberforce in the *Ailsa Craig* case.

In holding that the relevant condition was ineffective to limit the appellants' liability for a breach of contract caused by their negligence, Kerr LJ applied the principles stated by Lord Morton giving judgment of the Privy Council in *Canada Steamship Lines Ltd* v *R*. Kerr LJ stated correctly that this case was also referred to by Lord Fraser in the *Ailsa Craig* case. He omitted, however, to notice that, as appears from the passage from Lord Fraser's speech which I have already cited, the whole point of Lord Fraser's reference was to express his opinion that the very strict principles laid down in the *Canada Steamship Lines* case as applicable to exclusion and indemnity clauses cannot be applied in their full rigour to limitation clauses. Lord Wilberforce's speech contains a passage to the like effect, and Lord Elwyn-Jones, Lord Salmon and Lord Lowry agreed with both speeches. Having once reached a conclusion in the instant case that the relevant condition unambiguously limited the appellants' liability, I know of no principle of construction which can properly be applied to confine the effect of the limitation to breaches of contract arising without negligence on the part of the appellants. In agreement with Lord Denning MR, I would decide the common law issue in the appellants' favour.

The statutory issue turns, as already indicated, on the application of the provisions of the modified s55 of the Sale of Goods Act 1979, as set out in para 11 of Sch 1 to the Act. The 1979 Act is a pure consolidation. The purpose of the modified s55 is to preserve the law as it stood from 18 May 1973 to 1 February 1978 in relation to contracts made between those two dates. The significance of the dates is that the first was the date when the Supply of Goods (Implied Terms) Act 1973 came into force containing the provision now re-enacted by the modified s55, the second was the date when the Unfair Contract Terms Act 1977 came into force and superseded the relevant provisions of the 1973 Act by more radical and far-reaching provisions in relation to contracts made thereafter.

The relevant subsections of the modified s55 provide as follows:

"(1) Where a right, duty or liability would arise under a contract of sale of goods by implication of law, it may be negatived or varied by express agreement, ... but the preceding provision has effect subject to the following provisions of this section

...

(4) In the case of a contract of sale of goods, any term of that or any other contract exempting from all or any of the provisions of s13, 14, or 15 above is void in the case of a consumer sale and is, in any other case, not enforceable to the extent that it is shown that it would not be fair or reasonable to allow reliance on the term.

(5) In determining for the purpose of subs (4) above whether or not reliance on any such term would be fair or reasonable regard shall be had to all circumstances of the case and in particular to the following matters: (a) the strength of the bargaining positions of the seller and buyer relative to each other, taking into account, among other things, the availability of suitable alternative products and sources of supply; (b) whether the buyer received an inducement to agree to the term or in accepting it had an opportunity of buying the goods or suitable alternatives without it from any source of supply; (c) whether the buyer knew or ought reasonably to have known of the existence and extent of the term (having regard, among other things, to any previous course of dealing between the parties), (d) where the term exempts from all or any of the provisions of s13, 14 or 15 above if some condition is not complied with, whether it was reasonable at the time of the contract to except that compliance with that condition would be practicable; (e) whether the goods were manufactured, precessed, or adapted to the special order of the buyer

...

(9) Any reference in this section to a term exempting from all or any of the provisions of any section of this Act is a reference to a term which purports to exclude or restrict, or has the effect of excluding or restricting, the operation of all or any of the provisions of that section, or the exercise of a right conferred by any provi-

sion of that section, or any liability of the seller for breach of a condition or warranty implied by any provision of that section ..."

The contract between the appellants and the respondents was not 'consumer sale', as defined for the purpose of these provisions.

The effect of cl3 of the relevant condition is to exclude, inter alia, the terms implied by ss13 and 14 of the Act that the seeds sold by description should correspond to the description and be of merchantable quality and to substitute therefor the express but limited obligations undertaken by the appellants under cll 1 and 2. The statutory issue, therefore, turns on the words in s55(4) "to the extent that it is shown that it would not be fair or reasonable to allow reliance on" this restriction of the appellants' liabilities, having regard to the matters referred to in subs (5).

This is the first time your Lordships' House has had to consider a modern statutory provision giving the court power to override contractual terms excluding or restricting liability, which depends on the court's view of what is "fair and reasonable". The particular provision of the modified s55 of the 1979 Act which applies in the instant case is of limited and diminishing importance. But the several provisions of the Unfair Contract Terms Act 1977 which depend on "the requirement of reasonableness", defined in s11 by reference to what is "fair and reasonable", albeit in a different context, are likely to come before the courts with increasing frequency. It may, therefore, be appropriate to consider how an original decision what is "fair and reasonable" made in the application of any of these provisions should be approached by the appellate court. It would not be accurate to describe such a decision as an exercise of discretion. But a decision under any of the provisions referred to will have this in common with the exercise of a discretion, that, in having regard to the various matters to which the modified s55(5) of the 1979 Act, or s11 of the 1977 Act direct attention, the court must entertain a whole range of considerations,

put them in the scales on one side or the other and decide at the end of the day on which side the balance comes down. There will sometimes be room for a legitimate difference of judicial opinion as to what the answer should be, where it will be impossible to say that one view is demonstrably wrong and the other demonstrably right. It must follow, in my view, that when asked to review such a decision on appeal, the appellate court should treat the original decision with the utmost respect and refrain from interference with it unless satisfied that it proceeded on some erroneous principle or was plainly and obviously wrong.

Turning back to the modified s55 of the 1979 Act, it is common ground that the onus was on the respondents to show that it would not be fair or reasonable to allow the appellants to rely on the relevant conditions as limiting their liability. It was argued for the appellants that the court must have regard to the circumstances as at the date of the contract, not after the breach. The basis of the argument was that this was the effect of s11 of the 1977 Act and that it would be wrong to construe the modified s55 of the Act as having a different effect. Assuming the premise is correct, the conclusion does not follow. The provisions of the 1977 Act cannot be considered in construing the prior enactments now embodied in the modified s55 of the 1979 Act. But, in any event, the language of the subss (4) and (5) of that section is clear and unambiguous. The question whether it is fair or reasonable to allow reliance on a term excluding or limiting liability for breach of contract can only arise after a breach. The nature of the breach and the circumstances in which it occurred cannot possibly be excluded from "all circumstances of the case" to which regard must be had.

The only other question of construction debated in the course of the argument was the meaning to be attached to the words "to the extent that" in subs (4) and, in particular, whether they permit the court to hold that it would be fair and reasonable to allow partial reliance on a limitation clause and, for example, to decide in the instant case that the respondents should recover, say, half their consequential damage. I incline to the view that, in their context, the words are equivalant to "in so far as" or "in circumstance in which" and do not permit the kind of judgment of Solomon illustrated by the example.

But for the purpose of deciding this appeal I find it unnecessary to express a concluded view on this question.

My Lords, at long last I turn to the application of the statutory language to the circumstances of the case. Of the particular matters to which attention is directed by para (a) to (e) of s55(5), only those in paras (a) to (c) are relevant. As to para (c), the respondents admittedly knew of the relevant condition (they had dealt with the appellant for many years) and, if they had read it, particularly cl2, they would, I think, as laymen rather than lawyers, have had no difficulty in understanding what it said. This and the magnitude of the damages claimed in proportion to the price of the seeds sold are factors which weigh in the scales in the appellants' favour.

The question of relative bargaining strength under para (a) and of the opportunity to buy seeds without limitation of the seedsman's liability under para (b) were interrelated. The evidence was that a similar limitation of liability was universally embodied in the terms of trade between seedsmen and farmers and had been so for very many yeras. The limitation had never been negotiated between representative bodies but, on the other hand, had not been the subject of any protest by the National Farmers' Union. These factors, if considered in isolation, might have been equivocal. The decisive factor, however, appears from the evidence of four witnesses called for the appellants, two independent seedsmen, the chairman of the appellant company, and a director of a sister company (both being wholly-owned subsidiaries of the same parent). They said that it had always been their practice, unsuccessfully attempted in the instant case, to negotiate settlements of farmers' claims for damages in excess of the price of the seeds, if they thought that the claims were "genuine" and "justified". This evidence indicated a clear recognition by seedsmen in general, and the appellants in particular, that reliance on the limitation of liability imposed by the relevant condition would not be fair or reasonable.

Two further factors, if more were needed, weigh the scales in favour of the respondents. The supply of autumn, instead of winter, cabbage seed was due to the negligence of the appellants' sister company. Irrespective of its quality, the autumn variety supplied could not, according to the appellants' own evidence, be grown commercially in East Lothian. Finally, as the trial judge found, seedsmen could insure against the risk of crop failure caused by suuply of the wrong variety of seeds without materially increasing the price of the seeds.

My Lords, even if I felt doubts about statutory issue, I should not, for the reasons explained earlier, think it right to interfere with the unanimous original decision of that issue by the Court of Appeal. As it is, I feel no such doubts. If I were making the original decision, I should conclude without hesitation that it would not be fair or reasonable to allow the appellants to rely on the contractual limitation of their liability.'

Comment

See also *Ailsa Craig Fishing Co Ltd v Malvern Fishing Co Ltd* [1983] 1 WLR 964.

Granville Oil & Chemicals Ltd v Davis Turner & Co Ltd [2003] 2 Lloyd's Rep 356 Court of Appeal (Potter and Tuckey LJJ, Hart J)

• *Exclusion clauses – Unfair Contract Terms Act 1977 – reasonableness*

Facts

The appellant Davis Turner (DT) brought an appeal against the decision, at first instance, of Behrens J who held that cl 30(B) of the British International Freight Association (BIFA) Standard Trading Conditions (1989 edition), which had been incorporated into a contract, had satisfied the test of reasonableness under the Unfair Contract Terms Act 1977. Clause 30 of the BIFA Standard Trading Conditions state:

'(A) Any claim by the customer against the company arising in respect of any service provided for the customer or which the company has undertaken to provide should be made in writing and notified to the company within 14 days of the date upon which the customer became or should have become aware of any event or occurrence alleged to give rise to such claim and any claim not made and notified as aforesaid shall be deemed to be waived and absolutely barred except where the customer can show that it was impossible for him to comply with this time limit and that he has made the claim as soon as it was reasonably possible for him to do so.
(B) Notwithstanding the provisions of subpara(A) above the company shall in any event be discharged of all liability whatsoever howsoever arising in respect of any service provided to the customer or which the company has undertaken to provide unless suit be brought and written notice thereof given to the company within nine months from the date of the event or occurrence alleged to give rise to the cause of action against the company.'

On 27 October 1999, DT agreed to carry a consignment of paint from Kuwait and deliver the paint to the warehouse of Granville Oil & Chemicals Ltd (GOC). In order for DT to perform their side of the bargain they had to collect and pack the paint into two shipping containers in Kuwait. DT then transported the paint by sea to Southampton and then arranged for the containers to be transported by road to their final destination. On 4 November, DT were to arrange insurance for the consignment against all risks in transit as part of the agreement. DT collected and delivered the paint on 11 January 2000. Upon inspection of the goods, GOC found them to be damaged and made a claim against DT for £27,673.00, which complied with the time

scale outlined in cl 30(A) above. DT responded by contacting the insurance company and making a claim on behalf of GOC. Between 21 January and 27 June DT discussed the claim with the underwriters and eventually the underwriters rejected the claim under an 'excepted peril' limitation within the insurance policy. However, GOC were not informed that the claim had been rejected until 22 August. Under cl 30(B) GOC had to commence proceedings within nine months, and this right expired on 3 August. GOC commenced proceedings on 15 November 2001. The judge at first instance found the clause had been incorporated into the contract. The issue of whether this clause was fair and reasonable remained; to find it fair and reasonable would bar GOC from making a claim under the provisions of the Unfair Contract Terms Act 1977. Behrens J found the clause did not satisfy the reasonableness test under the 1977 Act and that the time bar was ineffective to bar GOC's claim. Thus, DT appealed.

Held

Tuckey LJ outlined the provisions of the Act and made specific reference to s3. The decision of this case was based upon the interpretation of 'reasonableness' as defined under s11:

'(1) In relation to a contract term the requirement of reasonableness for the purposes of this part of the Act ... is that the term shall have been a fair and reasonable one to be included having regard to the circumstances where were, or ought reasonably to have been, known to or in the contemplation of the parties when the contract was made ...
(5) It is for those claiming that a contract term ... satisfies the requirement of reasonableness to show that it does.'

Guidance is given in Sch 2 of the Act on the application of the reasonableness test, which makes reference to the following:

'... (a) the strength of the bargaining positions of the parties ...

(c) whether the [respondent] knew or ought reasonably to have known of the existence and extent of the term (having regard, among other things, to any custom of the trade and any previous course of dealing between the parties)

(d) … whether it was reasonable at the time of the contract to expect that compliance with that condition would be practicable.'

Tuckey LJ found DT to have been in breach of contract by damaging the goods and failing to provide adequate insurance. However, as cl 30(B) restricted their liability in such instances the Act applied to that term in question.

Tuckey LJ considered whether GOC were aware of the clause and its implications and referred to the evidence submitted by DT's Managing Director, Mr Stephenson, who was of the opinion that many freight forwarding companies were members of BIFA and contracted on their conditions. He was also of the opinion that the limitation period was a fair and reasonable time period and allowed for adequate time to investigate any potential claim. However, Mr Patrick, GOC's export administration manager, denied any knowledge of cl 30(B); even though he had used freight forwarders at least 30 or 40 times a month. Reference was made to *Schenkers* v *Overland Shoes Ltd* [1998] 1 Lloyd's Rep 498 which involved BIFA conditions and the dictum of Pill LJ, at p506:

'The current [BIFA] conditions date from 1989 when earlier conditions were revised. They now form the basis of the standard trading conditions of many associations throughout the world. The conditions represent three years of hard work between interested bodies including the British Shippers Council, which included importers and exporters and included a wide range of UK manufacturers … They seek to balance the interests of all parties and in my view, have long been accepted as reasonable and fair.'

Having considered the arguments placed before him Tuckey LJ found that this was a commercial contract between commercial parties of equal bargaining strength. The respondent was in a position, if he so wished, to contract on alternative conditions to those set out by BIFA and to make their own insurance arrangements. It was on this basis that Tuckey LJ believed Behrens J reached the wrong decision; cl 30(B) was reasonable as between the contracting parties at the time when the contract was made.

Comment

This was a commercial contract and the Court made its decision based upon the respective bargaining strength of the parties. Tuckey LJ found the parties to have individually negotiated the terms in question and confirmed they satisfied the test of 'fairness and reasonableness' under the Unfair Contract Terms Act 1977. However, there are proposals to change the legal rules that currently control standard term contracts. One of the changes being proposed is based upon the premise that a standard term contract within a commercial contract is not individually negotiated. The suggested proposal is to bring such contracts in line with consumer contracts, which are given additional protection under the governance of the Unfair Terms in Consumer Contracts Regulations 1999. The proposal stems from the Law Commission Consultation Paper on Unfair Terms in Contracts (Law Com No 166) to adopt a similar approach when dealing with business contracts that have been made on standard forms, and whether or not the term is one regularly used by the proponent. The Consultation Paper is likely to merge these two pieces of legislation and reflect the position of consumers and businessmen alike, whilst considering the bargaining position of the parties.

Hollier v *Rambler Motors (AMC) Ltd* [1972] 2 WLR 401 Court of Appeal (Salmon and Stamp LJJ and Latey J)

• *Exemption clause – previous dealings*

Facts

The plaintiff sent his motor car to the defendants' garage for repairs. There had been three or four previous such transactions over a period of five years and, on at least two occasions, the plaintiff had signed an invoice containing an exemption clause in favour of the defendants, but on this occasion did not. The car was damaged by fire caused by the defendants' negligence.

Held

There was not sufficient previous course of dealing between the parties to impart the exemption clause into the present oral contract.

Salmon LJ:

'I am bound to say that ... I do not know of any other case in which it had been decided, or even argued, that a term could be implied into an oral contract on the strength of a course of dealing (if it can be so called) which consisted, at the most, of three or four transactions over a period of five years.'

Comment

Applied: *McCutcheon* v *David MacBrayne Ltd* [1964] 1 WLR 125. Distinguished: *Kendall (Henry) & Sons* v *William Lillico & Sons Ltd* [1968] 3 WLR 110. See also *Spurling (J)* v *Bradshaw* [1956] 2 All ER 121; *Hardwick Game Farm* v *Suffolk Agricultural Association* [1969] 2 AC 31 and *Hire Corporation Ltd* v *Ipswich Plant Hire Ltd* [1975] QB 303.

Interfoto Picture Library Ltd v *Stiletto Visual Programmes Ltd*
[1988] 2 WLR 615 Court of Appeal (Dillon and Bingham LJJ)

• *Condition printed on delivery note – effect*

Facts

The defendant advertising agency telephoned the plaintiff library of photographic transparencies, with which they had not dealt before, inquiring as to the availability of photographs of a certain period. In response, on 5 March the plaintiffs sent 47 transparencies packed in a bag with a delivery note which clearly specified that the transparencies were to be returned by 19 March. Under the heading 'Conditions', which was printed prominently in capitals, the delivery note set out nine conditions in four columns. Condition 1 stated that all transparencies were to be returned within 14 days and that 'a holding fee of £5 plus VAT per day will be charged for each transparency which is retained by you longer than the said period of 14 days'. The defendants accepted delivery, bit it was unlikely that they read any of the conditions: they did not use any of the transparencies, but put them to one side and forgot them, eventually returning them on 2 April. The plaintiffs sued for £3,783.50, being the amount of the holding charge calculated in accordance with condition 2. The trial judge decided in their favour: the defendants appealed.

Held

The appeal would be allowed and the defendants ordered to pay on a quantum meruit of £3.50 per transparency per week for retention beyond a reasonable period, ie, 14 days from the defendants' receipt of the transparencies.

Dillon LJ:

'Counsel for the plaintiffs submits that *Thornton* v *Shoe Lane Parking Ltd* [1971] 1 All ER 686 was a case of an exemption clause and that what their Lordships said must be read as limited to exemption clauses and in particular exemption clauses which would deprive the party on whom they are imposed of statutory rights. But what their Lordships said was said by way of interpretation and application of the general statement of the law by Mellish LJ in *Parker* v *South Eastern Rly Co* (1877) 2 CPD 416 and the logic of it is applicable to any particularly onerous clause in a printed set of conditions of the one contracting party which would not be generally known to the other party.

Condition 2 of these plaintiffs' conditions is in my judgment a very onerous clause. The defendants could not conceivably have known, if their attention was not drawn to the clause, that the plaintiffs were proposing to charge a "holding fee" for the retention of the transparencies at such a very high and exorbitant rate.

At the time of the ticket cases in the last century it was notorious that people hardly ever troubled to read printed conditions on a ticket or delivery note or similar document. That remains the case now. In the intervening years the printed conditions have tended to become more and more complicated and more and more one-sided in favour of the party who is imposing them, but the other parties, if they notice that there are printed conditions at all, generally still tend to assume that such conditions are only concerned with ancillary matters of form and are not of importance. In the ticket cases the courts held that the common law required that reasonable steps be taken to draw the other parties' attention to the printed conditions or they would not be part of the contract. It is in my judgment a logical development of the common law into modern conditions that it should be held, as it was in *Thornton* v *Shoe Lane Parking Ltd,* that, if one condition in a set of printed conditions is particularly onerous or unusual, the party seeking to enforce it must show that that particular condition was fairly brought to the attention of the other party.

In the present case, nothing whatever was done by the plaintiffs to draw the defendants' attention particularly to condition 2; it was merely one of four columns' width of conditions printed across the foot of the delivery note. Consequently condition 2 never, in my judgment, became part of the contract between the parties.'

L'Estrange v *Graucob (F) Ltd*
[1934] 2 KB 394 Court of Appeal (Scrutton and Maughan LJJ)

• *Exemption clause – sale of automatic machine*

Facts
The plaintiff purchased an automatic machine from the defendants by a contract contained in the defendants' written 'Sale Agreement' which she signed. The machine proved faulty and the defendants sought to rely on an exemption clause in the agreement.

Held
Having signed the agreement, the plaintiff was bound by it.

Scrutton LJ:

'In this case the plaintiff has signed a document headed "Sales Agreement" which she admits had to do with an intended purchase and which contained a clause excluding all conditions and warranties. That being so, the plaintiff, having put her signature to the document, and not having been induced to do so by any fraud or misrepresentation, cannot be heard to say that she is not bound by the terms of the document because she did not read them.'

Mitchell (George) (Chesterhall) Ltd v *Finney Lock Seeds Ltd*

See *George Mitchell (Chesterhall) Ltd* v *Finney Lock Seeds Ltd*, above.

Olley v *Marlborough Court Ltd*
[1949] 1 KB 532 Court of Appeal (Bucknill, Singleton and Denning LJJ)

• *Hotel – notice in bedroom*

Facts
The plaintiffs arrived at a hotel, booked in at reception and paid in advance. They went up to their room where a notice purported to exempt the proprietors for articles lost or stolen unless handed to the manageress for safe custody. During their stay some clothing was stolen from their room.

Held

The contract had been concluded when the plaintiffs booked and paid for their room and the defendants could not unilaterally vary the contract to include as a term the notice in the bedroom, which the plaintiffs only saw at a later stage.

Denning LJ:

'The only other point in the case is whether the hotel company are protected by the notice which they put in the bedrooms, "The proprietors will not hold themselves responsible for articles lost or stolen, unless handed to the manageress for safe custody". The first question is whether that notice formed part of the contract. Now people who rely on a contract to exempt themselves from their common law liability, must prove that contract strictly. Not only must the terms of the contract be clearly proved, but also the intention to create legal relations – the intention to be legally bound – must also be clearly proved. The best way of proving it is by a written document, signed by the party to be bound. Another way is by handing him, before or at the time of the contract, a written notice specifying its terms and making it clear to him that the contract is on those terms. A prominent public notice which is plain for him to see when he makes the contract, or an express oral stipulation would, no doubt, have the same effect. But nothing short of one of these three ways will suffice. It has been held that mere notices put on receipts for money do not make a contract. (See *Chapelton* v *Barry Urban District Council*). So also, in my opinion, notices put up in bedrooms do not of themselves make a contract. As a rule, the guest does not see them until after he has been accepted as a guest. The hotel company no doubt hopes that the guest will be bound by them, but the hope is vain unless they clearly show that he agreed to be bound by them, which is rarely the case.'

Photo Production Ltd v *Securicor Transport Ltd* [1980] 2 WLR 283
House of Lords (Lords Wilberforce, Diplock, Salmon, Keith of Kinkel and Scarman)

- *Exemption clause – fundamental breach*

Facts

The plaintiffs employed the defendants to provide security services at their factory, including night patrols. While on such a patrol, an employee of the defendants deliberately lit a small fire, which got out of control and completely destroyed the factory and its contents, of value £615,000. The defendants in their defence, relied on an exemption clause which provided that 'under no circumstances' were the defendants to 'be responsible for any injurious act or default by any employee ... unless such act or default could have been foreseen and avoided by the exercise of due diligence on the part of the [defendants] as his employer; nor, in any event, [were the defendants to] be held responsible for ... any loss suffered by the [plaintiffs] through ... fire or any other cause, except in so far as such loss [was] solely attributable to the negligence of the [defendants'] employees acting within the course of their employment ...' The Court of Appeal followed and applied *Harbutt's Plasticine* and found for the plaintiffs.

Held

There was no rule of law preventing the defendants from relying on the clause and, on its true construction, it exempted them from liability.

Lord Wilberforce:

'There are further provisions limiting, to stated amounts, the liability of Securicor, on which it relies in the alternative if held not to be totally exempt.

It is first necessary to decide on the correct approach to a case such as this, where it is sought to invoke an exception or limitation clause in the contract. The approach of Lord Denning MR in the Court of Appeal was to consider first whether the breach was "fundamental". If so, he said, the court itself deprives the party of the benefit of an exemption or limitation clause. Shaw and Waller LJJ subsequently followed him in this argument.

Lord Denning MR, in this, was following the earlier decision of the Court of Appeal and, in particular, his own judgment in *Harbutt's Plasticine Ltd* v *Wayne Tank and Pump Co Ltd* [1970] 1 QB 447 …

My Lords, whatever the intrinsic merit of this doctrine, as to which I shall have something to say later, it is clear to me that so far from following this House's decision in the *Suisse Atlantique Case*, it is directly opposed to it and that the whole purpose and tenor of the *Suisse Atlantique Case* was to repudiate it. The lengthy and perhaps, I may say, sometimes indigestible speeches of their Lordships, are correctly summarised in the headnote –

> "(3) That the question whether an exception clause was applicable where there was a fundamental breach of contract was one of the true constructions of the contract."

That there was any rule of law by which exception clauses are eliminated, or deprived of effect, regardless of their terms, was clearly not the view of Viscount Dilhorne, Lord Hodson or myself. The passages invoked for the contrary view of a rule of law consists only of short extracts from two of the speeches, on any view, a minority …

Much has been written about the *Suisse Atlantique Case*. Each speech has been subjected to various degrees of analysis and criticism, much of it constructive. Speaking for myself, I am conscious of imperfections of terminology, though sometimes in good company. But I do not think that I should be conducing to the clarity of the law by adding to what was already too ample a discussion, a further analysis which, in turn, would have to be interpreted. I have no second thoughts as to the main proposition that the question whether, and to what

extent, an exclusion clause is to be applied to a fundamental breach, of a breach of a fundamental term, or, indeed, to any breach of contract, is a matter of construction of the contract. Many difficult questions arise and will continue to arise in the infinitely varied situations in which contracts come to be breached: by repudiatory breaches, accepted or not, anticipatory breaches, by breaches of conditions or of various terms and whether by negligent or deliberate action, or otherwise. But there are ample resources in the normal rules of contract law for dealing with these, without the super-imposition of a judicially invented rule of law. I am content to leave the matter there with some supplementary observations.

1. The doctrine of "fundamental breach", in spite of its imperfections and doubtful parentage, has served a useful purpose. There were a large number of problems, productive of injustice, in which it was worse than unsatisfactory to leave exception clauses to operate. Lord Reid referred to these in the *Suisse Atlantique Case*, pointing out at the same time that the doctrine of fundamental breach was a dubious specific. But since then, Parliament has taken a hand: it has passed the Unfair Contract Terms Act 1977. This Act applies to consumer contracts and those based on standard terms and enables exception clauses to be applied with regard to what is just and reasonable. It is significant that Parliament refrained from legislating over the whole field of contract. After this Act, in commercial matters generally, when the parties are not of unequal bargaining power and when risk are normally borne by insurance, not only is the case for judicial intervention undemonstrated, but there is everything to be said, and this seems to have been Parliament's intention, for leaving the parties free to apportion the risks as they think fit and for respecting their decisions …

2. *Harbutt's Plasticine Ltd* v *Wayne Tank and Pump Co Ltd* must clearly be overruled. It would be enough to put that on its radical inconsistency with the *Suisse Atlantique Case*. But even if the matter were res integra, I would find the decision to be

based on unsatisfactory reasoning ... Similarly, *Charterhouse Credit Co Ltd* v *Tolly* must be overruled, though the result might have been reached on construction of the contract.

3. I must add to this, by way of exception to the decision not to "gloss" the *Suisse Atlantique*, a brief observation on the deviation cases, since some reliance has been placed on them, particularly on the decision of this House in *Hain Steamship Co Ltd* v *Tate & Lyle Ltd* (so earlier than the *Suisse Atlantique*) in the support of the *Harbutt* doctrine. I suggested in the *Suisse Atlantique* that these cases can be regarded as proceeding on normal principles applicable to the law of contract generally, viz that it is a matter of the parties' intentions whether and to what extent clauses in shipping contracts can be applied after a deviation, ie a departure from the contractually agreed voyage or adventure. It may be preferable that they should be considered as a body of authority sui generis, with special rules derived from historical and commercial reasons. What, on either view, they cannot do is to lay down different rules as to contracts generally from those later stated by this House in *Heyman* v *Darwins Ltd*. The ingenious use by Donaldson J in *Kenyon, Son & Craven Ltd* v *Baxter Hoare & Co Ltd* of the doctrine of deviation in order to reconcile the *Suisse Atlantique* case with *Harbutt's Case*, itself based in part on the use of the doctrine of deviation, illustrates the contortions which that case has made necessary and would be unnecessary if it vanished as an authority.

4. It is not necessary to review fully the numerous cases in which the doctrine of fundamental breach has been applied or discussed. Many of these have now been superseded by the Unfair Contract Terms Act 1977. Others, as decisions, may be justified as depending on the contract (*Levison* v *Patent Steam Carpet Cleaning Co Ltd*) in the light of well-known principles such as that stated in *Alderslade* v *Hendon Laundry Ltd*.

In this situation, the present case has to be decided. As a preliminary, the nature of the contract has to be understood. Securicor undertook to provide a service of periodical visits for a very modest charge, which works out at 26p per visit. It did not agree to provide equipment. It would have no knowledge of the value of Photo Productions' factory; that, and the efficacy of their fire precautions, would be known to Photo Productions. In these circumstances, nobody could consider it unreasonable that as between these two equal parties, the risk assumed by Securicor should be a modest one and that Photo Productions should carry the substantial risk of damage or destruction.

The duty of Securicor was, as stated, to provide a service. There must be implied an obligation to use care in selecting their patrolmen, to take care of the keys and, I would think, to operate the service with due and proper regard to the safety and security of the premises. The breach of duty committed by Securicor lay in a failure to discharge this latter obligation. Alternatively, it could be put on a vicarious responsibility for the wrongful act of Musgrove, viz starting a fire on the premises; Securicor would be responsible for this on the principle stated in *Morris* v *C W Martin & Sons Ltd*. This being the breach, does condition 1 apply? It is drafted in strong terms: "Under no circumstances, any injurious act or default by any employee". These words have to be approached with the aid of the cardinal rules of construction that they must be read contra proferentem and that in order to escape from the consequences of one's own wrongdoing, or that of one's servants, clear words are necessary. I think that these words are clear. Photo Productions in fact relied on them for an argument, that since they exempted from negligence, they must be taken as not exempting from the consequence of deliberate acts. But this is a perversion of the rule that if a clause can cover something other than negligence, it will not be applied to negligence. Whether, in addition to negligence, it covers other, eg deliberate acts, remains a matter of construction, requiring, of course, clear words. I am of the opinion that it does and, being free to construe and apply the clause, I must hold that liability is excluded. On this part of the case

I agree with the judge and adopt his reasons for judgment. I would allow the appeal.'

Comment
Applied: *Suisse Atlantique Société d'Armement Maritime SA v NV Rotterdamsche Kolen Centrale* [1966] 2 WLR 944. Overruled: *Harbutt's Plasticine Ltd v Wayne Tank and Pump Co Ltd* [1970] 2 WLR 198. Applied in *Mitchell (George) (Chesterhall) Ltd v Finney Lock Seeds Ltd* [1983] 3 WLR 163 and *Aforos Shipping Co SA v Pagnan, The Aforos* [1983] 1 WLR 195.

See also *Levison v Patent Steam Carpet Cleaning Co Ltd* [1977] 3 WLR 90 which demonstrates a fundamental breach.

R & B Customs Brokers Co Ltd v United Dominions Trust Ltd
See SALE OF GOODS, Chapter 5, above.

Saunders v Anglia Building Society
[1970] 3 WLR 1078 House of Lords (Viscount Dilhorne, Lords Reid, Hodson, Wilberforce and Pearson)

• *Mistake – plea of non est factum*

Facts
The plaintiff, executrix of Mrs Gallie, a widow aged 84, ran a boarding house in Essex with the assistance of her nephew. Her nephew had possession of the deeds of the house and she was quite content that he should use them to raise money if he so wished, so long as she could stay in the house for the rest of her life. Lee, a friend of the nephew, was a man heavily in debt. Lee had a document of sale drawn up in respect of the house and took it to Mrs Gallie for her to sign. The nephew acted as witness. When she asked what the document was, she was told by Lee that it was a deed of gift in favour of the nephew. Lee paid Mrs Gallie nothing, but raised a loan for himself on the strength of the document. When he defaulted on one of the mortgages,

the building society sought to recover possession and the plaintiff raised the defence of non est factum.

Held
The building society would succeed.

Lord Reid:

'The existing law seems to me to be in a state of some confusion. I do not think that it is possible to reconcile all the decisions, let alone all the reasons given for them. In view of some general observations made in the Court of Appeal I think that it is desirable to try to extract from the authorities the principles on which most of them are based. When we are trying to do that my experience has been that there are dangers in there being only one speech in this House. Then statements in it have often tended to be treated as definitions and it is not the function of a court or of this House to frame definitions; some latitude should be left for future developments. The true ratio of a decision generally appears more clearly from a comparison of two or more statements in different words which are intended to supplement each other.

The plea of non est factum obviously applies when the person sought to be held liable did not in fact sign the document. But at least since the sixteenth century it has also been held to apply in certain cases so as to enable a person who in fact signed a document to say that it is not his deed. Obviously any such extension must be kept within narrow limits if it is not to shake the confidence of those who habitually and rightly rely on signatures when there is no obvious reason to doubt their validity. Originally this extension appears to have been made in favour of those who were unable to read owing to blindness or illiteracy and who therefore had to trust someone to tell them what they were signing. I think that it must also apply in favour of those who are permanently or temporarily unable through no fault of their own to have without explanation any real understanding of the purport of a particular document, whether that be from defective education, illness or innate incapacity.

But that does not excuse them from taking such precautions as they reasonably can. The matter generally arises where an innocent third party has relied on a signed document in ignorance of the circumstances in which it was signed, and where he will suffer loss if the maker of the document is allowed to have it declared a nullity. So there must be a heavy burden of proof on the person who seeks to invoke this remedy. He must prove all the circumstances necessary to justify its being granted to him, and that necessarily involves his proving that he took all reasonable precautions in the circumstances. I do not say that the remedy can never be available to a man of full capacity. But that could only be in very exceptional circumstances; certainly not where his reason for not scrutinising the document before signing it was that he was too busy or too lazy. In general I do not think that he can be heard to say that he signed in reliance on someone he trusted. But, particularly when he was led to believe that the document which he signed was not one which affected his legal rights, there may be cases where this plea can properly be applied in favour of a man of full capacity.

The plea cannot be available to anyone who was content to sign without taking the trouble to try to find out at least the general effect of the document. Many people do frequently sign documents put before them for signature by their solicitor or other trusted advisers without making any enquiry as to their purpose or effect. But the essence of the plea non est factum is that the person signing believed that the document he signed had one character or one effect whereas in fact its character or effect was quite different. He could not have such a belief unless he had taken steps or been given information which gave him some grounds for his belief. The amount of information he must have and the sufficiency of the particularity of his belief must depend on the circumstances of each case. Further the plea cannot be available to a person whose mistake was really a mistake as to the legal effect of the document, whether that was is own mistake or that of his adviser. That has always been the law and in this branch of the law at least I see no reason for any change.

We find in many of the authorities statements that a man's deed is not his deed if his mind does not go with his pen. But that is far too wide. It would cover cases where the man had taken no precautions at all, and there was no ground for his belief that he was signing something different from that which in fact he signed. I think that it is the wrong approach to start from that wide statement and then whittle it down by excluding cases where the remedy will not be granted. It is for the person who seeks the remedy to show that he should have it.

Finally, there is the question to what extent or in what way must there be a difference between that which in fact he signed and that which he believed he was signing. In an endeavour to keep the plea within bounds there have been many attempts to lay down a dividing line. But any dividing line suggested has been difficult to apply in practice and has sometimes led to unreasonable results. In particular I do not think that the modern division between the character and the contents of a document is at all satisfactory. Some of the older authorities suggest a more flexible test so that one can take all factors into consideration. There was a period when here as elsewhere in the law hard and fast dividing lines were sought, but I think that experience has shown that often they do not produce certainty but do produce unreasonable results.

I think that in the older authorities difference in practical result was more important than difference in legal character. If a man thinks that he is signing a document which will cost him £10 and the actual document would cost him £1,000 it could not be right to deny him this remedy simply because the legal character of the two was the same. It is true that we must then deal with questions of degree but that is a familiar task for the courts and I would not expect it to give rise to a flood of litigation.

There must I think be a radical difference

between what he signed and what he thought he was signing – or one could use the words "fundamental" or "serious" or "very substantial". But what amounts to a radical difference will depend on all the circumstances. If he thinks he is giving property to A whereas the document gives it to B the difference may often be of vital importance, but in the circumstances of the present case I do not think that it is. I think that it must be left to the courts to determine in each case in light of all the facts whether there was or was not a sufficiently great difference. The plea non est factum is in sense illogical when applied to a case where the man in fact signed the deed. But it is none the worse for that if applied in a reasonable way.'

Comment
Approved: *Foster* v *Mackinnon* (1869) LR 4 CP 704. Overruled: *Carlisle and Cumberland Banking Co* v *Bragg* [1911] 1 KB 489. Applied in *United Dominions Trust Ltd* v *Western* [1976] QB 513 and *Avon Finance Co Ltd* v *Bridger* [1985] 2 All ER 281.

St Albans City and District Council v International Computers Ltd
[1996] 4 All ER 481 Court of Appeal (Nourse and Hirst LJJ, Sir Iain Glidewell

• *Exclusion/limitation clause – Unfair Contract Terms Act 1977 – meaning of Goods under s60(1) of the Sale of Goods Act 1979*

Facts
The defendants/appellants (International Computers Ltd) supplied software to operate a computer system (hardware) which was to be used in the collection of the community charge by the plaintiff/respondent (St Albans City and District Council). The software turned out to be faulty and resulted in a loss of revenue. The plaintiff was granted a licence to use the software under the defendant's patent/copyright.

International Computers Ltd (ICL) appealed against the measure of damages in consequence of loss suffered by St Albans City District Council (St Albans). Due to an error in the software St Albans lost £484,000 between 1990 and 1991 and also had to pay a net sum of £685,000 by way of increase precept payments to the county council. St Albans were able to cut its losses for the year 1990–91 by increasing the community charge in 1991–92. St Albans commenced proceeding against ICL for breach of contract, claiming the total loss caused by the faulty software. ICL's contention was that St Albans did not suffer a loss of revenue as they were able to recoup this loss by increasing the community charge between the period 1991–92 and that St Albans had not suffered any loss through breach of contract.

At first instance St Albans were awarded damages and no distinction was drawn between the lost revenue that was recouped and the precept payments made to the county council. ICL appealed against this award.

ICL attempted to limit their liability through a number of exclusion/limitation clauses contained within their tender. Under the heading 'ICL Statement' the appellants warranted that the equipment and software to be supplied would be as described and of merchantable quality, but went on to say:

'None of the statements contained in this document constitutes representations for which ICL can accept liability and St Albans must satisfy themselves that the equipment and programs are fit for the purposes to which they will be put.'

ICL also attempted to limit their liability in clause 9, which was headed 'ICL's Liabilities', which provided in sub-clause (c) the following:

'... ICL's liability will not exceed the price or charge payable for the item of equipment, program or service in respect of which the liability arises or £100,000 (which ever is the lesser). Provided that in no event will ICL be liable for: (i) loss resulting from any defect or deficiency which ICL shall have physically remedied at its own expense within a reasonable time; or (ii) any indirect or consequential loss or loss of business or profits sustained by the Customer; or (iii) loss which could have been avoided by the Customer following ICL's reasonable advice and instructions.'

It was found at first instance the contract incorporated ICL's general conditions for the supply of equipment, programmes and services. The appeal related to the reasonableness of these clauses and whether or not they were covered by the Unfair Contract Terms Act 1977.

Held

On the question of damages Nourse LJ dealt with the distinction of damages, stating:

> 'In my view, the distinction must be made. Once it is made, it is seen that the £685,000 is recoverable and the £484,000 is not. This is the most important and difficult question in the case. In the end I have come to a clear opinion in regard to each of the two amounts … If the software had not been faulty, the plaintiffs would not have to pay out the £685,000. Having paid it out, they were unable to recover it from the county council or any other third party … they can recover the £685,000 from the defendant … they cannot recover the £484,000 from the defendant. The effect of the recovery would be to relieve the chargepayers of an obligation to which they were always subject or, if you prefer, to give them a bonus to which they were not entitled. They have not been out of pocket. The plaintiffs, on the other hand, are entitled to recover interest on the £484,000 for the year 1990–91.' (p489)

With regard to the exclusion/limitation clauses Nourse LJ found St Albans had contracted with ICL on their written standard terms of business and was covered by s3(1) of the Unfair Contract Terms Act (UCTA) 1977, and ICL were not able to rely upon the limitation clause contained within clause 9(c) unless they satisfied the requirements of reasonableness under UCTA 1977. Nourse LJ considered guidelines on reasonableness and

the case of *George Mitchell (Chesterhall) Ltd v Finney Lock Seeds Ltd* [1983] 2 AC 803 and struck down the limitation clause confirming the decision by the court of first instance. Nourse LJ considered the principles applied in *George Mitchell* and took into consideration that ICL were insured for an aggregate sum of £50 million worldwide and the limitation clause was nominal in comparison to the potential risks involved.

One of the issues discussed by the Court was whether or not the contract between the appellants and the respondent was a contract for the sale of goods. A contract for the sale of goods is governed by the Sale of Goods Act 1979 and would have implied terms to quality and fitness for purpose into the contract. For this to have been possible the contract would have to be covered by s2(1) of the 1979 Act which provides:

> 'A contract of sale of goods is a contract by which the seller transfers or agrees to transfer the property in the goods to the buyer for a money consideration called the price.'

In this instance the wording 'sale of goods' and what is meant by 'goods' needed to be examined and goods is defined by s61(1) as:

> 'Goods includes all personal chattels other than things in action and money, and in Scotland, all corporeal moveable except money; and in particular, "goods" includes emblements, industrial growing crops and things attached to or forming part of the land which are agreed to be severed before sale or under the contract of sale.'

The Court discussed this section in relation to the legal status of computer software. Sir Iain Glidewell considered the issue, at p493, to whether or not software would constitute goods under the 1979 Act. He found that the disk, which contains the programme, was within the definition of goods under the 1979 Act. A defective disk could be dealt with under this legislation as being in breach of the implied terms as to quality and fitness for purpose. However, he found the programme itself was not within the meaning of the definition and that the programme, in this instance, had been transferred from the disk onto the computer (hardware) and as there was no sale of goods, there were no implied terms as to quality and fitness for purpose. However, at common law the court did imply a term that the programme would be reasonably fit for its purpose. The basis upon which the court justified implying a term into a contract, which had not been expressly agreed between the parties, was on the dicta of Lord Pearson in the case of *Trollope & Colls Ltd* v *N W Metropolitan Regional Hospital Board* [1973] 1 WLR 601. At p609 he stated:

'An unexpressed term can be implied if and only if the court finds that the parties must have intended that term to form part of their contract; it is enough for the court to find that such a term would have been adopted by the parties as reasonable men if it had been suggested to them; it must have been a term that went without saying, a term which, though tacit, formed part of the contract which the parties made for themselves.'

Therefore, the Court found in the absence of any express term as to quality and fitness for purpose the contract was subject to an implied term. The programme would be reasonably fit for its purpose and as it was incapable of achieving its purpose International Computers Ltd were in breach of this implied term.

Comment
The case illustrates the approach of the courts when dealing with limitation clauses and reasonableness under the Unfair Terms Act 1977, and also the definition of 'goods' under the Sale of Goods Act 1979 and its application to software and hardware. This latter point has now, to an extent, been clarified when dealing with computer software.

Thornton v *Shoe Lane Parking Ltd*
[1971] 2 WLR 585 Court of Appeal (Lord Denning MR, Megaw LJ and Sir Gordon Willmer)

• *Automatic car park – notice*

Facts
A notice displayed at the entrance to a car park stated 'All cars parked at owners risk'. The plaintiff approached the car park, took a ticket dispensed by an automatic machine and entered. The ticket stated that it was 'issued subject to the conditions of issue as displayed on the premises'. These conditions, displayed inside the car park, purported to exempt the defendants from liability for damage to cars, or any injury to the customer howsoever caused. When the plaintiff went to collect his car he was injured in an accident, partly caused by the defendants' negligence.

Held
The exemption clause was not a term of the contract and it did not, therefore, enable the defendants to escape liability.

Lord Denning MR:

'We have been referred to the ticket cases of former times from *Parker* v *South Eastern Ry Co* to *McCutcheon* v *David MacBrayne Ltd*. They were concerned with railways, steamships and cloakrooms, where booking clerks issued tickets to customers who took them away without reading them. In those cases, the issue of the ticket was regarded as an offer by the company. If the customer took it and retained it without obligation, his act was regarded as an acceptance of the offer: see *Watkins* v *Rymill* and *Thompson* v *London, Midland and Scottish Ry Co*. These cases were based on the theory that the customer, on being handed the ticket, could refuse it and decline to enter into a contract on those terms. He could ask for his money back. That theory was, of course, a fiction. No customer in a thousand ever read the conditions. If he had stopped to do so, he would have missed the train or the boat.

None of those cases has any application to a ticket which is issued by an automatic machine. The customer pays his money and gets a ticket. He cannot refuse it. He cannot get his money back. He may protest to the machine, even swear at it; but it will remain unmoved. He is committed beyond recall.

He was committed at the very moment when he put his money into the machine. The contract was concluded at that time. It can be translated into offer and acceptance in this way. The offer is made when the proprietor of the machine holds it out as being ready to receive the money. The acceptance takes place when the customer puts his money into the slot. The terms of the offer are contained in the notice placed on or near the machine, stating what is offered for the money. The customer is bound by those terms as long as they are sufficiently brought to his notice beforehand, but not otherwise. He is not bound by the terms printed on the ticket if they differ from the notice, because the ticket comes too late. The contract has already been made: see *Olley* v *Marlborough Court Ltd*. The ticket is no more than a voucher or receipt for the money that has been paid (as in the deckchair case, *Chapelton* v *Barry Urban District Council*), on terms which have been offered and accepted before the ticket is issued. In the present case, the offer was contained in the notice at the entrance, giving the charges for garaging and saying, 'At owners' risk', ie at the risk of the owner so far as damage to the car was concerned. The offer was accepted when the plaintiff drove up to the entrance and, by the movement of his car, turned the light from red to green and the ticket was thrust at him. The contract was then concluded and it could not be altered by any words printed on the ticket itself. In particular, it could not be altered so as to exempt the company from liability for personal injury due to their negligence.

... the customer is bound by the exempting condition if he knows that the ticket is issued subject to it; or, if the company did

what was reasonably sufficient to give him notice of it. Counsel for the defendants admitted here that the defendants did not do what was reasonably sufficient to give the plaintiff notice of the exempting condition. That admission was properly made. I do not pause to enquire whether the exempting condition is void for unreasonableness. All I say is that it is so wide and so destructive of rights that the court should not hold any man bound by it unless it is drawn to his attention in the most explicit way. It is an instance of what I had in mind in *J Spurling Ltd* v *Bradshaw*. In order to give sufficient notice, it would need to be printed in red ink with a red hand pointing to it, or something equally startling.

However, although reasonable notice of it was not given, counsel for the defendants said that this case came within the second question propounded by Mellish LJ, namely that the plaintiff 'knew or believed that the writing contained conditions'. There was no finding to that effect. The burden was on the defendants to prove it, and they did not do so. Certainly there was no evidence that the plaintiff knew of this exempting condition. He is not, therefore, bound by it ... the whole question is whether the exempting condition formed part of the contract. I do not think it did. The plaintiff did not know of the condition, and the defendants did not do what was reasonably sufficient to give him notice of it.'

Comment
See *Spurling (J) Ltd* v *Bradshaw* [1956] 1 WLR 461 which discusses the issues of exemption clauses and reasonable notice, and *New Zealand Shipping Co Ltd* v *A M Satterthwaite and Co Ltd* [1974] 2 WLR 865.

8   The Passing of Property

Abdulrahaman Abdulrazaq v Modena Sportswagen Handels GmbH and Others [2003] EWHC 284 Queen's Bench Division (Eady J)

- *Transfer of title under s25(1) Sale of Goods Act 1979 – implied agency*

Facts
The facts of this case are complicated and involved a number of parties in relation to the purchase of a black Ferrari 456 GTM. There were four defendants in total involved in the sale of a Ferrari and then a sub-sale to the claimant. The claimant then placed the Ferrari with two of the defendants for safekeeping, who later refused to release the vehicle. To discuss the facts of this case it is necessary to divide up the role of each defendant and explain the complainant's contention to the facts in question.

The first defendant, Modena Sportswagen Handels GmbH (MSH), entered into an agreement with the second defendant, Prince Malik Ado-Ibrahim (PMA), to purchase a Ferrari in July 1999. Payment for the Ferrari was to be made by a number of instalments. In November 1999 the claimant, Abdulrahman Abdulrazaq (AA), entered into an agreement with the second defendant (PMA) to purchase the Ferrari. Payment was to be made as follows: the claimant was to part-exchange his blue Ferrari (valued at $90,000) and make it available for collection by the first defendant (MSH) in Paris, plus pay $20,000 in respect of import taxes for the blue Ferrari. The claimant also handed over $40,000 in cash to the second defendant (PMA). The second defendant then gave the Ferrari to the claimant.

The second defendant failed to meet the payments owed to the first defendant and as a direct result the first defendant took steps to repossess the Ferrari from the claimant. The claimant resisted repossession by depositing the Ferrari with Hssam Yeganeh and Hassan Yeganneh, the third and fourth defendants, who later refused to deliver the Ferrari at a later date.

The claimant sought a declaration that ownership of the Ferrari had been transferred to him, and any dispute between the first defendant and second defendant was nothing to do with the claimant. MSH counterclaimed for the balance owed on the Ferrari from the claimant. This claim involved MSH alleging there was a valid contract between MSH and the claimant. MSH believed the second defendant (PMA) acted as his agent, who brought about the contract between MSH and the claimant.

Held
Eady J examined the facts and found there was no evidence to support the claim that PMA acted as an agent and the counterclaim failed. Eady J then looked at the facts supporting the claimant's argument and s25(1) of the Sale of Goods Act 1979, which states:

> 'Where a person having bought or agreed to buy goods obtains, with the consent of the seller, possession of the goods or the documents of title to the goods, the delivery or transfer by that person, or by a mercantile agent acting for him, of the goods or documents of title, under any sale, pledge, or other disposition thereof, to any person receiving the same in good faith and without notice of any lien or right of the original seller in respect of the goods, has the same effect as if the person making the delivery or transfer were a mercantile agent in possession of the goods or documents of title with the consent of the owner.'

Eady J also considered the provisions of s27(3) of the Hire Purchase Act 1964, which deals specifically with the protection of a purchaser of a motor vehicle subject to a hire purchase agreement and sold on to an innocent third party. It states:

'Where the person to whom the disposition referred to in subs(1) … is made (the "original purchaser") is a trade or finance purchaser, then if the person who is the first private purchaser of the motor vehicle after that disposition (the "first private purchaser") is a purchaser of the vehicle in good faith without notice of the relevant agreement, the disposition of the vehicle to the first private purchaser shall have effect as if the title of the creditor to the vehicle had been vested in the debtor immediately before he disposed of it to the original purchaser.'

Thus, Eady J was of the opinion that the deciding factor of this case was whether or not the claimant acted in 'good faith' and 'without notice'. There were a number of issues that suggested the claimant may have 'turned a blind eye' and the burden of proving good faith and the absence of notice was placed directly on the claimant. However, Eady J was persuaded to accept the claimant's argument and that he had discharged the burden of proving good faith and lack of notice. Therefore, judgment was given for the claimant and he was entitled to the declaration sought.

Comment

This case demonstrated a clear interpretation of the legislation involved, and the application of the law to the facts. Although the legal rules relating to agency were briefly explained and there was no finding of an agency relationship between the parties, there was scope, arguably, to extend this discussion through additional case law given the facts in question. See further *Shogun Finance Ltd* v *Hudson* [2003] 3 WLR 1371.

Aluminium Industrie Vaassen BV v *Romalpa Aluminium Ltd* [1976] 1 WLR 676 Court of Appeal (Megaw, Roskill and Goff LJJ)

- *Aluminium foil – passing of property*

Facts

The plaintiffs, a Dutch company, sold aluminium foil to the value of £122,239 to the defendants, an English company, whose bankers appointed a receiver on 1 November, 1974. The plaintiffs purported to incorporate their general selling terms and conditions in the contract, in particular Clause 13 stated that: 'ownership of the foil passed to the purchaser when all debts owing to AIV were met'; the material should be stored in such a way to show it is clearly the property of AIV; further if the materials are made into any other objects, AIV has the ownership of these as surety for full payment of debts owing to AIV; the purchaser keeps these objects as fiduciary owner for AIV; if sold the purchaser shall hand over to AIV any claims he has against the buyer emanating from this transaction.

The plaintiffs sued in respect of foil in the defendant's possession and in respect of proceeds of sale by the defendants.

Held

The plaintiffs were entitled to succeed.

Roskill LJ:

'As to incorporation of the said terms and conditions, I agree entirely with the conclusion of Moccata J that those conditons clearly applied by course of dealing to the contract in question. All parties knew precisely of the terms of business. Once this is accepted, there is no real dispute that the result of clause 13 is that the plaintiffs are the owners of the remaining unsold aluminium foil held by the receiver.

I now turn to the question of whether the plaintiffs have a right to trace and recover the proceeds of the defendant's sub-sales. We must examine the principle established in *Re Hallett's Estate* (1880) 13 Ch 696.

There is no difficulty regarding the funds being mixed since the receiver has kept them separate. Further it makes no difference, according to *Re Hallett's Estate* whether the sale by a trustee or beneficiary was a rightful or wrongful sale In any event, the defendants were entitled to sell here and the critical question is whether there was here the required fiduciary relationship. Without clause 13 it would have been a simple contractual relationship. But clause 13 plainly provides otherwise: the sellers retained property until *all* owing had been paid. The second part of clause 13 is far more detailed because of its complexity. In its context, it is clear that the business purpose of this clause was to secure the sellers, as far as possible against the risks of non-payment after parting with possession of the goods, whether or not they retained their identity. The second part clearly contemplates the creation of a fiduciary relationship in relation to mixed goods …the assignment provisions are clearly designed to give the sellers an additional security to recover debts otherwise payable to the buyers but not paid to them by the sub-purchasers if any indebtedness is outstanding …

… There is no contractual difficulty that the appellants sold as principals within their implied authority from the respondents which they were selling as agents for the respondents to whom they remained fully accountable, similarly to the position of agent and principal.

Thus the respondents are entitled to trace the proceeds – clause 13 was clearly designed to deal with the possibility of insolvency.'

Comment
Distinguished in *Tatung (UK) Ltd v Galex Telesure Ltd* (1989) 5 BCC 325 and *Pfeiffer (E) Weinkellerei-Weineinkauf GmbH & Co v Arbuthnot Factors Ltd* [1988] 1 WLR 150.

Armour v Thyssen Edelstahlwerke AG [1990] 3 WLR 810 House of Lords (Lords Keith of Kinkel, Griffiths, Oliver of Aylmerton, Goff of Chieveley and Jauncey of Tullichettle)

• *Steel strip – reservation of right of disposal*

Facts
The defendants carried on business in Germany as manufacturers and suppliers of steel. The defendants had for a considerable time pursued a course of business with Carron & Co Ltd (C), whereby the defendants sold steel strip to C for use in its engineering processes. The contracts of sale were stated to be subject to the defendants' standard conditions of sale; one such clause of which provided: 'All goods delivered by us remain our property … until all debts owed to us … are settled'. C went into receivership owing £71,769 to the defendants. A large amount of steel strip was found at the works of C; some had been cut ready for use and some was as it was when delivered. The defendants claim that ownership and property in the steel still vested in them was challenged by the receivers who claimed it to be part of C's assets and as such available to other creditors as well as the defendants.

Held
By the terms of the contract of sale the defenders had reserved the right of disposal of the steel strip until fulfilment of the condition that all debts due to them by C had been paid and by virtue of ss17 and 19(1) of the Sale of Goods Act 1979 the property in the goods had not passed to C until that condition had been complied with. Accordingly, in the circumstances, the defenders were entitled to decree for payment as concluded for in their counterclaim, ie the invoice price of the steel strip.

Lord Keith of Kinkel:

'Section 17 of the Sale of Goods Act 1979 provides:

"(1) Where there is a contract for the sale of specific or ascertained goods the property in them is transferred to the buyer at such time as the parties to the contract intend it to be transferred.
(2) For the purpose of ascertaining the intention of the parties regard shall be had to the terms of the contract, the conduct of the parties and the circumstances of the case."

In the present case the parties in the contract of sale clearly expressed their intention that the property in the steel strip should not pass to Carron until all debts due by it to the appellants had been paid. In my opinion there are no grounds for refusing to give effect to that intention.

Further, s19(1) of the same Act provides:

"Where there is a contract for the sale of specific goods or where goods are subsequently appropriated to the contract, the seller may, by the terms of the contract or appropriation, reserve the right of disposal of the goods until certain conditions are fulfilled; and in such a case, notwithstanding the delivery of the goods to the buyer, or to a carrier or other bailee or custodier for the purpose of transmission to the buyer, the property in the goods does not pass to the buyer until the conditions imposed by the seller are fulfilled."

Here the appellants, by the terms of the contract of sale, have in effect reserved the right of disposal of the steel strip until fulfilment of the condition that all debts due to them by Carron have been paid. By virtue of this enactment, that has the effect that the property in the goods did not pass to Carron until that condition had been fulfilled. Counsel for Carron argued that the word "conditions" in s19(1) must be read as excluding any condition which has the effect of creating a right of security over the goods. I am, however, unable to regard a provision reserving title to the seller until payment of all debts due to him by the buyer as amounting to the creation by the buyer of a right of security in favour of the seller. Such a provision does in a sense give the seller security for the unpaid debts of the buyer. But it does

so by way of a legitimate retention of title, not by virtue of any right over his own property conferred by the buyer.'

Comment
See also *Tatung (UK) Ltd* v *Galex Telesure Ltd* (1989) 5 BCC 325 and *Pfeiffer (E) Weinkellerei-Weineinkauf GmbH & Co* v *Arbuthnot Factors Ltd* [1988] 1 WLR 150 which demonstrates when the courts are prepared to treat a reservation clause as a registrable charge.

Atari Corp (UK) Ltd v *Electronics Boutique Stores (UK) Ltd* [1998] 1 All ER 1010 Court of Appeal (Auld, Phillips and Waller LJJ)

• *Sale or return – notice of rejection*

Facts
Atari, the respondents, supplied goods to Electronics, the appellants, on a sale or return basis (SOR). An arrangement had been agreed between the parties which allowed the appellants to order goods on a SOR until the 31 January 1996. The appellants sent a letter to the respondents in December 1995 informing them some of the goods were not selling well and they intended not to stock them any longer, and a full list of the goods would be forwarded to the respondents once all stock had been returned by the appellants' stores to their central warehouse. The respondents did not believe the letter constituted a formal notice to reject the goods as it did not specifically state which goods were being rejected and because the goods to be returned were not made available for return at the same time as the notice.

Held
The Court of Appeal found the letter to be an unequivocal rejection and not just an intention to reject the goods. The making of a list was to assist with the return of the goods and was secondary to the rejection. Their Lordships

found the letter was sufficient to identify the goods generically as long as the generic description enabled the goods to be identified with certainty, which in this instance was in fact the case. It was reasonable, given that the goods were held by various stores, to give notice exercising the right to reject the goods and only then to give the seller a reasonable opportunity to collect the goods after a reasonable laps of time. On this basis the Court held the letter to be a valid notice of rejection of such unsold goods that were deemed to be part of the SOR agreement and allowed the appeal.

Comment
The Sale of Goods Act 1979, s18 rule 4 gives guidance on contracts of sale or return and the Court of Appeal appears to have implemented rule 4 producing a logical conclusion.

Borden (UK) Ltd v *Scottish Timber Products Ltd* [1981] Ch 25 Court of Appeal (Buckley, Bridge and Templeman LJJ)

• *Chipboard resin – reservation of title clause*

Facts
The plaintiffs, Borden, were the suppliers of resin for use in the manufacture of chipboard; the second defendant was the manager of STP and receiver since 16 September, 1977. Resin was provided on standard conditions.

'2. *Risk and Property*
Property in goods supplied hereunder will pass to the customer when (a) the goods subject of the contract and (b) all other goods the subject of any other contract between the company and the customer which at the time of payment of the full price of the goods sold under the contract, have been delivered to the customer and paid for in full.'

Resin was delivered between 14 February and 16 September 1977 but not all of it was paid

for. A statement of agreed facts stated that as STP had only limited storing space, it was inevitable that it would need to use any resin delivered into its tanks within two days, at the most, of each delivery.

Two (relevant) points of law were tried as preliminary issues.

1. Did Borden have any proprietary interest at common law in any chipboard manufactured by STP using the resin supplied by Borden?
2. What right, if any, has Borden on the principle in *Re Hallett's Estate* (1880) 13 ChD 696 to trace their resin into its proceeds of sale?

Judge Rubin QC decided both points in favour of the plaintiffs. The defendants appealed.

Held
The appeal would be allowed.

Bridge LJ:

'As soon as the resin was used in the manufacturing process, it ceased to exist as resin, and accordingly the title to the resin simply disappeared …
  To take an example: cattle are sold to a farmer, or fuel to a steel manufacturer, in each case with a reservation of title clause, but on terms which permit the farmer to feed the cattle cake to his herd and the steelmaker to fuel his furnaces, before paying the purchase price. It is conceded that in these cases the seller cannot trace into the cattle or the steel – the difference is that the goods have been consumed. Once this is conceded I find it impossible to draw an intelligible line of distinction in principle which would give the plaintiffs a right to trace the resin into the chipboard in the present case. What has happened here is much more akin to the process of consumption than any simple process of admixture of goods. Alternatively, if one could trace here one could trace the fuel in the steelmaking process.'

Comment
See also *Re, Bond Worth Ltd* [1980] Ch 228

which discusses beneficial and equitable ownership when using a retention of title clause.

Carlos Federspiel & Co SA v *Charles Twigg & Co Ltd* [1957] 1 Lloyd's Rep 240 High Court (Pearson J)

• *Goods never delivered – passing of property*

Facts

By a contract dated 16 June, 1953, the plaintiffs ordered a number of cycles and tricycles from the defendant company, which order was accepted. On 28 July a receiver was appointed to the defendant company which continued to trade. On 17 November a compulsory winding-up order was made and the company went into liquidation. The goods had been paid for by the plaintiffs on 1 July, 1953, but were never delivered. The plaintiffs claimed that the goods were appropriated to the contract and that the property had passed to them. Further, they said they had been deprived of the opportunity of selling the goods at a profit and claimed damages for this. The plaintiffs had previously claimed delivery of the goods from the receiver, but this had not been done on the basis that the goods had not been appropriated to the contract and property had not passed in them. There was, therefore, no authority for the receiver to deliver them to the plaintiffs. The defendant company took no part in this action which resolved itself in a contest between the plaintiffs and the receiver.

Held

The goods had not been appropriated to the contract and the property in them had not passed to the plaintiffs at the time of the winding-up. Judgment would therefore be entered for the defendants.

Pearson J:

'The issues are (1) whether ownership of the goods passed from the defendant company and (2) if so, whether there is any additional

liability for loss of profit. The relevant provisions of s18 (particularly Rule 5) and 20 are cited. Two old cases are referred to as a basis for discussion of the meaning of appropriation. In *Mirabita* v *Imperial Ottoman Bank* (1878) 3 Ex D 164 at p 172, Cotton LJ says there must be an appropriation of the specific chattels in which the property is to pass, and nothing must remain to be done in order to pass it. So in the case of such a contract, delivery by vendor to common carrier is an appropriation sufficient to pass the property. In *Wait* v *Baker* (1848) 2 Ex 1, Baron Parke said the contract would be satisfied by the delivery of any 500 quarters of corn of the character agreed in the contract. But this is not enough to pass property. Delivery to a carrier would, since from that point the carrier acts as the buyer's agent... The law of England requires a bargain with a specific article.

Throughout the correspondence which can be said to be of contractual effect, the emphasis is on shipment as indicating the intention of the parties that shipment should be a decisive act of performance by the seller. Looking at the correspondence as a whole, it is in my view an fob contract. In the absence of any further development normally under an fob contract, the property passes on shipment; Erle J in *Browne & Another* v *Hare & Another* (1859) 4 H & N 822 at p829.

Then there is the case of *Stock* v *Inglis* 10 App Cas 263. The question of the passing of property was important in determining whether the buyer had an insurable interest in the relevant goods. It was not decided in that case that with specific goods fob meant more than merely that the shipper had to put them on board at his expense – the risk passes at that moment as well. There is no authority or commercial practice which suggests that the position should be any different with goods which have not been ascertained. Thus, risk passes on shipment. Other authorities including the more recent case of *Colley* v *Overseas Exporters* [1921] 3 KB 302 confirm that risk actually passes on a true fob contract when the goods are put on board.

Undoubtedly the contract in this case contained some cif feature but it is unnecessary to look any further into that because if it were a true cif contract the property would, if anything, pass later than under an fob contract. So in this contract, it was expected that ownership would pass on shipment. Anything done to the goods before the time of shipment should be regarded as preparation for shipment rather than appropriation to the contract.

In all the correspondence the important element was clearly that of shipment. Was there any appropriation of the goods to the contract by the sellers with the consent of the buyers after the conclusion of the contract and before the receiver's first letter of October 2nd, 1953?

In *Mucklow* v *Mangles* (1808) 1 Taunt 318 Heath J said that ..."if the thing be in existence at the time of the order, the property of it passes by the contract, but not so where the subject is to be made".

There follows a series of old cases ending in *Pignataro* v *Gilroy* [1918] 1 KB 459 where it was held that property had passed, because in effect there was nothing remaining for the seller to do.

The following principles emerge as to appropriation.

1. The element of common intention has always to be borne in mind. Mere setting apart of the goods the seller expects to use in performance of the contract is not enough – he could always use other goods in performance of this contract. There must be an intention to attach the contract irrevocably to those goods, so that those goods and no others are the subject of the sale and become the property of the buyer.

2. Appropriation is made by agreement of the parties.

3. An appropriation by the seller with the assent of the buyer, may be said always to involve an actual or constructive delivery. If the seller retains possession he does so as bailee for the buyer.

4. Section 20 of the Act should be remembered whereby the ownership and the risk are normally associated. So if the goods are still at the seller's risk that is prima facie an indication that the property had not passed to the buyer.

5. The appropriating act is usually the last act to be performed by the seller.

Applying those principles to the present case, the intention was that the ownership should pass on shipment; there is no evidence of an agreement to a change of ownership before the time of shipment; there is no actual or constructive delivery – no suggestion of the seller becoming a bailee for the buyer; no suggestion of the goods being at the buyer's risk at any time before shipment; finally, the last two acts to be performed by the seller, ie sending the goods to Liverpool and having the goods on board, were not performed. There was, therefore, no appropriation of these goods and the action fails. The question of damages does not fail to be considered.'

Comment
See also *Healey* v *Howlett & Sons* [1917] 1 KB 337 and *Wardar's (Import and Export) Co Ltd* v *W Norwood & Sons Ltd* [1968] QB 663 which gives a comparative discussion on appropriation, transfer of title and risk.

Forthright Finance Ltd v *Carlyle Finance Ltd* [1997] 4 All ER 90 Court of Appeal (Stuart-Smith LJ, Pill LJ and Phillips LJ)

• *Distinction between a conditional sale agreement and a hire purchase agreement in relation to s25 of the Sale of Goods Act 1979*

Facts
Forthright Finance owned a Ford motor car which they delivered to a dealer, Fernland Limited, a company which dealt in motor cars under the trade name of Senator, under an agreement described as a hire purchase agreement. The agreement gave the dealer an option to purchase the car upon the last instalment being made, thus passing title to the dealer. The dealer gave possession to a customer, a

Mr Griffiths, who took the car under a conditional sale agreement, which was financed by Carlyle Finance Ltd, to whom it was purported to transfer ownership. Neither the court of first instance nor the Court of Appeal disputed Mr Griffiths's title to the car, Phillips LJ stating (at p92):

> 'It is common ground that Mr Griffiths acquired a good title pursuant to the provisions of Pt III (ss27–29) of the Hire Purchase Act 1964 (title to motor vehicles on hire purchase or conditional sale).'

The proceedings between the two finance companies are based upon whether or not the agreement between Forthright Finance and the dealer, Senator, was a hire purchase agreement or a conditional sale agreement. At first instance the judge held the agreement to be a hire purchase agreement. This finding meant the dealer (hirer) did not have a good title to pass to Carlyle and title remained with Forthright. As a consequence Carlyle was found liable in conversion to Forthright to the sum of £12,943 plus interest.

Carlyle appealed against this decision, claiming the original agreement between Forthright and the dealer was not a hire purchase agreement but a conditional sale agreement, as the dealer had 'agreed to buy' the car under the terms of the original agreement. This approach would convert the dealer into a buyer in possession under s25 of the Sale of Goods Act 1979 and having been placed in possession of the car, with the consent of the seller, the dealer was then in a position to pass good title to Carlyle under s25(1) of the said Act, which provides:

> 'Where a person, having bought or agreed to buy goods obtains, with the consent of the seller, possession of the goods or the documents of title to the goods, the delivery or transfer by that person, or by a mercantile agent acting for him, of the goods or documents of title, under any sale, pledge, or other disposition thereof, to any person receiving the same in good faith and without notice of any lien or other right of the original seller in respect of the goods, has the

same effect as if the person making delivery or transfer were a mercantile agent in possession of the goods or documents of title with the consent of the owner.'

The interpretation of this section allows a second buyer, in this instance Carlyle, provided the requirements of s25 are fulfilled, to take priority over Forthright's claim to the car.

Held
The Court of Appeal found the agreement to be a conditional sale in substance and form since the dealer was obliged to pay all the contractual instalments to become the owner of the car. The Court found the option not to take title, in this instance, did not affect the true nature of the agreement.

Comment
The essential difference between finding the agreement to be one of sale and not hire purchase dictates the purchaser is obliged to pay the price in full. The reality of this transaction was that the purchaser was committed to pay and the inclusion of the option not to take title was unlikely. The wording of the original agreement had been structured to avoid the operation of s25 but did not succeed in this instance.

Section 25 would not usually apply to hire purchase agreements and conditional sale agreements, which are regulated by the Consumer Credit Act 1974. In this instance, the latter was placed outside the 1974 Act because the purchase price, then, was outside the control of the legislation and, arguably, due to Senator, the original debtor, being a corporate body (company).

Freeman v Walker and Others
[2001] EWCA Civ 923 Court of Appeal (Dyson LJ and Wall J)

• *Hire purchase agreement – s27 Hire Purchase Act 1964*

Facts
This was an appeal by the third defendant

from an order made by Reading County Court on the 25 February 2000. The third defendant was a Mr Walton (W), a motor dealer who had purchased a Bentley car for £83,500, having borrowed £75,000 from a Finance Co (IHF Ltd) through a hire purchase (HP) agreement.

W sold the Bentley car to the second defendant, a Mr Brice (B), who was also a motor dealer, whilst the car was still subject to the HP agreement. B sold the car to the first defendant, a Mr Walker (WK), who was also a car dealer. WK sold the car to the claimant (at first instance), Mr Freeman (F), who, it transpired, was a private purchaser.

At first instance a consent judgment was entered by which F recovered £49,000 plus costs against WK, and WK was awarded £49,000, plus costs against B. That left B's claim against W. The judge awarded B £42,425 plus B's costs against W.

It is against this background the appeal arose from the court of first instance on the legal basis that s27 of the Hire Purchase Act 1964 gives absolute protection to the first private purchaser of a motor vehicle which is subject to a HP agreement. The first private purchaser will acquire good title to the motor vehicle providing he acquired it in good faith. Based upon this contention F would have been the first private purchaser of the car and the court of first instance had proceeded on the basis that F had not acquired a good title to the motor vehicle.

Held

It was successfully argued that F did acquire a good title by reason of s27(3) of the Hire Purchase Act 1964 and on that basis F did not have a valid claim against WK, as he (F) had suffered no loss. Therefore, WK should not have settled the claim against him by agreeing to pay F. As a direct result of this finding WK would have no claim against B, on the basis that WK had suffered no loss. Consequently, from this chain of events, B would have no claim against W because B had suffered no loss. This finding was based upon the premise that F did not have to be compen-

sated having obtained what he bargained for, namely ownership (title) of the Bentley.

It was found on the evidence presented to the Court that s27(1) of the Hire Purchase Act 1964 had been satisfied and that the first instance court had made its judgment without s27(3) of the Hire Purchase Act 1964 being brought to the attention of the trial judge.

Comment

Section 27 of the Hire Purchase Act is not to be overlooked as a statutory exception to the nemo dat quod non habet rule.

Michael Gerson (Leasing) Ltd v *Wilkinson* [2000] 1 All ER 148 Court of Appeal (Pill and Clarke LJJ, Bennett J)

• *Sale of Goods Act 1979 – ss 24 and 25, transfer of property*

Facts

This was an appeal by the respondent who claimed damages for conversion against both appellants. The action was in relation to ownership of various items consisting of heavy plant and machinery, which were formerly owned by a third party, Emshelf (E). In 1995 the third party sold equipment (the whole goods) to the respondent Gerson (G) under a sale and leaseback agreement which allowed E to remain in physical possession of the equipment (the whole goods) at all times. Subsequently E, without the authority of G, sold part of the goods (part goods) to the respondent, State (S), also under a leaseback agreement, again allowing E to remain in physical possession. S later terminated the lease with E and sold the part goods to Sagebush (SB). SB in turn sells the part goods to Wilkinson (W), an innocent purchaser.

Based upon the facts presented to the court, it was found that there was a delivery and a redelivery of the goods to E, by reason of s24 of the Sale of Goods Act 1979 (seller in possession). It was found that S became the owner of the part goods having acquired them in good faith and without notice of the sale from E to G, under the leaseback agreement. This allowed S to pass title to SB who in turn passed title to W, who the court found to be a purchaser of good faith and without notice of the leaseback agreement, and acquired a good title to the part goods.

Regarding the leaseback agreement for the whole goods between E and G, E did not maintain payment on the lease and as a direct result G terminated the lease and sold the whole goods to SB. G claims that property was not to pass to SB until all the money had been paid and that no contract had been agreed. SB rejected this argument claiming to be a buyer in possession under s25 the Sale of Goods Act 1979 and was able to sell the whole goods on to W and pass good title.

Held

The Court of Appeal examined the evidence and it was revealed that G negotiated the sale of the whole goods to SB by fax and was not intended to be an offer and therefore no acceptance could have taken place. The fax simply stated 'I am willing to make an outright sale for £319,000 plus VAT.' It was not couched in terms of an offer and instead was an invitation to treat. Indeed, there was no contract by the sending and receipt of the reply fax. Thus, SB did not at any stage obtain a good title to the whole goods as there was no contract with G and, therefore, SB could not pass title to W. As a direct result s25 of the Sale of Goods Act 1979 (buyer in possession), upon which W relied upon to give him good title, failed.

G's appeal against W for the whole goods, which depended upon there being a contract between G and SB or upon s25(1) of the Sale of Goods Act 1979, succeeded. However, the appeal by G for the part goods, against S and W, was unsuccessful. It follows that W, although found to be an innocent purchaser, was liable in conversion, except for the part goods.

Comment

This case confirms the current principles in contract law when dealing with offer and acceptance, when compared to mere negotiations. It also reinforces the rules laid down under ss24 and 25 of the Sale of Goods Act 1979 when establishing whether or not a seller or buyer in possession may pass good title to an innocent purchaser in good faith.

Mitsui & Co Ltd v *Flota Mercante Grancolombiana SA, The Ciudad de Pasto and the Ciudad de Neiva* [1989] 1 WLR 1145 Court of Appeal (Purchas and Staughton LJJ, Sir George Waller)

• *Frozen prawns – passing of property*

Facts

The plaintiffs bought 2,426 cartons of prawns from a Colombian company and they were shipped fob by the sellers from Colombia to Japan on the defendants' vessels. The bills of lading provided that the goods were deliverable to the order of the sellers and 80 per cent of the purchase price was paid before shipment by a letter of credit. On arrival, the prawns were found to be damaged and the question arose, inter alia, as to whether the plaintiffs had title to sue the defendants in tort.

Held

They did not as, on the facts, the presumption in s19 of the Sale of Goods Act 1979 had not been displaced.

Staughton LJ:

'Counsel for the [defendants] argues that the property passed to [the plaintiffs] only when the remaining 20 per cent of the price was paid. As there is no evidence that this occurred before the damage, he submits that the claim in tort must fail.

The Sale of Goods Act 1979 supplies part of the answer. Section 16 provides:

"Where there is a contract for the sale of unascertained goods no property in the goods is transferred to the buyer unless and until the goods are ascertained."

There is no evidence that the goods in this case were ascertained when the contract of sale was made, or as I think at any time before shipment. But on shipment they were ascertained.

Section 17 provides:

"(1) Where there is a contract for the sale of specific or ascertained goods the property in them is transferred to the buyer at such time as the parties to the contract intend it to be transferred.
(2) For the purpose of ascertaining the intention of the parties regard shall be had to the terms of the contract, the conduct of the parties and the circumstances of the case."

Although the contract in this case was, in all probability, for a sale of unascertained goods, it is agreed that s17 applied once the goods had been ascertained. The court accordingly has to resolve the problem by the means set out in s17(2).

"Unless a different intention appears, the following are rules for ascertaining the intention of the parties as to the time at which the property in the goods is to pass to the buyer."

The relevant rule in this case is r5 …

In this case prima facie [the sellers] did not conditionally appropriate the goods to the contract, but reserved a right of disposal. That appears from s19 …

Here by the bills of lading the goods were deliverable to the order of the sellers; consequently the prima facie presumption is that they reserved the right of disposal. Unless the presumption is displaced, that has the result that the property did not pass to the buyers until the condition imposed by the sellers was fulfilled. That condition was, presumably, that the balance of the price be paid.

The question then is whether that presumption is displaced …

It seems to me that in the ordinary way a seller will not wish to part with the property in his goods if they are shipped overseas until he has been paid in full …

Of course, the seller may choose to give credit, but I would not readily infer that he intended to do so. I find it difficult to draw any distinction for this purpose between a seller who has received 80 per cent of the price in advance and one who has received, say, 40 per cent, or none.

Nor can I attach much weight to the fact that the balance of the price was (as I assume) payable by letter of credit. Even the most copper-bottomed letter of credit sometimes fails to produce payment for one reason or another; and the seller who has a letter of credit for 100 per cent of the price will nevertheless often retain the property in his goods until he has presented the documents and obtained payment. If only 20 per cent is outstanding his worries will be less, but they may not have disappeared altogether.

One must, of course, pay attention to the position of [the plaintiff] since it is the common intention of the parties which must be ascertained. They had paid 80 per cent of the price and would be anxious to obtain some security. But it seems to me that they had already been content to assume that risk. They had advanced the 80 per cent as a matter of trust, with no security so far as the evidence goes, or none that I can discern, up to the time of shipment. I can see no very powerful argument that, between the time of shipment and the presentation of the bills of lading under the letter of credit for payment of the remaining 20 per cent, they intended to acquire the property in the goods to safeguard their advance.

Looking at the case as a whole I consider that the presumption in s19 is not displaced. As counsel for the shipowners observed … if the parties wanted it to be displaced all they had to do was arrange that [the sellers] should insert the name of [the plaintiffs] as consignee in the bills of lading. [The sellers] did not do that. They took bills of lading to their own order and, therefore, in accordance with the presumption they retained the property in the goods until the balance of the price was paid. It is not proved that this occurred before the goods were damaged. Consequently the claim fails …

I would ... enter judgment for the defendants.'

Nanka-Bruce v *Commonwealth Trust Ltd* [1926] AC 77 Privy Council (Lords Atkinson, Shaw and Parmoor)

- *Sale of cocoa – passing of property*

Facts
The appellant was a planter and shipper of cocoa at Accra. The respondents were general exporters and importers. One Laing (a co-defendant with the respondents) had previously bought cocoa from the appellant. The appellant claimed damages for conversion for 160 bags of cocoa from the respondents. The appellant entered into a general arrangement with Laing for cocoa at 59 shillings per 60lbs for resale by Laing to other merchants, who would weigh them. It was only then that the amount payable was ascertained. The goods were despatched under a consignment note made out in favour of Laing. He then so Laing. He then sold them to the respondents and handed the consignment note to their representatives. The respondents then took delivery of the goods and credited Laing with the price. The courts found that Laing acted dishonestly, and that the respondents were quite honest and that they purchased goods for the value and without any notice of any objection to, or defect in, the title of Laing, or the contract under which he had acquired the goods. The appellant attacked this finding as being erronous in law, alleging that the weight of goods must be treated as having been a condition precedent to an operative sale.

Held
The appeal should be disallowed.

Lord Shaw:

'It was not a condition precedent. The testing was merely to see whether the goods fitted the weights as represented.
    This was clear from the case of *Cundy* v

Lindsay 3 App Cas 459. In that case Lords Cairns LC said that the purchaser of a chattel takes the chattel as a general rule subject to what may turn out to be a certain infirmities in the title. If he obtains title which is good against all the world, but if he does not purchase the chattel in market overt and if it turns out that the chattel has been found by the person who professed to sell it, the purchaser will not obtain a title good against the real owner. If it turns out that the chattel has been stolen by the person who professed to sell it, by a de facto contract, ie a contract which has purported to pass the property to him from the owner of the property, there the purchaser will obtain a good title, even although afterwards it should appear that there were circumstances connected with that contract which would enable the original owner of the goods to reduce it, and to set it aside. This is because these circumstances, enabling the original owner of the goods to reduce the contract and to set it aside, will not be allowed to interfere with a title for valuable consideration obtained by some third party during the interval while the contract remains unreduced.
    Applying this it is clear these goods were de facto sold to Laing by the appellant and bought in good faith by the respondents.'

Poole v *Smith's Car Sales (Balham) Ltd* [1962] 1 WLR 744 Court of Appeal (Ormerod, Willmer and Danckwerts LJJ)

- *Cars supplied 'on sale or return' – passing of property*

Facts
The plaintiff was a motor car dealer. He employed one Donald Savage. They had a loose association which was something less than a partnership. As the plaintiff was going away on holiday in August, he left two Vauxhall cars, a Velox and a Wyvern, to Donald Savage to deal with – there was no room for them on his premises. Donald came to an arrangement with his brother, Colin, who

worked for the defendants, whereby the two cars went into the possession of the defendants at their showroom. Here the evidence conflicts: Savage says the arrangement was one of sale or return. Mr Smith, a director of the defendant firm, seems to accept this, but the judge seems to have come to the conclusion that it was a more nebulous arrangement whereby the defendants merely provided 'house room' for the cars – if they sold them, all well and good; if not, they would be returned. No difficulty arises from the Velox for which the plaintiffs were paid £200. The agreed minimum for the Wyvern was £325. By October the plaintiff began to enquire why the car had not been returned, and asked for its return. Colin Savage repeatedly told him that he had a customer for the car and a deposit pending the conclusion of the sale. The plaintiff, being rather tired of this, wrote an ultimatum on 7 November, stating that the car had been left with the defendants on sale or return; it had not been returned, and if it was not returned by the 10 November the £325 was to be paid and the car deemed to be sold. The deadline passed and the car was not returned. The plaintiff claimed, inter alia, £325, the price of goods sold and delivered.

Held

His action would be successful.

Ormerod LJ:

'On the uncontested evidence, the contract was clearly one of sale or return. We then turn to the provisions of ss18, and Rule 4 (which are recited). The defendant has argued that a different intention has been shown again the evidence is against this.

So we are thrown back on Rule 4. By the rule, if the parties have fixed a time for the property to pass, then the property will pass at that time. No time had been fixed here. Failing that, it is a question of fact whether a reasonable time has passed on the expiry of which the property passed. On the affidavit of Smith, it seems clear that by early October 1960 there was no reasonable prospect of selling the car and instructions

had in fact been given for its return. Further, I take judicial knowledge of the fact that the market, after the holiday period from July to September, is less good. This assists as to what is a reasonable time.

I am fully satisfied that a reasonable time had certainly expired by November and thus by operation of s18 property passed to the defendants. If so, what happended afterwards is of no consequence. Further, it does not avail the defendants that they may not have been entirely responsible for the failure to return within a reasonable time. The contractual liability is theirs and they have failed to perform it.'

Wilmer LJ:

'I agree. As to what is a reasonable time, the rule in *Moss* v *Sweet* (1851) 16 QB 493 says that what is a reasonable time is a question of fact which must depend on the particular circumstances of the particular case.

In particular, I am swayed by the evidence of Mr Donald Savage to the effect that the whole arrangement was designed to tide over the holiday period while he would be away. That in itself suggests two or three weeks would have been a reasonable time.

Secondly, a second-hand car, already four years old, would be likely to depreciate rapidly – making a long time unlikely and unreasonable. Then there are the repeated requests for return indicating at least the plaintiffs' view that a reasonable time had elapsed. Finally, the other car, the Velox, was sold and paid for in September. It is also significant that no reply was ever made to the plaintiff's letter of 7 November.

Any later attempts to return the car was too late; property had passed and the plaintiff was entitled to reject the car and claim the value. This decision is not based on the fact that the car was damaged or had travelled an additional 1,600 miles. Even if the car had been returned in perfect condition its purported return would have been too late; by that time property had passed.'

Comment

See also *Weiner* v *Harris* [1910] 1 KB 285.

Stapylton, Fletcher Ltd, Re; Ellis, Son and Vidler Ltd, Re [1994] 1 WLR 1181 Chancery Division (Baker J)

- *Sale of goods – ascertainment – passing of property*

Facts

Both Stapylton, Fletcher Ltd and Ellis, Son & Vidler Ltd held stocks of wine for customers in return for rental fees. Stocks of wine were kept, either in a duty-paid warehouse or in a bonded warehouse; the wine was stored according to type (vintage etc), but was not marked with customers' names. A very accurate index was kept, showing wine as allocated to customers and continually updated as shipments were made to customers.

Both companies went into receivership shortly after B's company took over. By that time much of the wine, especially that belonging to E Ltd, had been moved to B's personal residence and the index had been largely lost. The receivers sought directions from the court as to whether property had passed. The question of ascertainment under ss16–18 Sale of Goods Act 1979 arose.

Held

That if a number of identical cases of wine were kept in store for specific customers, the owner of each having been noted in an index, then, regardless of the fact that the crates themselves were not marked, property passed to the customer. This was true even if the wine was not immediately appropriated to the customer and continued to be stored in the warehouse. Property passed according to common intention.

However, in the instance of wines ordered by customers in advance which were still in France (in some cases not even harvested or bottled), even if paid for in full, property did not pass at the point at which the company went into receivership; the wine was still generic and, even though subject to a contract of sale, was not at that point ascertainable. No property, or equity, passed to customers.

Judge Paul Baker QC:

'In summary, on the facts here, I conclude that if a number of cases or bottles of identical wine are held, not mingled with the trading stock, in store for a group of customers, those cases or bottles will be ascertained for the purposes of s16 of Sale of Goods Act [1979], even though they are not immediately appropriated to each individual customer. Property will pass by common intention and not pursuant to s18 rule (5).'

Comment

The findings of the court in this case are not new, but it provides useful and up-to-date support for the arguments as to time of ascertainment. See also *Karlshamns Oljefabriker* v *Eastport Navigation Corp, The Elafi* [1982] 1 All ER 208.

Underwood Ltd v *Burgh Castle Brick and Cement Syndicate* [1922] 1 KB 343 Court of Appeal (Bankes, Scrutton and Atkin LJJ)

- *Condensing engine – passing of property*

Facts

On 19 February 1920, the plaintiffs agreed to sell to the defendants a condensing engine to be delivered 'free on rail' in London. On that date the engine was a trade fixture in Millwall. It weighed 30 tons and was bolted to a concrete flooring in which it had become embedded by its own weight. Before delivery it had to be separated and dismantled. On 24 April 1920, the defendants gave written instructions to have the engine sent to Yarmouth. On 6 August 1920, the bedplate was accidentally broken while the main body of the engine was being loaded onto a railway truck. The defendants after inspection refused to accept it. The plaintiffs sued for the price (£650) of goods bargained and sold. The defendants were successful before Rowlatt J in pleading that the property in the engine had not at the date of the accident passed to them.

Held

The plaintiffs' appeal would be dismissed.

Bankes LJ:

'Considering the risk and expense involved in dismantling and moving the engine I have no hesitation in holding that the property was not to pass until the engine was safely placed on rail in London. An elaborate discussion of the rules in s18 of the Sale of Goods Act 1893 is unnecessary since these do not apply if a different intention appears as it does here, assuming for the moment that the machine was in a deliverable state when it was fixed in position in Millwall.

The appellants contended that where a specific article is complete in itself, ie where nothing more has to be done to make it an engine, it is then in a deliverable state within the meaning of s18, rule 1. I do not accept the test of mere "completeness" for deliverable state. It depends on the actual state of the goods at the date of the contract and the state in which they are to be delivered by the terms of the contract. The amount of trouble and money expended to put this engine on rail means that the subject matter could not have been in a deliverable state.'

Scrutton LJ:

'I think the question is quite simply answered by s18, rule 2 which states that "where the seller is bound to do something to the goods for the purpose of putting them in a deliverable state, the property does not pass until such a thing be done ..."

The appellants say the aspect of delivery is immaterial. The definition of "deliverable state" by s62 as "a state in which the buyer is bound to take delivery' cannot apply to this case where the buyers find an engine so firmly attached that up to two weeks' work is required to put in on rail. I decide this case on s18, rule 2 but do not dissent from the way Bankes LJ came to the same decision.'

Ward (RV) Ltd v *Bignall* [1967] 1 QB 534 Court of Appeal (Sellers, Diplock and Russell LJJ)

• *Sale of motor cars – passing of property*

Facts

The defendant contracted to buy a Ford Zodiac and a Vanguard Estate car from the plaintiffs for a total price of £850. A £25 deposit was paid, and the plaintiffs retained possession pending payment. Subsequently, the defendant declined to pay on the grounds that there had been a misrepresentation as to the date of manufacture of the Vanguard. He offered to buy the Zodiac alone for £500, but the plaintiffs rejected this and wrote saying if they were not paid they would sell both cars and claim damages for the difference. The Vanguard was sold for £350. A claim for the balance was successful in the county court, the Zodiac being unsold. No finding as to the passing of property was made. The defendant appealed. The plaintiffs contended property had passed to the defendant and that under s48(3) of the 1893 Act their resale had not effected any rescission of the contract and so they had properly been awarded damages.

Held

The appeal would be allowed.

Sellers LJ:

'The plaintiffs' proper remedy and action in the court below was damages for non-acceptance. All the defendant had done was to put down £25 which does not go a long way towards passing the property. The balance had not been paid; no inquiries had been made about the log book; no arrangements for removal or insurance had been made. Thus property had not passed and the correct action was for damages for non-acceptance.

The plaintiffs now say that the property was in the defendants since the time of making the contract. As a binding contract has been established the plaintiffs were unpaid sellers and by s39(1)(c) of the Act they had a right of resale as limited by the Act. [Section 48 is then recited.]

The question on this part of the appeal is therefore whether, if the property passed on sale, the unsold Zodiac remains the buyer's property so that the plaintiffs' action is for the price or whether by the sale of the Vanguard the plaintiffs have rescinded the whole contract on the buyer's breach so that the ownership of the Zodiac reverted to them and in effect their remedy is for damages for non-acceptance. Section 48 is quite clear that the property reverts on such a re-sale and the seller retains the proceeds whether they be greater or less than the contractual price. The seller then re-sells as owners and the second buyer gets good title by subs (2).

On this view of the law, the plaintiffs cannot recover the price of the Zodiac, which is their property, but only the loss sustained by the buyer's default. The result is that the plaintiffs have judgment for £850 less £25 deposit, less £350 for the Vanguard, less £450 agreed value of the Zodiac, plus cost of advertising the Zodiac in an attempt to re-sell (£22 10s). This comes to £47 10s.'

Diplock LJ:

'... If the seller's only right at the date of the issue of the writ was for damages for non-acceptance, I would agree with Sellers LJ.

... The seller's primary duty under the contract was to deliver both cars to the buyer. If he delivered only one, the buyer would be entitled to reject it; s30(1). By his conduct in selling the Vanguard the unpaid seller put it out of his power to perform his primary obligation under the contract.

He thereby elected to treat the contract as rescinded.

The property in the Zodiac thereby reverted to him and his only remedy against the buyer after the date of sale of the Vanguard was for damages for non-acceptance of the two cars of which the prima facie measure is the difference between the contract price and their market value at the date of sale of the Vanguard.'

Comment
Overruled: *Gallagher* v *Shilcock* [1949] 2 KB 765.

9   Risk, Impossibility and Frustration

Blackburn Bobbin Co Ltd v *T W Allen and Sons Ltd* [1918] 2 KB 467
Court of Appeal (Pickford, Bankes and Warrington LJJ)

- *Frustration – outbreak of war*

Facts
In 1914 the defendants agreed to sell to the plaintiffs a quantity of birch timber, which the defendants obtained through import. Delivery was due to commence in July and cease in November. War broke out in August 1914, before any deliveries had been made and imports of timber stopped. The plaintiff claimed damages for breach of contract. The defendant alleged the dissolution of the contract by the war.

Held
The plaintiff was entitled to damages.

Pickford LJ:

'Why should a purchaser of goods, not specific goods, be deemed to concern himself with the way in which the seller is going to fulfil his contract by providing the goods he has agreed to sell? The seller in this case agreed to deliver the timber free on rail at Hull and it was no concern of the buyers as to how the sellers intended to get the timber there. I can see no reason for saying – and to free the defendants from liability this would have to be said – that the continuance of the normal mode of shipping the timber from Finland was a matter which both parties contemplated as necessary for the fulfilment of the contract. To dissolve the contract, the matter relied on must be something which both parties had in their minds when they entered into the contract, such as, for instance, the existence of the music hall

in *Taylor* v *Caldwell*, or the continuance in readiness of the vessel to perform the contract, as in *Jackson* v *Union Marine Insurance Co*. Here there is nothing to show that the plaintiffs contemplated and there is no reason why they should be deemed to have contemplated that the sellers should continue to have the ordinary facilities for despatching the timber from Finland. As I have said, that was a matter which, to the plaintiffs, was wholly immaterial. It was not a matter forming the basis of the contract they entered into.'

Couturier v *Hastie* (1856) 9 Ex 102
Court of Exchequer Chamber (Coleridge, Maule, Cresswell, Wightman, Williams, Talfourd and Compton JJ)

- *Mistake – right to repudiate contract*

Facts
The contract was for the purchase of a quantity of Indian corn 'when shipped' on the 'Kezia Page' from Salonica to a safe port in the United Kingdom. The ship left Salonica, but because of the weather, had to put into Tunis Bay, where the cargo was found to have fermented and had to be sold.

Held
The contract could be repudiated.

Coleridge J:

'… For the plaintiffs it was contended that the parties plainly contracted for the sale and purchase of goods … that a vendor of goods undertakes that they exist and that they are capable of being transferred … and that as the goods in question had been sold and delivered to other parties before the contract in question was made, there was nothing on which it could operate ...

On the other hand, it was argued that this was not a mere contract for the sale of an ascertained cargo, but that the purchaser bought the adventure and took upon himself all risks from the shipment of the cargo ... it appears to us that the contract in question was for the sale of a cargo supposed to exist and to be capable of transfer and that inasmuch as it had been sold and delivered to others by the captain before the contract in question was made, the plaintiffs cannot recover in this action ...'

Comment
This decision was affirmed (1856) 5 HL Cas 673) by the House of Lords. See also *McRae v Commonwealth Disposals Commission* (1950) 84 CLR 377. Also see *Great Peace Shipping Ltd v Tsavliris Salvage (International) Ltd, The Great Peace* [2002] 4 All ER 689 Court of Appeal.

Demby Hamilton & Co Ltd v Barden [1949] 1 All ER 435 High Court (Sellers J)

• *Apple juice – delayed delivery*

Facts
A manufacturer contracted to supply thirty tons of apple juice in accordance with sample to a wine merchant, to be delivered in weekly truckloads. He crushed the apples, put the juice in casks, and kept it pending delivery. It was found as a fact that it would have been difficult to supply juice complying with the sample unless all the apples had been crushed at one time and that the juice was rightly and reasonably kept for the fulfilment of the contract, but that the property had not passed to the buyer. After 20.5 tons had been delivered no further deliveries were made through the delay of the buyer, in breach of contract, despite requests for delivery instructions from the seller, and in due course the undelivered

juice went bad. It was found that delivery had been delayed through the fault of the buyer within the Sale of Goods Act, s20. The seller sued for damages for breach of contract or for the price of goods sold.

Held
The action would be successful.

A good delivery, which would have avoided all loss, was delayed through the fault of the buyer.

The seller had goods ready for delivery and had to keep them ready for delivery as and when the buyer proposed to take them. The sellers could not dispose of these goods while they still had an outstanding obligation to keep them at the disposal of the buyer and to deliver them when requested. In both a practical and business sense the loss was caused by the buyers and the risk therefore had to fall on them. See also *Sterns Ltd v Vickers Ltd* [1923] 1 KB 78.

McRae v Commonwealth Disposals Commission (1951) 84 CLR 377 High Court of Australia (Dixon, Fullagar and McTiernan JJ)

• *Contract – purchase of non-existent tanker*

Facts
The defendants invited tenders for an oil tanker, loaded with oil, lying on Jourmand Reef off Papua. The plaintiff's tender was accepted and he incurred considerable expense in going to retrieve the vessel and its contents. There was no ship to be found where the vessel was supposed to be – and no place known as Jourmand Reef. The plaintiff claimed, inter alia, damages for breach of contract.

Held
He was entitled to succeed.

Dixon and Fullagar JJ:

'The position ... may be summed up as follows: It was not decided in *Courturier* v *Hastie* that the contract in that case was void. The question whether it was void or not did not arise. If it had arisen, as in an action by the purchaser for damages, it would have turned on the ulterior question whether the contract was subject to an implied condition precedent. Whatever might then have been held on the facts of *Courturier* v *Hastie*, it is impossible in this case to imply any such term. The terms of the contract and the surrounding circumstances clearly exclude any such implication. The buyers relied upon, and acted upon, the assertion of the seller that there was a tanker in existence. It is not a case in which the parties can be seen to have proceeded on the basis of a common assumption of fact so as to justify the conclusion that the correctness of the assumption was intended by both parties to be a condition precedent to the creation of contractual obligation. The officers of the Commission made an assumption, but the plaintiffs did not make an assumption in the same sense. They knew nothing except what the Commission had told them. If they had been asked, they would certainly not have said: "Of course, if there is no tanker, there is no contract". They would have said: "We shall have to go and take possession of the tanker. We simply accept the Commission's assurance that there is a tanker and the Commission's promise to give us that tanker." The only proper construction of the contract is that it included a promise by the Commission that there was a tanker in the position specified. The Commission contracted that there was a tanker there ... If, on the other hand, the case of *Couturier* v *Hastie* and this case ought to be treated as cases raising a question of "mistake", then the Commission cannot in this case rely on any mistake as avoiding the contract, because any mistake was induced by the serious fault of their own servants, who asserted the existence of a tanker recklessly and without any reasonable ground. There *was* a contract, and the Commission contracted that a tanker existed in the position specified. Since there was no such tanker, there has been a breach of contract, and the plaintiffs are entitled to damages for that breach.

Before proceeding to consider the measure of damages one other matter should be briefly mentioned. The contract was made in Melbourne, and it would seem that its proper law is Victorian law. Section 11 of the Victorian Goods Act 1928, corresponds to s6 of the English Sale of Goods Act 1893, and provides that "where there is a contract for the sale of specified goods, and the goods without the knowledge of the seller have perished at the time when the contract is made the contract is void". This has been generally supposed to represent the legislature's view of the effect of *Couturier* v *Hastie*. Whether it correctly represents the effect of the decision in that case or not, it seems clear that the section has no application to the facts of the present case. Here the goods never existed and the seller ought to have known that they did not exist.'

10 The Transfer of Title by a Non Owner

Folkes v *King* [1923] 1 KB 282
Court of Appeal (Bankes and Scrutton LJJ and Eve J)

* *Car sold by agent at less than specified price – title*

Facts
The owner of a motor car delivered it to a mercantile agent for sale. The owner stipulated and the agent agreed that the car should not be sold at less than a specified price without the owner's permission. The agent intended from the beginning to sell the car immediately for the best price he could get and to use the proceeds for his own purposes. On the same day he received the car he sold it for less than the specified price to a purchaser who bought it in good faith and without notice of the agent's fraud. The agent misappropriated the proceeds. The car was subsequently bought by the defendant. The owner sued the defendant for detinue. Judgment was given for the plaintiff; the defendant appealed.

Held
The appeal would be allowed.

Bankes LJ:

'The whole case turns on whether or not the car was obtained by the agent with the plaintiff's consent. The question is whether under the circumstances the plaintiff did intend to pass the property in the car to the agent Hudson or to give him the necessary authority to pass the property in it to a purchaser ... if he did then Hudson could not have been convicted of larceny of the car and the plaintiff must fail; *Whitehorn's Case* [1911] 1 KB 463 ... It seems to me that where the owner of the goods intends to confer a power to pass the property it is a case of

obtaining goods by false pretences ... if he gives, and intends to give that power, and the power is exercised, the person who takes under the execution of the power obtains the property, not against, but by the authority of, the original owner and none the less because the authority was obtained by fraud ... The plaintiff's claim must therefore fail.'

Comment
See also the decision of *Pearson* v *Rose & Young* [1951] 1 KB 275 which compares a dishonest mercantile agent and *Stadium Finance Ltd* v *Robbins* [1962] 2 QB 664 which examines s2(1) of the Factors Act 1889.

Mercantile Credit Co Ltd v *Hamblin* [1965] 2 QB 242 Court of Appeal (Sellers, Pearson and Salmon LJJ)

* *Authority to sell car – estoppel by negligence*

Facts
One Phelan was an apparently respectable motor dealer with authority from the plaintiff finance company to arrange hire purchase transactions with their firm. The defendant, who had done previous business with Phelan, wanted to raise a loan of £1,000 on the security of her car and approached Phelan for this purpose. Phelan promised to make inquiries asking the defendant to sign forms in blank which she apparently thought were mortgage documents, but were in fact standard hire purchase application forms. In return Phelan gave the defendant a blank cheque to be later made out for the exact sum of the loan. Phelan completed the HP forms in the normal way with the plaintiff company stating that he had absolute title to the car. The defendant never

received any money. She claimed inter alia 'non est factum' because she did not understand the nature of the documents she had signed. The plaintiffs claimed they had title to the car 'inter alia' since the defendant was estopped either by negligence or conduct by asserting otherwise (s21 Sale of Goods Act 1893). The plaintiff had acted in good faith throughout.

Held
The title to the car remained in the defendant.

Pearson LJ:

> On estoppel, the plaintiff must establish that the defendant had a duty of care to the plaintiff company; that she was in breach of that duty and that the breach was the proximate cause of any loss sustained by the plaintiffs. There was a sufficient relationship of proximity between the defendant and any persons who might advance her money on the security of the car to impose on her a duty of care with regard to the preparation and custody of contractual documents in respect of such a loan and thus the defendant owed the plaintiff that duty in this case. But on the fact of the case she was not in breach of that duty because of her acquaintance with Phelan whose blank cheque must have led her to believe she was entitled to rely on the arrangement she thought she was making to be carried out. Thus it was not negligent of her to leave the forms in blank with him. But even if the defendant had been negligent in leaving the documents signed in blank with Phelan, Phelan's fraud, the proximate cause of the plaintiff's loss, was not a foreseeable result of her actions.

Salmon LJ:

> 'The plaintiffs rely on *Eastern Distributors Ltd* v *Goldring* [1957] 2 QB 600 which is in fact very different from the present case. There the customer had expressly authorised the filling of the hire purchase forms and was a party to the fraudulent misrepresentation. Neither of those factors exist in the present case ... The doctrine of estoppel by negligence as applied to documents signed

> in blank is in general confined to negotiable instruments, but this is by no means an exhaustive rule.'

Comment
See *Eastern Distributors Ltd* v *Goldring* [1957] 2 QB 600 which discuses the legal rules that deal with apparent authority and passage of title.

Moorgate Mercantile Co Ltd v *Twitchings* [1977] AC 890 House of Lords (Lords Wilberforce, Salmon, Edmund-Davies, Fraser of Tullybelton and Russell of Killowen)

• *Estoppel by negligence and representation*

Facts
The plaintiff finance company let a car on hire-purchase to one McLorg, paid partly in cash the rest to be by instalments. The plaintiffs belonged to an organisation known as HP Information Ltd (HPI), 98 per cent of hire purchase (HP) agreements being registered wth HPI for the purposes of preventing fraud. As a matter of practice finance companies would almost invariably register agreements but it was not a condition of membership. HPI issued search vouchers on the following conditions.

1. All information supplied was given to the best knowledge and belief of HPI according to the information contained in its records.
2. That HPI did not warrant or guarantee that it had a complete record of every vehicle which was the subject of an HP agreement or that it had a complete up to date record of those vehicles which were at one time but had subsequently ceased to be the subject of an HP agreement.
3. That HPI did not accept liability for any action arising out of any information given.

Because of an oversight the agreement

between McLorg and the plaintiffs was not registered. McLorg offered the car to a dealer, a member of HPI, saying falsely he was the defendant and that the car was not subject to any HP agreement. HPI stated that the car was not registered with them. In consequence of this the defendant bought the car and later resold it. The plaintiffs were successful in their claim for conversion but the Court of Appeal reversed the decision on the grounds that they were estopped from asserting their title against the defendant. The plaintiffs appealed.

Held (Lords Wilberforce and Salmon dissenting)
The appeal would be allowed.

Lord Edmund-Davies:

'(1) Estoppel by representation
HPI quite clearly stated they were not guaranteeing that there was not in existence an HP Agreement in relation to the car. As Geoffrey Lane LJ put it ... "the assertion was only that no such agreement had been communicated to them. The dealer in the end has to rely on his assessment of the customer's honesty, and if he misjudges it, it is that misjudgment brought about by the customer's dishonesty which is the real and proximate cause of his loss". Even if they were acting as agents the representation fell far short of that which could lead to an estoppel.

(2) Estoppel by negligence
This requires the existence of a duty of care. The plaintiffs were under no legal duty to the defendant to register or take reasonable care in registering with HPI the hire purchase agreement despite the fact that both parties were members of HPI. Although the primary purpose of HPI was to protect finance companies it did not follow that companies who were members were under any obligation to make use of the facilities provided by HPI ...'

Oppenheimer v *Attenborough & Son*
[1908] 1 KB 221 Court of Appeal (Lord Alverstone CJ, Buckley and Kennedy LJJ)

• *Diamonds pledged – trade custom*

Facts
The plaintiff sued for the return of diamonds from the defendant pawnbrokers which were alleged to have been wrongfully pledged with the defendants for about £1,200. One Schwabacher, who had originally traded as a diamond merchant in that name, was in the habit of pledging diamonds with the defendants. In 1906 he came to the plaintiff receiving diamonds on the pretext of possible sale to named firms. The plaintiff gave him diamonds and a commission note. In fact Schwabacher pledged them with the defendants, who refused to deliver them up. Evidence was given at trial that a broker employed to sell diamonds had *no* authority to pledge them – his was unheard of in the trade. Channell J found that the diamonds were in the possession of Schwabacher, a mercantile agent, with the consent of the plaintiff, that the defendants had accepted the pledge in good faith – and that the general authority under the Factors Act 1889 is not limited by particular trade custom. Judgment was given for the defendants; the plaintiff appealed.

Held
The appeal would be dismissed.

Lord Alverstone CJ:

'We ought not to hold that the words in s2(1) of the Act were meant to deprive the pledges of the protection given by former acts solely on the ground that the mercantile agents had acted contrary to a trade custom I think that Channell J was right in holding that evidence of this custom was not admissable to defeat the protection otherwise given by the Act ...

In my opinion the words "acting in the ordinary course of business of a mercantile agent" mean that the person must act in the transaction as a mercantile agent would act if he were carrying out a transaction which he was authorised by his masters to carry out. There is not evidence to suggest Schwabacher was not acting in the ordinary course etc …

Phillips v *Brooks Ltd* [1919] 2 KB 243 High Court (Horridge J)

• *Contract induced by fraud – property passed?*

Facts

North entered the shop of the plaintiff jeweller and selected an emerald ring. When writing a cheque (which he signed 'George Bullough') he said: 'You see who I am; I am Sir George Bullough' and he gave the plaintiff an address in St James' Square. The plaintiff had heard of Sir George Bullough as a man of means and a directory told him that Sir George lived at the address North had given. The plaintiff allowed North to take the ring (as it was, he said, his wife's birthday tomorrow), but the cheque was returned marked 'No account' and North was subsequently convicted of obtaining the ring by false pretences. Meanwhile, though, he had pledged the ring with the defendant pawnbrokers and the plaintiff now sought its return.

Held

His action would fail.

Horridge J:

'I think the seller intended to contract with the person present, and there was no error as to the person with whom he contracted, although the plaintiff would not have made the contract if there had not been a fraudulent misrepresentation … In this case there was a passing of the property and the purchaser had a good title, and there must be judgment for the defendants, with costs.'

Comment

Followed in *Lewis* v *Averay* [1971] 3 WLR

603 and *Dennant* v *Skinner* [1948] 2 KB 164. Distinguished in *Ingram* v *Little* [1960] 3 WLR 504. See also *Shogun Finance Limited* v *Hudson* [2003] 3 WLR 1371 which applied the principle of *Cundy* v *Lindsay* (1878) 3 App Cas 459.

Shaw v *Metropolitan Police Commissioner* [1987] 1 WLR 1332 Court of Appeal (Fox, Lloyd and Stocker LJJ)

• *Title to car – agreement to sell*

Facts

Mr Natalegawa owned a car which he wanted to sell. He allowed Mr London to have possession of it and also gave him a letter which said: 'This letter serves to certify that I, ADH Natalegawa have sold the [car] to Mr Jonathan London of [address] and from the date shown below no longer have any legal responsibility connected with that car'. Mr London agreed to sell the car to Mr Shaw and another, motor dealers. Mr Shaw paid by banker's order but this was never paid – in other words there was an agreement to sell between Mr London and Mr Shaw, but the agreement never became a sale because the price was not paid. The question arose whether Mr Shaw or Mr Natalegawa owned the car.

Held

The car belonged to Mr Natalegawa. Despite the letter, Mr London had not 'bought or agreed to buy' the car himself within s25 of the Sale of Goods Act 1979 and s21 of the 1979 Act did not apply as there had merely been an agreement to sell.

Lloyd LJ:

'The crucial factor in the present case is that the plaintiffs [Mr Shaw and his associate] did not buy the car. They agreed to buy it. It was expressly, and in my view rightly, conceded that the property in the car was not intended to pass until Mr London was paid. So when Mr London went into the bank to cash the banker's draft, the moment had not yet come when the property was to pass from Mr London to the plaintiffs. That moment never did come ... The meaning of the word "sold" in the phrase "where goods are sold" in s21 of the 1979 Act does not appear to have been considered in any decided case ... On principle it seems to me that s21 does not apply to an agreement to sell.'

Staffs Motor Guarantee Ltd v *British Wagon Co Ltd* [1934] 2 KB 305 High Court (MacKinnon J)

• *Sale of lorry subject to hire-purchase agreement*

Facts
Heap, a motor dealer, and the defendant finance company entered into a transaction whereby Heap sold a lorry to the defendants who let it back to him on hire purchase. Heap, who at no time had given up possession, fraudulently sold it to the plaintiffs who bought in good faith being unaware of the previous transactions between Heap and the finance company. Heap defaulted on his payments. The defendants took possession of the lorry and refused to deliver it to the plaintiffs at their request. The plaintiffs sued the defendants for delivery up of the lorry or damages for its detention.

Held
Their action would fail.

MacKinnon J:

'The plaintiffs put their claim first on the ground that the document of hire purchase between Heap and the defendant ought to be treated in reality as a bill of sale ... a mere loan to be repaid by instalments. Following *Yorkshire Railway Wagon Co* v *Maclure* (1882) 21 Ch D 309 the circumstances of the transaction was in fact what it purported to be, ie a valid hire purchase agreement, not a bill of sale to secure the repayment of a loan by the defendants to Heap.

Following *Oppenheimer* v *Frazer and Wyatt* [1907] 2 KB 50, Heap was not in possession of the lorry as a "mercantile agent" within the meaning of the Factors Act 1889 s2(1), but as a bailee. Thus the sale of the lorry by him to the plaintiff was not rendered valid as against the defendants by s2(1). From the Oppenheimer case, the claimant must be able to assert not only that the goods were in the man's possession as a mercantile agent, but also that they were entrusted by the owner to him as a mercantile agent.

The plaintiffs further claim by s25(1) of the Sale of Goods 1893 that Heap was a person who 'having sold goods, continues or is in possession of the goods' after the transaction between him and the defendants had been completed by the agreement for the hire purchase. Heap was not such a person; rather he was as I have stated above, a bailee. Thus the delivery or transfer by him of that lorry under the sale by him to the plaintiffs had not by virtue of that section, the same effect as if it had been authorised by the defendants, and was not thereby rendered valid as against the defendants.'

Comment
Not followed in *Worcester Works Finance Ltd* v *Cooden Engineering Ltd* [1972] 1 QB 210. Disapproved in *Pacific Motor Auctions Pty Ltd* v *Motor Credits (Hire Finance) Ltd* [1965] AC 867.

Stevenson v *Beverley Bentinck Ltd* [1976] 1 WLR 483 Court of Appeal (Lord Denning MR, Roskill and Browne LJJ)

• *Purchaser of a car a 'private purchaser'?*

Facts
On 16 February 1973 a Mr Roberts got a second-hand Jaguar on hire-purchase from the defendant finance company. Roberts ceased to make the payments and on 14 January 1974

purported to sell the car to the plaintiff, who bought it in good faith and without notice of the HP agreement. At the time of the purchase the plaintiff was employed full-time in a manufacturing company – in his spare time he carried on a business buying vehicles for resale. The car in question was for his own use and not for resale. In March 1974 the defendants repossessed the car under the terms of the HP agreement and re-sold it. The plaintiff sued for conversion, claiming that as 'private purchaser' within s29(2) of the Hire-Purchase Act 1964 who had bought the car in good faith, he had acquired a good title thereto under s27(2) of the 1964 Act. The judge dismissed the action. On appeal, the issued related to whether the plaintiff was not a private purchaser since at the time of purchase he carried on the business of purchasing motor vehicles for the purpose of offering or exposing them for sale or whether he was since he had bought the car in his private capacity and not for the purposes of his business.

Held

The appeal would be dismissed. The plaintiff was not a 'private purchaser' and he was therefore not entitled to the protection afforded by s27(2) of the 1964 Act.

Lord Denning MR:

'Section 29(2) defines trade or finance purchases as "a purchaser who, at the time of the disposition made to him, carries on a business which consists, wholly or partly – (a) of purchasing motor vehicles for the purpose of offering or exposing them for sale" … a private purchaser … does not carry on any such business. The judge found the plaintiff did prima facie come within the definition of "trade or finance purchaser", but this car was not bought by way of that business but for his own purposes. Professor Goode has said that such a person would purchase "not in the course of his business" but the Act does not contain any such words so I disagree. Neither can I accept that he must be acting as a trade purchaser at the very moment of the disposition. The trade

purchaser can protect himself by contacting the Hire Purchase Information Service: see *Moorgate Mercantile Co* v *Twitchings* [1976] QB 225.'

Comment

Moorgate Mercantile Co v *Twitchings* was reversed on appeal ([1977] AC 890) by the House of Lords.

Ward (RV) Ltd v *Bignall*

See SALE OF GOODS, Chapter 8, above.

Worcester Works Finance Ltd v *Cooden Engineering Ltd* [1972] 1 QB 210 Court of Appeal (Lord Denning MR, Phillimore and Megaw LJJ)

• *Cheque dishonoured – title to car*

Facts

The defendants sold a car to one Griffiths for £525, which was paid by cheque. Griffiths then purported to sell the car to the plaintiffs as part of a hire purchase transaction under which one Millerick was to hire it with a view to purchase. Griffiths remained in possession of the car. Millerick never received it. Griffiths' cheque was later dishonoured and Cooden Engineering repossessed the car. After they discovered its whereabouts through the Hire Purchase Information Bureau, the plaintiffs claimed against the defendants to recover it, alternatively for £315 damages for conversion, being the amount unpaid on the hire purchase agreement.

Held

By virtue of s25(1) of the Sale of Goods Act 1893, the defendants had a good defence.

Lord Denning MR:

'The defendants rely on s25(1) of the Sale of Goods Act 1893 ie that Mr Griffiths was a person who having sold goods to Worcester Finance, continued in possession of them;

his disposition therefore, they alleged, had the same effect as if the person making it was expressly authorised by the owner to make the same. It is accepted that Griffiths was a person "having sold goods" to the finance company under s25(1). The question is whether Griffiths is one who "continues in possession" of the goods. The plaintiffs, relying on *Staffs Motor Guarantee Ltd* v *British Wagon Co Ltd* [1934] 2 KB 305, applied in *Eastern Distributors* v *Goldring* [1957] 2 All ER 52 contends that such a person must continue in possession lawfully as seller and not bailee. But those cases were disapproved by the Privy Council *Pacific Motor Auctions* v *Motor Credits* [1965] 2 All ER 105. I take the view that the authority of the Privy Council, although not binding, makes us able to depart from previous decisions of this court which have been disapproved. The words "continues in possession" refer to the continuity of physical possession regardless of any private transaction between seller and purchaser which might alter the legal title under which the possession was held. It is sufficient if he remains in possession of the goods that he has sold to the purchaser ... if there is a substantial break in the continuity ... then the the the section might not apply.

Regarding the interpretation of "disposition" that is to be interpreted widely to include all acts by which a new interest (legal or equitable) in the property is effectually created. Nor do I have any doubt about the good faith of the defendants: they simply retook a car for which they had been given a dud cheque.'

Megaw LJ:

'The Factors Act and the Sale of Goods Act are for many purposes to be treated as one code. But in the Sale of Goods Act the words "with the consent of the owner" have been omitted by the legislature. Thus if here the possession is the possession of a trespasser, it is irrelevant that that is possession which is not with the consent of the owner

...

On the other matters I agree.'

Comment

Not followed: *Staffs Motor Guarantee Ltd* v *British Wagon Co Ltd* [1934] 2 KB 305 and *Eastern Distributors Ltd* v *Goldring* [1957] 2 QB 600.

11 Real Remedies

Booth Steamship Co Ltd v *Cargo Fleet Iron Co Ltd* [1916] 2 KB 570
Court of Appeal (Lord Reading CJ, Warrington LJ and Scrutton J)

- *Goods stopped in transit – liability*

Facts
The defendants carried on the business of a manufactring company. Certain goods were sold to a Company A which were to be delivered in one of the plaintiffs' ships to place R, in Brazil. The voyage would end at a place S and passage would then be made by lighter to R. Before the ship carrying the goods arrived the defendants heard of A Company's financial difficulties and gave notice to the plaintiffs stopping the goods in transit. The goods would not be landed unless duty was paid upon them. When the plaintiffs' agents at S received the notice from the defendants they said that they (the defendants) should pay all freight charges and were further told by the plaintiffs that they would land them on their account; but the defendants declined responsibility. In the subsequent action, the plaintiffs argued that, because the goods had been stopped in transit, the defendants were liable for all and any charges upon the goods. At the time of trial no duty or landing charges had been paid.

Held
The defendants were liable in damages for the loss created by their exercise of the stop notice.

Lord Reading CJ:

'By s44 of the [Sale of Goods Act 1893] when the buyer becomes insolvent, the unpaid vendor has the right to resume pos-session of the goods so long as they are in course of transit, and he has rights of sale under s48. The method of effecting the right of stoppage is by taking actual possession of the goods, or by giving notice of the claim to the carrier or other bailee in whose possession the goods are: s46(1). The statute thus gives two ways of effecting stoppage. The first is by taking actual possession, and the second by notice of claim, the latter ... being a relaxation of the old rule that required actual possession to be taken. To get actual possession of goods carried the vendor must discharge the shipowner's lien (if any) for freight. Therefore satisfaction of the lien for freight must have been and still is an integral part of the stoppage of goods in transitu by the method of taking actual delivery – until that time there is a right in the unpaid vendor to resume the possession on arrival if he can. If the stoppage is by means of notice given, the vendor, upon arrival of the goods, is in the same position as if he had taken actual possession of the goods – that is to say, he is the sole person entitled, and, as I think, obliged, to take or order delivery of the goods. He cannot get actual possession unless he is ready and willing to discharge the lien for freight. I am, therefore, of opinion that a notice of stoppage given during the transit, and persisted in upon arrival of the goods, involves an obligation upon the vendor to discharge the shipowner's lien for freight – that is, to pay the freight due in respect of the goods carried. To get the goods he must free them from the lien.

There being, then, an obligation upon the vendor to take delivery and discharge the lien by paying the freight, it follows that, if he repudiates the obligation and so conducts himself as to prevent the shipowner completing his voyage and earning his freight, an action can be maintained by the shipowner against the vendor for damages for the breach of the obligation created by the notice to take actual possession of the goods upon arrival, and to discharge the shipowner's lien for the freight in respect of the goods. The damages may be the equivalent of the freight.

Having arrived at this conclusion, it must now be considered whether in the present case the plaintiffs' right of action is defeated by their failure to complete the voyage ... [The trial judge] decided, without determining whether or not there would otherwise have been a right of action in the plaintiffs, that they would not recover because they had not proved that the defendants had prevented the completion of the voyage. With all respect to the learned judge I cannot arrive at the same conclusion, having regard to my view of the legal position of the defendants. In my judgment, when the goods arrived at [S] the plaintiffs were ready and willing, then and at all material times, to complete the voyage and carry the goods to [R]. The obstacle to the continuance of the voyage was the non-payment of the duty and the repudiation by the defendants of all responsibility for freight, charges, or expenses. For the reasons already given, I think this was a repudiation of their obligation to take delivery, and that they were bound to provide the duty, or to make arrangements for its payment, so as to enable the voyage to be completed. As they refused, the goods were landed and are still at [T]. In my opinion, the plaintiffs are entitled in these circumstances to treat the voyage as completed, and to recover, as damages for the breach of obligation, the full amount of freight which they would have earned had the voyage been completed ... They claim, and I think rightly, to be placed in the same position as if the vendors had discharged their obligation and enabled the voyage to be continued to [R]. It is immaterial that, after the repudiation by the defendants, the plaintiffs acted in their own interests and for their own protection as regards the freight.'

Lyons (JL) & Co Ltd v *May & Baker Ltd* [1923] 1 KB 685 High Court (Sherman J)

• *Rejection by buyer after price paid*

Facts
On 8 June 1922, the plaintiffs sold to a third party, P, 16 tons of acid crystals ex wharf. Cash would be paid against delivery and the total price would be £195.1s.4d. which was accordingly paid. On 13 June P re-sold the crystals to the defendants on the same terms but at a higher price. The goods were duly delivered and on 17 June the defendants rejected them on quality grounds. Similarly the third party rejected them and passed the rejection on to the plaintiffs. On 29 June the defendants issued a writ against the third party for repayment of the sum paid. The plaintiffs stated that they would take back the crystals and return the cheque against a delivery order for the goods, and P said he would similarly return the goods and return the cheque. P gave the defendants a cheque for the sum paid to him. A delivery note was given to the plaintiffs by P who received it from the defendant and they in turn gave P a cheque for the sum repaid to them. These cheques were honoured when presented at the bank, but the cheques that P gave to the defendants were dishonoured. In July 1977, a receiving order was made against P and the plaintiffs demanded through the delivery note the return of the crystals. The defendants refused to give up the goods because their cheque given by P had been dishonoured. The defendants in their turn claimed a lien over the goods in their possession until they had been paid and the plaintiffs brought an action claiming a declaration that the property in the goods was with them.

Held
The plaintiffs' claim would succeed.

Sherman J:

'When the goods were rejected by P and defendants, then the property re-invested in the plaintiffs. There is no right for the defendants to retain possession until they have been paid in the same way that there is a right for a seller of goods to retain them until the whole price has been paid under Sale of Goods Act 1893.'

Ward (RV) Ltd **v** *Bignall*

See SALE OF GOODS, Chapter 8, above.

12 Personal Remedies of the Seller

Charter v Sullivan [1957] 2 WLR 528 Court of Appeal (Jenkins, Hodson and Sellers LJJ)

• *Repudiation of contract – measure of damages*

Facts
The plaintiff dealer agreed to sell a Hillman Minx motor car to the defendant. Subsequently he received a letter from the defendant refusing to complete the purchase, but seven to ten days later he resold the car to another purchaser (Mr Wigley) at the same manufacturers' fixed price. The plaintiff's sales manager said in evidence 'can sell all Hillman Minx we can get'.

Held
The plaintiff was entitled to nominal damages only for the defendant's breach of contract.

Jenkins LJ:

'The matter … stands thus. If the defendant had duly performed his bargain, the plaintiff would have made on that transaction a profit of £97.15s. The calculation accordingly starts with a loss of profit through the defendant's default, of £97 15s. That loss was not cancelled or reduced by the sale of the same car to Mr Wigley, for, if the defendant had duly taken and paid for the car which he agreed to buy, the plaintiff could have sold another car to Mr Wigley, in which case there would have been two sales and two profits …

The matter does not rest there. The plaintiff must further show that the sum representing the profit which he would have made if the defendant had performed his contract has in fact been lost. Here I think he fails, in view of [the sales manager's] evi-

dence to the effect that the plaintiff could sell all the Hillman Minx cars he could get.

I have already expressed my opinion as to the meaning of this statement. It comes, I think, to this, that, according to the plaintiff's own sales manager, the state of trade was such that the plaintiff could always find a purchaser for every Hillman Minx car he could get from the manufacturers; and if that is right it inevitably follows that he should the same number of cars and made the same number of fixed profits as he would have sold and made if the defendant had duly carried out his bargain.

Upjohn J's decision in favour of the plaintiff dealers in *Thompson* v *Robinson* was essentially based on the admitted fact that the supply of the cars in question exceeded the demand, and his judgment leaves no room for doubt that, if the demand had exceeded the supply, his decision would have been the other way.'

Comment
Distinguished: *Thompson (WL) Ltd* v *R Robinson (Gunmakers) Ltd* [1955] 2 WLR 185.

Millett v Van Heek & Co [1921] 2 KB 369 Court of Appeal (Bankes, Warrington and Atkin LJJ)

• *Anticipatory breach – assessment of damages*

Facts
The plaintiff cotton waste merchant agreed to sell waste to the defendants, cotton spinners and manufacturers in Holland, subject to government export permission. After part of the waste had been delivered, in 1917, permission

112

for further export was withheld: the parties agreed that deliveries would be resumed when a reasonable time had elapsed after the removal of the embargo. In 1918 the plaintiffs repudiated the contract and the defendants accepted the repudiation. The embargo was removed in 1919. The plaintiffs sought a declaration that the contract had been, or could be, determined: the defendants counterclaimed for damages for breach of contract.

Held

The defendants' counterclaim would be successful.

Atkin LJ:

'I think that the construction of s51(3) of the Sale of Goods Act, 1893, which the defendants contend for, would, if it were admitted, introduce a very serious anomaly into the administration of the law relating to the sale of goods, because the position is this: It is admitted that, if a contract is made for the sale of goods deliverable in the future by specified instalments at specified dates, and before the time has arrived for performance the contract is repudiated, and the repudiation is accepted, the damages have to be measured in reference to the dates on which the contract ought to have been performed. That is beyond controversy ... and it was the law at the time when the Sale of Goods Act 1893 was passed; and there is no reason to suppose that the Act intended to alter it ...

Therefore, if it was such a contract for delivery by fixed instalments at fixed times, then, although the action is brought in respect of the accepted repudiation, the damages would have to be assessed with reference to those fixed times. But it is said that, if no times have been expressed in the contract, and the contract is such as would be construed by law as a contract for delivery by reasonable instalments over a reasonable time, even though those times might be ascertained as a question of fact by the jury, the plaintiff suing may not merely have an option, but is compelled to fix his damages in reference to the market price at the time when the repudiation takes place. That, I

think, would introduce an anomaly entirely without any kind of principle. I am satisfied that the Act never intended to make that distinction, or to vary what was the rule of law at the time when it was passed, a rule which has been recorded in countless decisions since the doctrine of repudiation of contract received its development in *Frost* v *Knight* (1872) LR 7 Exch III, namely, that the damages are to be fixed in reference to the time for performance of the contract subject to questions of mitigation ...

Whether [the Divisional Court] are right in saying that a contract for delivery within a reasonable time is not a contract for delivery at a fixed time, I say nothing. I wish to reserve the point ... It is difficult to see why it should be said that the contract for delivery at times which can be determined by a jury is not a contract for delivery at fixed times. It seems to me that a meaning could be given to the words, "if no time was fixed," by reading them as referring to a contract such as to deliver goods on demand or to deliver goods as required by the purchaser. It might well be argued that that would give a meaning to the words in question. However, I do not wish to determine the question ...'

Otis Vehicle Rentals Ltd (Formerly Brandrick Hire (Birmingham) Ltd) v Ciceley Commercials Ltd [2002] EWCA Civ 1064 Court of Appeal (Peter Gibson and Potter LJJ, Sir Murray Stuart-Smith)

• *Section 49(1) Sale of Goods Act 1979 – action for the price of goods sold*

Facts

The appeal by the appellant, Ciceley Commercials Ltd, was based upon the interpretation of s49(1) of the Sale of Goods Act 1979. The appellant sold commercial vehicles and the respondent (Otis) were engaged in the business of selling and letting such vehicles. Under the terms of the agreement the respondent purchased 14 Mercedes Benz tractor units (the vehicles) from the appellant with the use of credit from Mercedes Benz Finance Limited (MBFL). Thus, in effect the vehicles were sold to MBFL and hired to Otis until the final payment would transfer ownership to Otis. Payments were to be made monthly to MBFL and the final payment, for each vehicle, was to be an increased payment, known in the trade as a 'balloon' payment. This was a common clause to be included, particularly when the property in question was subject to a buy-back agreement which would usually operate as the source of income to cover this inflated final payment under the finance agreement.

Certain issues in respect of liability had been previously agreed and were reflected in the amended pleadings on 3 October 2000. In the course of the oral negotiations from about July 1994 between the parties it was agreed:

'a) that if the plaintiff (respondent) entered into a hire purchase agreement with a finance company in respect of the said tractor units (for the purpose of which the defendant (appellant) would sell the tractor units to the finance company) the defendant would repurchase the said vehicles from the plaintiff at the plaintiff's option after either two or three years;
b) that the repurchase price would be either 60 per cent or 45 per cent of the purchase price of each vehicle depending on whether it was after two or three years.'

Three years later Otis notified the appellant in writing they wished to exercise the buy-back agreement and the repurchase of each Tractor unit would be £19,153.53p. However, the appellant responded by denying the vehicles had ever been the subject of a buy-back agreement and refused to repurchase them at the said price. This resulted in Otis successfully requesting an extended 12 months to pay off the outstanding debt to MBFL by refinancing the balloon payments payable on each vehicle. Thus, Otis continued to lease out the vehicles and eventually sold off all 14 vehicles

between June 1999 and April 2000 to meet his obligations to MBFL.

Otis commenced an action against the appellant under s49(1) of the Sale of Goods Act 1979, which provides:

'Where, under a contract of sale, the property in the goods has passed to the buyer and he wrongfully neglects or refuses to pay for the goods according to the terms of the contract, the seller may maintain an action against him for the price of the goods.'

Otis claimed they were ready, willing and able to deliver the vehicles to the appellant and the appellant was indebted to them for the price of the vehicles, plus interest amounting to £315,075.57p; they supported this argument using s49(2) of the Sale of Goods Act 1979, which provides:

'Where, under a contract of sale, the price is payable on a day certain irrespective of delivery and the buyer wrongfully neglects or refuses to pay such a price, the seller may maintain an action for the price, although the property in the goods has not passed and the goods have not been appropriated to the contract.'

The appellant believed the claim should have been for breach of contract and an award of damages in the sum of £150,003.91p.

Held

Potter LJ examined the effect of s49(1) in light of the circumstances and was of the opinion that by allowing recovery of the price (debt) the court would in effect be granting specific performance in circumstances where damages would be an adequate remedy. He believed the appellants' ground for appeal was justified: it was wrong to have given judgment for the price under the buy-back agreement, instead of awarding damages.

Potter LJ was mindful of the balloon payment, which was to be met through the buy-back agreement, as such an arrangement would indemnify the respondent. However, such an arrangement would involve the appellant paying either MBFL or the respondent to ensure the hire purchase agreements were met and title was allowed to pass to the respondent and then back to the appellant. Such an agreement (a buy-back agreement), which was to take place three years from the original contract, did not comply with s49(2): it could not be ascertained that the price was to be payable on a day certain irrespective of delivery. Also, Potter LJ made it clear that even if s49(2) had been complied with, the seller's right to sue for the price would also depend upon his continuing willingness to deliver the goods: in this instance the goods had been sold, leaving a claim for damages. Thus, the appeal was allowed and damages substituted the original award.

Comment

This case clearly shows the difference between suing for the price of the goods or for damages. Under the former the price is due and there is no need to mitigate any loses; whereas, with the latter, the claimant must not only mitigate their losses but also demonstrate that their damages are not too remote. It was easy to see why Otis elected to sue for the price instead of damages, as the latter offers a secure and favourable position in comparison to damages.

13 Remedies of the Buyer I: The Right to Reject the Goods

Lyons (J L) & Co Ltd v *May & Baker Ltd*

See SALE OF GOODS, Chapter 11, above. Also note the Sale and Supply of Goods to Consumers Regulations 2002, which came into force on 31 March 2003. The Regulations apply to a number of different situations when goods have been sold to a consumer. For example, they apply when a consumer purchases goods from a trader or enters into a hire purchase transaction. However, they do not apply, generally, to the supply of services or to goods sold at auction that a consumer was allowed to attend. The Regulations allow for a full refund if faulty goods are returned within a reasonable period of time. However, what is a reasonable time has not been defined, but it is implied this would be a short period of time. Furthermore, a consumer is given additional rights under Part 5A of the Sale of Goods Act 1979. The amendment reverses the burden of proof when a consumer returns goods within the first six months from the date of sale and requests either a repair, replacement or a partial or full refund. In such cases the consumer does not have to prove that the goods were faulty at the time of sale. Instead, it will be assumed that the goods were faulty and it is for the retailer to rebut this presumption and prove that the goods were satisfactory at the time of sale (see Part 5A Additional Rights of Buyer in Consumer Cases, Statutory Instrument 2002, No 3045, s3).

14 Remedies of the Buyer II

Coastal (Bermuda) Petroleum Ltd v VTT Vulcan Petroleum SA (No 2), The Marine Star [1994] 2 Lloyd's Rep 629 Queen's Bench Division (Mance J)

• *Sale of goods – non-delivery – assessment of damages*

Facts

The plaintiffs purchased, on 10/11 July 1991, 50–55,000 tonnes of fuel oil from the defendants. The contract was cif delivery to Aruba. Initially the defendants nominated the Marine Star or substitute, which was accepted by the plaintiffs. However, on the same day as the plaintiffs accepted nomination, the defendants purported to withdraw the Marine Star and substitute another ship. The substitution was never made and a fortnight later the plaintiffs treated the contract as repudiated and claimed damages. They claimed to have sustained damages (a) by reason of loss of profits (they had agreed to sell on the oil) and (b) because of liability to Aruba for non-delivery.

Held

There was clearly repudiation of contract. As to assessment of damages, the plaintiffs had established that there was, at the relevant time, no available market to buy substitute oil. The defendants' argument that such loss of profits could not have been envisaged was dismissed. Quite clearly, the exact size of the profit might vary, but 'selling on' was so normal a practice that it would be within the contemplation of the parties at the time of making the contract. The argument by the defendants that the plaintiffs could have relied on a force majeure clause to defeat any claim from Aruba for non-delivery was dismissed. Claims by Aruba

for loss of yield at the refinery (because they had to buy in a different, inferior oil) was set at 30 cents a barrel. The defendants were liable for both forms of damages: loss of profits and payment to be made by plaintiffs for non-delivery.

Mance J:

'In my judgment it was within the assumed scope of both parties' contemplation when the plaintiffs contracted to buy E4 (oil) from the defendants that the plaintiffs could make a profit from resale and delivery of such E4 to Coastal Aruba on a broadly back-to-back basis and there was nothing about the size of any profit, in the light of such variations as there were on resale, to take it outside the scope of their contemplation.'

Comment

This case provides further support for the argument that in industries where sub-selling or selling-on is commonly practised; both parties can be assumed to have this 'in contemplation' at the time of making the contract. There is no need for one party to mention it specifically to the other. See also *Vitol SA v Norelf Ltd* [1995] 3 WLR 549.

Leaf v International Galleries

See SALE OF GOODS, Chapter 3, above.

Sealace Shipping Co Ltd v Oceanvoice Ltd, The Alecos M [1991] 1 Lloyd's Rep 120 Court of Appeal (Neill, Ralph Gibson and McCowan LJJ)

• *Breach of contract – measure of damages*

Facts

The parties contracted for the sale and purchase of The Alecos M, together with its spare propeller. The vessel did not have a spare propeller and the buyers claimed damages for breach of contract. The arbitrator awarded them the propeller's scrap value: on appeal, Steyn J awarded the reasonable cost of replacing the spare propeller, a larger sum.

Held

The arbitrator's decision would be restored. Neill LJ acknowledged that it might sound suprising to hear that a spare propeller had no more than scrap value, but as he understood the award, the arbitrator had reached that conclusion, not because he had applied some wrong principle of law, but because he had decided as a matter of fact that in the particular circumstances of the case the commercial value of that spare propeller on that ship was no more than its scrap value. His award could only be read as meaning that he had asked the question: what had those buyers really suffered as a result of the non-delivery of that spare propeller with that vessel? And he had given the answer: they had lost its scrap value which in the circumstances had been the only value which it had for them.

Shearson Lehman Hutton Inc v *Maclaine Watson & Co Ltd (No 2)* [1990] 1 Lloyd's Rep 441 High Court (Webster J)

• *Breach of contract – measure of damages*

Facts

Between 25 July and 30 September 1985 Shearsons and Maclaines made with each other a series of contracts concerning the buying and selling of tin. The contracts were divided into 'cash and carries' and 'general trades'. On 24 October 1985 trading in the tin market on the London Metal Exchange was suspended. Shearson bought an action against Maclaine and others alleging breach of contract. The question arose, inter alia, as to the assessment of damages and in particular the definition of the term 'available market'. On the issue of damages, Shearsons claimed that the measure of damages was that prescribed by s50(3) of the Sale of Goods Act 1979, ie the prima facie difference between the contract price and the market or current prices on 12 March. Alternatively, they claimed that the measure was that presented by s50(2) which would be the difference between the contract price and the prices at which they sold the tin plus carrying and other costs.

Held

Shearsons were entitled to damages based on the fair market or current price at the time of the breach.

Section 50(3), under the rubric 'Damages for non-acceptance', provides:

> 'Where there is an available market for the goods in question the measure of damages is prima facie to be ascertained by the difference between the contract price and the market or current price at the time or times when the goods ought to have been accepted or (if no time was fixed for acceptance) at the time of the refusal to accept.'

The object of the provision is to avoid uncertainty by the arbitrary insertion, into the assessment of damages, of a presumption that if there is an available market the plaintiff seller can obtain the market or current price of the goods on the date of the breach, that his damages are to be measured by reference to that price whether or not it would have been reasonable or sensible for him to have waited before going into the market and selling the goods, and that neither party is to be adversely affected by price fluctuations either before or after the date of the breach. Because of this the requirements of reasonable mitigation, which would ordinarily apply to a claim for damages, do not apply when the measure of damages is governed by s50(3).

Webster J's view was that the subsection contemplates a hypothetical sale by a hypothetical seller of the amount in question of the goods in question.

It was Webster J's view that the expression 'prima facie' in the subsection could affect the literal application of the words which follow it.

The evidence established that it would have been impossible to sell the greater part of the standard tin on 12–13 March to consumers of tin (as distinct from merchants), and that a better price would have been obtained if the sale were to have been negotiated over a few days than if it had taken place all within 24 hours, ie by the end of 13 March. The central issues, therefore, were first whether given the proper meaning of 'available market', that there was an available market on 12–13 March (on which dates most consumers would not have been accessible to a seller of 7,755 tonnes of standard tin) and second what Webster J called the 'appropriate price' issue whether to determine the market or current price on 12–13 March it was necessary to consider only prices at which the tin could have been negotiated and sold on that day or whether it was permissible to consider the price which could have been negotiated over a slightly longer period. The Judge referred to 12–13 March because the time for delivery expired at midnight on 12 March, so 13 March would have been the first date on which Shearsons could have sold the tin.

If the seller actually offers the goods for sale there is no available market unless there is one actual buyer on that day at a fair price; that if there is no actual offer for sale, but only a notional or hypothetical sale for the purposes of s50(3), there is no available market unless on that day there are in the market sufficient traders potentially in touch with each other to evidence a market in which the actual or notional seller could if he wished sell the goods: see *ABD (Metals and Waste) Ltd* v *Anglo Chemical and Ore Co Ltd* [1955] 2 Lloyd's Rep 456 at 466 per Sellers LJ and *Charter* v *Sullivan* [1957] 2 QB 117.

On the 'appropriate price' issue, Webster J's view was that where there is no actual sale,

the market price must be a fair market price for the total quantity of goods assuming them to have been sold by a seller on the relevant date – however it might be unfair to the defendant purchaser to confine the price so established to the price obtainable if an actual sale had to be concluded on that day, so it is permissible to take into account the price which would be negotiated within a few days with persons who were members of the market on that day and who could not be taken into account as potential buyers on the day in question only because of difficulties of communication. For that purpose it has to be assumed that the price remained constant during the period of the negotiations. Further, the expression 'prima facie' enabled the court, practically (in a case where it would be unfair to confine a notional sale to a sale which could only have been made on the day in question) to determine what would have been in substance a fair price on that day in all the circumstances.

Applying his conclusions the Judge found that there was an available market. The fact that all of the potential buyers would not have been immediately accessible to the notional seller on that very day did not mean that there was on that day no available market for the goods.

In determining the fair market or current price on 12–13 March 1986 for 7,755 tonnes of standard grade tin Webster J took into account both the price which would have been obtained if a sale had taken place all on 12–13 March, and the price which would have been obtained if it had taken place after negotiations of a few days up to a week, either before 12–13 March at a price fixed on that date and without reference to previous fluctuations, or on a sale or sales concluded up to a week after that date but on the assumption that the price had remained constant since 12–13 March. The Judge thought it was impossible, in the circumstances, to determine a fair market or current price without taking into account, inter alia, the evidence about both those prices. The fair market price could only be determined by reference to a range, and necessarily a fairly wide range, of possible prices; and the price which would have been obtained if the whole tonnage had to be sold on 13 March was relevant to the determination of that range.

15 Consumer Protection

Ashington Piggeries Ltd v *Christopher Hill Ltd*

See SALE OF GOODS, Chapter 5, above.

Balding v *Lew Ways Ltd* [1995] TLR 153 Queen's Bench Divisional Court (Pill LJ and Keene J)

• *Consumer protection – defence required to avoid conviction under Regulations*

Facts
The defendants Lew Ways Ltd had been acquitted by Towcester Justices of three specimen charges of providing toys which did not satisfy the essential safety requirements of the Toys (Safety) Regulations 1989. As a defence, under s39 Consumer Protection Act 1987, the defendants had argued that their toys satisfied the British Standard. This standard was inferior to that specified in the 1989 Regulations. It was clear that the managing director of the firm was aware of this. On appeal by way of case stated:

Held
In order to establish a defence under s39 to the offence of supplying a toy which did not satisfy the requirements of the 1989 Regulations, it was not sufficient to show compliance with the British Standard. It was necessary to show that all steps had been taken to avoid falling below the requisite standards of the Regulations (which were higher and more exacting than that established by the British Standard). The due diligence defence failed and the case was remitted to Towcester Justices.

Pill LJ:

'It was common ground before the present court that the offence was proved subject ot the statutory defence and that the elements were different from those required to comply with the regulations.

The issue before the court was whether the defence had been made out.

Section 39 of the 1987 Act provided: "(1) … in proceedings against any person for an offence to which this section applied it shall be a defence … to show that he took all reasonable steps and exercised all due diligence to avoid committing the offence".'

His Lordship referred to the test for all reasonable steps and all due diligence in *Amos* v *Melcon (Frozen Foods) Ltd* (1985) 149 JP 712.

'The requirement was to show due diligence in relation to the regulations, that is, steps toward avoiding falling below the standard required by regulations made under Parliamentary authority. Compliance with other standards would not show steps had been taken.'

Grant v *Australian Knitting Mills Ltd*

See SALE OF GOODS, Chapter 5, above.

MFI Furniture Centres Ltd v *Hibbert* [1996] COD 100 Queen's Bench Division (Balcombe LJ and Collins J)

• *Misleading indication of price – burden of proof*

Facts

The plaintiff company had been convicted (of two sample charges) under the Consumer Protection Act 1987 for indicating misleading prices. The appealed, by way of case stated from the decision of Newcastle Crown Court to dismiss their appeal against conviction, on the grounds that it was for the prosecution to produce 'an individual customer who had been misled' on each charge.

Held

There is nothing in ss20 or 21 of the 1987 Act (as to the meaning of 'misleading') which requires the prosecution to prove that a particular misleading indication of price misled any one particular person who was a potential customer. The appeal was dismissed.

Balcombe LJ:

> '... there was nothing in ss20 or 21 requiring the prosecutor to prove that a particular misleading indication of price had been given to a particular person who might wish to be supplied with the goods for his own private use or consumption. Indeed, if in every case the prosecutor had to lead evidence by an individual as well as establish that the indication was misleading, it might well deprive the section (s20) of much of its effect ...'

R v Piper [1995] TLR 134 Court of Appeal (Criminal Division) (Roch LJ, Scott Baker and Jowitt JJ)

• *Offences under the Trade Descriptions Act 1968 – particulars of the offence*

Facts

Piper appealed against his conviction under s14(1) Trade Descriptions Act 1968, for making in the course of his trade or business a statement which was reckless or false as to the provision of a trade or service. He had included on the letterhead of his business notepaper the logo of the Guild of Master Craftsmen. The appeal was made on the basis

that to thus misrepresent his status, did not necessarily amount to a statement as to provision of a service.

Held

In trying offences under s14(1) of the 1968 Act, it was desirable to confine the particulars of the offence to identifying the statement on which the prosecution relied. It had been argued that the basic statement complained of as being false and misleading was that Piper was a member of the Guild of Master Craftsmen and not as to any service he might supply. However, certain parts of s14 (s14(1)(a)(i)) covered the situation specifically and it was clear an offence had been committed. The complications arising could have been avoided, if the statement of offence and particulars had been more specific.

Lord Roch, delivering the judgment of the court:

> '(The Court of Appeal) is bound by the decision in *R v Breeze* ([1973] 1 WLR 994, 996): "... there is no reason for saying that a man carrying on business whose business is the provision of services does not commit an offence under s14(1)(a)(i) if he adopts to himself a personal qualification which he does not enjoy". The present case could not be distinguished from that authority on its facts.
>
> Nevertheless s14(1) covered much more directly the circumstances of this present case in subpara (iii). The subparagraphs in subs (1) of s14 overlapped and clearly there would be cases where the facts potentially fell within more than one of those subparagraphs.
>
> The complications which arose in the present case could be avoided if the statement of offence and the particulars of offence were confined in the way suggested.
>
> In the present case it would have sufficed had the particulars of offence been confined to the assertion that the appellant had recklessly made a statement which was false, namely that he was a member of the Guild of Master Craftsmen when he was not.'

Warwickshire County Council v *Johnson* [1993] 2 WLR 1 House of Lords (Lords Griffiths, Emslie, Roskill, Ackner and Lowry)

• *Meaning of the phrase 'in the course of any business of his' in the context of the Consumer Protection Act 1987*

Facts

The appellant was a branch manager of a retail electrical goods shop. He placed a notice in the window claiming to have goods £20 cheaper than rival firms, but refused to sell at £20 lower than a competitor's price for a TV set. Warwickshire County Council presented an information, under s20(1) of the CPA 1987, before local magistrates.

Held

In deciding whether the appellant was acting 'in the course of any business' the House of Lords ruled that this must mean a business of which the defendant is the owner, or in which he has a controlling interest. This did not apply here and the conviction should be set aside. The fact that it was Johnson's business as a manager to be responsible for such notices did not make him responsible under s20(1).

Lord Roskill (as to the phrase 'in the course of any business of his'):

'This involves treating the phrase "in the course of any business of his" as also appearing in the opening words of s40(1). This seems to me to make it impossible to relate those same words when they appear later in the subsection as applying to the "person" mentioned in the opening words. Thirdly and apart from these difficulties, as my noble and learned friend, Lord Ackner, pointed out during the argument, the defendant was charged with an offence against s20(1) and not with an offence against s40(1).

The obscurity of this language has puzzled commentators to whom it has seemed odd that when a misleading notice

or advertisement is published the person responsible for refusing to honour the advertisement, if an employee and not the owner of the business in question, is not guilty of an offence against s20(1). In commenting upon the decision of the Divisional Court in the present case [1992] Crim LR 644, 646-647, Professor JC Smith wrote in discussing the phrase "any business of his":

"The inconvenience of holding that the offence can be committed only by the owner of the business is obvious but what did the draftsman mean by this emphatic and inelegant phrase if he did not mean any business belonging to the defendant? Perhaps the answer to the difficulty is to be found in s40(1) ..."

He then set out the text of s40(1) and continued:

"There is an ambiguity here. Does 'any business of his' refer to a business of 'any person' or of 'some other person'? If the latter, we are no farther forward; but, if the former, there is no difficulty about convicting the employee. This assumes that the employer is guilty of the offence as well – ie that the offence is one imposing strict and vicarious liability."

Professor Smith thus highlights the problem of construction but does not resolve it. I have already indicated the impossibility of construing these words out of their natural order and the effect of the incorporation of s20(1) into s40(1).

... I have, in respectful agreement with Professor Smith, criticised the drafting of these sections and I share his particular criticism of the drafting of s40(1). As already stated it is now, within the limitations already mentioned, permissible to have regard to statements by a minister in Parliament in order to ascertain the true intention of ambiguous legislation the interpretation of which has become a matter of controversy.

As already stated at the report stage of the Bill which became the Consumer Protection Act 1987, the noble and learned Lord, Lord Morton of Shuna, moved an amendment to clause 20(1) of the Bill, as it then was, to delete the words "of his". At column 1140 of Hansard, vol 485, he said:

"The words 'of his' appear to be quite unnecessary and unnecessarily restrictive. What is to be the position of somebody who is giving a misleading price indication in the course of his employer's business, possibly unauthorised by his employer? Is that employee who is acting against instructions to be safe from prosecution? That is the way it reads. There does not appear to be a necessity for the words 'of his'. The sense would remain if it is just 'in the course of any business', which would restrict the subsection to a business use, so to speak, but allow the prosecution of somebody who might say, 'Well, it was not my business. I was acting for somebody else when I gave the misleading price.' "

The noble and learned Lord, Lord Denning added: "The words 'of his' are not only unnecessary but misleading." '

16 The Supply of Goods and Services Act 1982

Cronin (Trading as Cronin Driving School) v Customs and Excise Commissioners [1991] STC 333 Queen's Bench Division (Brooke J)

• *Supply of goods and services – supply of driving tuition – franchise agreements*

Facts
The plaintiff operated a franchise system, whereby he provided taxed, insured vehicles, advertising and general maintenance. The instructors paid for petrol and oil, and were able to advertise separately, book their own lessons, and use the cars for their private purposes. By the terms of the franchise, standard fees were charged and each instructor paid a fixed percentage to Cronin.

The question arose as to whether Cronin could be charged VAT as being the supplier of goods or services.

Held
Although the instructors were treated as self-employed for tax and NI purposes, they were not in business on their own account. Cronin was supplying a service of driving tuition to the public through the driving instructors and VAT was payable by him.

Esso Petroleum Ltd v Commissioners of Customs and Excise

See SALE OF GOODS, Chapter 1, above.

Rickards (Charles) Ltd v Oppenheim

See SALE OF GOODS, Chapter 4, above.

Wilson v Best Travel [1993] 1 All ER 353 Queen's Bench Division (Phillips J)

• *Implied terms – obligations of tour operator*

Facts
The plaintiff, on holiday in Greece, fell through a plate-glass balcony door at his hotel. The doors complied with Greek, but not British, safety standards. He argued that the tour operators were in breach of s13 of Supply of Goods and Services Act (SGSA) 1982 which was implied into the terms of the contract.

Held
Where tour operators check that local safety standards in respect of accommodation have been observed, they will normally have discharged their duty of care under the SGSA to the client. Note, however, that had the condition of the glass doors been obviously dangerous, notwithstanding that they complied with local safety standards, then the situation would have been different.

Wong Mee Wan v Kwan Kin Travel Services Ltd and Others [1995] 4 All ER 745 Privy Council (Lords Goff of Chieveley, Jauncey of Tullichettle, Slynn of Hadley, Nolan and Hoffmann)

• *Contract of service – implied term(s)*

Facts

The plaintiff's daughter bought a package tour of mainland China offered by the defendant, a Hong Kong travel agent. The tour brochure contained the terms of the contract which referred throughout to the tour group as 'we'. At the border, a local Chinese company took over responsibility for the group. On arrival at a lake, the group were told that the scheduled ferry had already left and they would make the crossing in a speedboat owned by the third defendant a small local firm. Three crossings were necessary to take the group across the lake, but after two crossings the driver of the boat refused to work longer. Another local employee agreed to stand in for him for the third crossing, in the course of which the boat collided with another and sank. The plaintiff's daughter was drowned. There was no doubt but that her death was caused by the negligence of the relief driver. What remained to be decided by the court was the extent to which liability should be allocated as between the various defendants.

Held

In the specific terms of the brochure the first defendant undertook to provide all the services listed, not merely arrange for them to be provided. This was the case even if some activities were to be provided by others. It was an implied term that services provided would be carried out with reasonable care and skill and this obligation continued even if some of the services were to be rendered by others and even if tortious liability existed on the part of those others. The first defendants were liable for breach of contract, because they had not carried out the provision of services with reasonable care and skill.

Lord Slynn delivered the judgment. At one point he said:

'Taking the contract as a whole their Lordships consider that the first defendant here undertook to provide and not merely to arrange all the services included in the programme, even if some activities were to be carried out by others. The first defen-

dant's obligation under the contract that the services would be provided with reasonable skill and care remains even if some of the services were to be rendered by others, and even if tortious liability may exist on the part of those others. It has not been suggested that Miss Ho Shui Yee was in contractual relations with the others.

In their Lordships' view it was an implied term of the contract that those services would be carried out with reasonable skill and care. That term does not mean, to use the words of Hodgson J in *Wall* v *Silver Wing Surface Arrangements Ltd*, that the first defendant undertook an obligation to ensure "the safety of all the components of the package". The plaintiff's claim does not amount to an implied term that her daughter would be reasonably safe. It is a term simply that reasonable skill and care would be used in rendering the services to be provided under the contract. The trip across the lake was clearly not carried out with reasonable skill and care in that no steps were taken to see that the driver of the speedboat was of reasonable competence and experience and the first defendant is liable for such breach of contract as found by the trial judge.

Their Lordships of course appreciate the desire of the Court of Appeal to avoid imposing a burden which is "intolerable" on package tour operators. It must, however, be borne in mind that the tour operator has the opportunity to seek to protect himself against claims made against him in respect of services performed by others negotiating suitable contractual terms with those who are to perform those services. He may also provide for insurance cover. He may include an appropriate exemption clause in his contract with the traveller. It also has to be borne in mind, in considering what is "tolerable" or reasonable between the parties, that a traveller in the position of Miss Ho Shui Yee could have no influence on the terms negotiated by the tour operator with third parties, and if injured by their lack of care would, if having no right against the package tour operator, be obliged to pursue a claim in a foreign country. The difficulty involved in doing so does not need to be elaborated. In considering what is or is not tolerable as between traveller and tour operator it is of some relevance to note the Package Travel, Package Holidays and Package Tours Regulations 1992, SI 1992/3288, made pursuant to Council Directive (EC) 90/314.'

Consumer Credit

1   Introduction

Helby v *Matthews*

See SALE OF GOODS, Chapter 1, above.

Liare v *Schurek* (1993) The Times 28 May Court of Appeal (Dillon, Mann and Steyn LJJ)

• *Credit agreements – private or one-off loan – within Consumer Credit Act 1974*

Facts

A motor vehicle dealer agreed to put a hire purchase agreement in his name on behalf of the plaintiff who wished to purchase a vehicle from the defendant but was unable to obtain credit.

The agreement was written on a used car sale invoice.

The first six months' payments were made, but then the plaintiff defaulted leaving 30 instalments unpaid.

The question arose as to whether there was a commercial agreement and, if so, whether it came within the Consumer Credit Act (CCA) 1974, as the motor vehicle dealer had no licence.

Held

If the agreement was made in the course of business it was an isolated transaction and was capable of coming within s189(2) CCA 1974. In this case by virtue of s189(2) CCA 1974 no licence was required.

But, since it was not clear whether as a question of fact it was in the course of business, or a private transaction, the case was remitted for rehearing.

2   Formation of the Contract

Dimond v *Lovell* [2000] 2 All ER 897 House of Lords (Lords Browne-Wilkinson, Nicholls of Birkenhead, Hoffmann, Saville of Newdigate and Hobhouse of Woodborough)

- *Hire agreement was a regulated agreement – regulated agreement not properly executed and unenforceable*

Facts

Mrs Vanessa Dimond was the innocent victim of a road traffic accident which involved Mr Lovell, the other driver. Mr Lovell ran into the back of Mrs Dimond's Suzuki Vitara when she was driving home from work. The Suzuki Vitara was eventually taken to a garage for repairs and while being repaired Mrs Dimond hired a Ford Mondeo, for eight days, from a car hire company called 1st Automotive Ltd. The total charge for the hire was £346.63p. Mr Lovell's insurers, Co-operative Insurance Society (CIS), were prepared to pay for the loss caused by their customer's negligent driving but contested the claim for the hire of the Ford Mondeo and that Mrs Dimond had not hired a suitable replacement vehicle. CIS claimed Mrs Dimond had failed to mitigate her loss and/or the hire agreement had given her additional benefits, which should have been considered when calculating her loss.

CIS argued the agreement between 1st Automotive Ltd and Mrs Dimond was a regulated agreement, as defined under s189 of the Consumer Credit Act (CCA) 1974, and the documentation did not contain all the prescribed terms, resulting in the agreement not being properly executed under s61. As direct result of not complying with the CCA 1974 the hire agreement between Mrs Dimond and

1st Automotive was unenforceable and Mrs Dimond had suffered no loss.

Their Lordships examined the definition of a 'regulated agreement' in s189(1) of the 1977 Act to mean 'a consumer credit agreement, or consumer hire agreement, other than an exempt agreement'. Thus, CIS were arguing the hire agreement was indeed a consumer credit agreement and that it was not an exempt agreement under s8(2) of the Act, which defines a 'consumer credit agreement' as:

> 'A consumer credit agreement is a personal credit agreement by which the creditor provides the debtor with credit not exceeding [a sum specified by regulation, which at the time of hiring the vehicle the sum was £15,000: see the Consumer Credit (Increase of Monetary Limits) Order (SI 1983/1878), which has since been increased to £25,000 by the Consumer Credit (Increase of Monetary limits Order 1998, SI 1998/996)].'

Their Lordships applied this definition to the terms of the hire agreement between Mrs Dimond and 1st Automotive in order to consider the argument put forward by CIS. Clause 5 of the said agreement provided:

> 'Where the hire is consequent upon the hirer's own vehicle being unroadworthy as a result of a road traffic accident: (i) the lessor will allow the hirer credit on the hire charges until such time as a claim for damages has been concluded against the party (hereinafter called the third party) that the hirer alleges is liable for damages arising out of the said accident.'

Their Lordships applied this clause in relation to s8(1) of CCA 1974 which defines a 'personal credit agreement' as 'an agreement between an individual ("the debtor") and any other person ("the creditor") by which the creditor provides the debtor with credit of any amount.' Credit for the purposes of a regulated agreement under the CCA 1974 is covered by s9(1) which 'includes a cash loan, and any other form of financial accommodation'.

1st Automative claimed the agreement was regulated under the CCA 1974. They further claimed the agreement was an exempt agreement under art 3(1)(a) of the Consumer Credit (Exempt Agreements) Order 1989 (SI 1989 No 869), which exempts certain consumer credit agreements by reference to the number of payments to be made by the debtor:

> '... the total number of payments to be made by the debtor does not exceed four, and those payments are required to be made within a period not exceeding 12 months beginning with the date of the agreement'.

However, the agreement between Mrs Dimond and 1st Automative was silent on the number of payments and that full payment should have been received within 12 months of the agreement.

Held

Their Lordships found the agreement between Mrs Dimond and 1st Automative was a regulated agreement under the CCA 1974, and was improperly executed and as a result unenforceable against Mrs Dimond. Their Lordships also considered s65(1) of the 1974 Act, which provides that an improperly executed agreement is enforceable against a debtor/hirer but only on the order of the court. However, their Lordships examined their judicial control in such matters under s127 CCA 1974 and found that subs(3) prevented them from making such an order: 'The court shall not make an enforcement order under s65(1) if s61(1)(a) [signing of agreements] was not complied with ... [the] regulations under s60(1)'. In this instance the agreement had not complied with s61(1)(a) and the agreement was irredeemably unenforceable.

Comment

Many insurance policies cover the damage to vehicles but do not cover the hire of a replacement vehicle whilst the damaged vehicle is being repaired. The services offered by 1st Automative have attempted to fill this gap in the market by providing a car on credit whilst the claim is being pursued. However, whilst filling this gap, arguably the rates being charged by such hire companies are above the market rates and has inevitably resulted in motor insurance companies, such as CIS, resisting such claims. This judgment will certainly send a message to all involved and will probably result in a change of practice.

Forthright Finance Ltd v *Ingate (Carlyle Finance Ltd, third party)*
[1997] 4 All ER 99 Court of Appeal (Staughton, Henry and Thorpe LJJ)

- *Consumer Credit Act 1974, s56 – antecedent negotiations*

Facts

The defendant, a Mrs Olive Ingate, purchased an Austin Metro in March 1990. The car was purchased using credit provided by the plaintiffs, Forthright Finance Ltd. One year after the purchase Mrs Ingate approached a car dealer, Matthew Phillipsons Ltd, and an agreement was reached allowing Mrs Ingate to buy a second hand Fiat Panda. The Austin Metro was to be used in part-exchange, having agreed the value of the car at £2,000. At this time £1,992 was still outstanding on the Austin Metro to Forthright Finance Ltd. A Mr Taylor, who was a sales manager for the car dealer, Matthew Phillipsons Ltd, informed Mrs Ingate that 'if she bought the Fiat Panda ouse they would take the Austin Metro in part-exchange. What is more, *they would discharge the balance of the money due for the Austin Metro to Forthright* (emphasis added)' (p101). Mrs Ingate purchased the Fiat Panda using credit provided by Carlyle Finance Ltd, the third party to the proceedings.

The Fiat Panda cost £2,995, a deposit of £1,000 was made and the amount left on credit was to be £1,995. In October 1991 the car dealer, Matthew Phillipsons Ltd, went into liquidation and it was found contrary to their agreement with Mrs Ingate that they had not discharged the £1,992 owed to Forthright Finance Ltd. This resulted in Forthright Finance Ltd successfully suing Mrs Ingate. However, execution of this judgment was stayed, pending the outcome the third party proceedings brought against Carlyle Finance Ltd under s56 of the Consumer Credit Act (CCA) 1974:

'In this Act "antecedent negotiations" means any negotiations with the debtor or hirer ... (b) conducted by a credit-broker in relation to goods sold or proposed to be sold by the credit-broker to the creditor before forming the subject matter of a debtor-creditor-supplier agreement within s12(a) ...' (p101)

Therefore, Mrs Ingate claimed the car dealer, Matthew Phillipsons Ltd, was acting as agent for Carlyle Finance Ltd and was liable for the false statement made by the agent during negotiations.

Staughton LJ examined the wording of the CCA 1974 and went beyond the Act to find the intention of the legislation by looking at the Tenth Report of the Law Reform Committee (*Innocent Misrepresentation*) (Cmnd 1782) (July 1962), which concluded (at para 20):

'We think, therefore, that it should be made clear in any legislation on this subject that where negotiations for a hire-purchase contract are in fact conducted by a dealer he shall, notwithstanding any agreement to the contrary, be deemed to be the agent of the finance company for the purpose of any representations in respect of the goods which are the subject matter of the contract.' (p104)

Staughton LJ referred to this (at p104) as 'the mischief which the Law Reform Committee detected; and the remedy which they proposed was an agency as to representations made in respect of goods.'

Held
It was upon the above reasoning that Staughton LJ allowed Mrs Ingate's appeal and found Carlyle Finance Ltd liable. He was of the opinion that:

'In my judgment the law is plain enough: one simply has to inquire whether all the negotiations form part of the one transaction as a matter of fact. The facts are plain enough to lead to that conclusion in this case.'

Comment
This was a complex case which appeared to have been two separate transactions but the Court of Appeal applied the CCA 1974 with its true intention: to protect consumers. Section 56 made the third party liable, in this instance, and discharged Mrs Ingate's liability.

Holwell Securities Ltd v Hughes
[1974] 1 WLR 155 Court of Appeal (Russell, Buckley and Lawton LJJ)

• *Offer and acceptance – mode of acceptance prescribed*

Facts
The plaintiffs were granted an option to purchase the defendant's freehold property and the agreement provided that the option was exercisable 'by notice in writing to the [defendant] at any time within six months from the date hereof ...' Within that time, the plaintiffs' solicitors wrote to the defendant giving notice of the exercise of the option. The letter was posted, properly addressed and prepaid, but it was never delivered.

Held
The option had not been validly exercised.

Lawton LJ:

'Now in this case, the "notice in writing" was to be one "to the Intending Vendor". It was to be an intimation to him that the grantee had exercised the option: he was the one who was to be fixed with the information contained in the writing. He never was, because the letter carrying the information went astray. The plaintiffs were unable to do what the agreement said they were to do, namely, fix the defendant with knowledge that they had decided to buy his property. If this construction of the option clause is correct, there is no room for the application of any rule of law relating to the acceptance of offers by posting letters since the option agreement stipulated what had to be done to exercise the option. On this ground alone I would dismiss the appeal.'

Comment
Distinguished: *Henthorn* v *Fraser* [1892] 2 Ch 27 and *Bruner* v *Moore* [1904] 1 Ch 305.

Mercantile Credit Co Ltd v *Hamblin*

See SALE OF GOODS, Chapter 10, above.

Wilson v *First County Trust* [2001] 2 WLR 302 Court of Appeal (Sir Andrew Morrit V-C, Chadwick and Rix LJJ)

• *Misstatements – unenforceable agreement under the Consumer Credit Act 1974*

Facts
The appellant, a consumer, claimed that the respondent, a pawnbroker, did not comply with ss60 and 61 of the Consumer Credit Act (CCA) 1974 and was seeking a declaration that the agreement was unenforceable by reason of s127(3) of the said Act.

In January 1999 the respondent agreed to lend the appellant £5,000 on the security of her car. The respondent charged a document fee of £250 in connection with the loan, which the appellant was unwilling or unable to pay at the time of the initial arrangement. Subsequently, the £250 was added to the amount of the loan. The agreement was a regulated agreement for the purposes of the CCA

1974 and stated that the total credit amounted to £5,250.

The main issue was whether or not the inclusion of the document fee, which amounted to £250, should have been added to the total charge for credit and as a result the amount of credit was misstated.

The Court examined the wording of s61(1) of the CCA 1974 which sets out three conditions which must be met in order for a regulated agreement to be treated as properly executed. In particular s61(1)(a) states that 'a document in the prescribed form itself containing all the prescribed terms and conforming to regulations under s60(1)'. In this context 'prescribed terms' would relate to paragraph 2 in Schedule 6 to the Consumer Credit (Agreement) Regulations 1983 (SI 1983/1553) which includes 'a term stating the amount of the credit'.

Held
Based upon the facts the amount of credit was misstated and it followed that the regulated agreement had not been properly executed. The consequences of this finding was that the agreement was unenforceable based upon the effect of s127(3) CCA 1974 which precludes enforcement of the agreement under s65 of the Act.

Comment
The Court of Appeal applied the letter of the law in complying with the spirit of the CCA 1974 – *truth in lending* – which adopts the principle of disclosure and requires businesses to ensure they reveal all the facts, for example in advertising, canvassing, quotations and the contents of credit agreements. This case demonstrates the Court of Appeal's willingness to address the inequality of bargaining power between a consumer and a trader who offers credit facilities to the consumer whilst not giving a true reflection of the credit agreement. See also *R* v *Modupe* (1991) The Times 27 February (CA) which also discusses the implications of non-compliance with the CCA 1974.

3   The Creditor's Obligations

Clough Mill Ltd v Martin [1985] 1 WLR 111 Court of Appeal (Sir John Donaldson MR, Oliver and Robert Goff LJJ)

- *Sale of yarn – reservation of title clause*

Facts
The sellers supplied yarn to the buyers who intended to use it for the manufacture of cloth. The contract provided, inter alia:

> 'Condition 12. However, the ownership of the material shall remain with the seller, which reserves the right to dispose of the material until payment in full for all the material has been received by it in accordance with the terms of this contract or until such time as the buyer sells the material to its customers by way of bona fide sale at full market value. If such payment is overdue in whole or in part the seller may (without prejudice to any of its other rights) recover or resell the material or any of it and may enter upon the buyer's premises by its servants or agents for that purpose. Such payments shall become due immediately upon the commencement of any act or proceeding in which the buyer's solvency is involved. If any of the material is incorporated in or used as material for other goods before such payment the property in the whole of such goods shall be and remain with the seller until such payment has been made, or the other goods have been sold as aforesaid, and all the seller's rights hereunder in the material shall extend to those other goods.'

The question arose whether this clause gave the sellers secured rights on the buyers' insolvency.

Held
The clause covered two separate matters. Firstly it allowed for retention of title to unused goods and secondly retention of title to newly created goods. The first of these objects is allowed by English law. The second point was smore difficult because the buyer may have added his own work and materials when creating new goods. Therefore the effect of the clause was to create a charge in favour of the sellers, with the buyers having legal title.

Robert Goff LJ:

> 'There has been a spate of decisions in recent years concerning these so-called *Romalpa* clauses. But it is of great importance to bear in mind that these cases have been concerned with different clauses, very often in materially different terms; that different cases have raised different questions for decision; and that the decision in any particular case may have depended on how the matter was presented to the court, and in particular may have depended on a material concession by counsel …
>
> In every case, we have to look at the relevant documents and other communications which have passed between the parties, and to consider them in the light of the relevant surrounding circumstances, in order to ascertain the rights and duties of the parties inter se, always paying particular regard to the practical effect of any conclusion concerning the nature of those rights and duties. In performing this task, concepts such as bailment and fiduciary duty must not be allowed to be our masters, but must rather be regarded as the tools of our trade. I for my part can see nothing objectionable in an agreement between parties under which A, the owner of the goods, gives possession of those goods to B, at the same time conferring on B a power of sale and a power to

consume the goods in manufacture, though A will remain the owner of the goods until they are either sold or consumed. I do not see why the relationship between A and B, pending sale or consumption, should not be the relationship of bailor and bailee, even though A has no right to trace the property of his goods into the proceeds of sale. If that is what the parties have agreed should happen, I can see no reason why the law should not give effect to that intention. I am happy to find that both Staughton J and Peter Gibson J, have adopted a similar approach in the recently reported cases of *Hendy Lennox (Industrial Engines) Ltd* v *Grahame Puttick Ltd* [1984] 1 WLR 485, and in *Re Andrabell Ltd* [1984] 3 All ER 407 ...

... The difficulty with the present conditions is that the retention of title applies to material, delivered and retained by the buyer, until payment in full for *all* the material delivered under the contract has been received by the seller. The effect is therefore that the seller may retain his title in material still held by the buyer, even if part of that material has been paid for. Furthermore, if in such circumstances the seller decides to exercise his rights and resell the material, question can arise as to (1) whether account must be taken of the part payment already received in deciding how much the seller should be entitled to sell, and (2) whether, if he does resell, he is accountable to the buyer either in respect of the part payment already received, or in respect of any profit made on the resale by reason of a rise in the market value of the material ...

I can see no reason why the retention of title in the first sentence of condition 12 should be construed as giving rise to a charge on the unused material in favour of the plaintiff ...

The buyer does not, by way of security, *confer* on the plaintiff an interest in the property defeasible upon the payment of the debt so secured. On the contrary, the plaintiff *retains* the legal property in the material ...

The difficulty of construing the fourth sentence as simply giving rise to a retention by the plaintiff of title to the new goods is that it would lead to the result that, upon the determination of the contract under which the original material was sold to the buyer, the ownership of the plaintiff in the new goods would be retained by the plaintiff, uninhibited by any terms of the contract which had then ceased to apply; and I find it impossible to believe that it was the intention of the parties that the plaintiff would thereby gain the windfall of the full value of the new product, deriving as it may well do not merely from the labour of the buyer but also from materials that were the buyer's, without any duty to account to the buyer for any surplus of the proceeds of sale above the outstanding balance of the price due by the buyer to the plaintiff. It follows that the last sentence must be read as creating either a trust or a charge. In my judgment, however, it cannot have been intended to create a trust ...

Is is difficult to see why, if the parties agree that the property in the goods shall vest in A, that agreement should not be given effect to. On this analysis, under the last sentence of the condition as under the first, the buyer does not *confer* on the seller an interest in property defeasible upon the payment of the debt; on the contrary, when the new goods come into existence the property in them ipso facto vests in the plaintiff, and the plaintiff thereafter retains its ownership in them, in the same way and on the same terms as the plaintiff retains its ownership in the unused material ...

Accordingly, consistent with the approach of Vinelott J to a similar provision in *Re Peachdart Ltd* [1984] 1 Ch 131, I have come to the conclusion that, although it does indeed do violence to the language of the fourth sentence of the condition, that sentence must be read as giving rise to a charge on the new goods in favour of the seller ...'

Helby v *Matthews*

See SALE OF GOODS, Chapter 1, above.

Leaf v *International Galleries*

See SALE OF GOODS, Chapter 3, above.

Mercantile Credit Co Ltd v *Hamblin*

See SALE OF GOODS, Chapter 10, above.

Rowland v *Divall*

See SALE OF GOODS, Chapter 4, above.

Shanklin Pier Ltd v *Detel Products Ltd* [1951] 2 KB 854 High Court (McNair J)

• *Paint suitable for piers – collateral warranty*

Facts
The defendants were manufacturers of paint, and they assured the plaintiffs that their paint was suitable for piers and would last seven years. In consequence the plaintiffs stipulated in their contract with a firm of painters that the defendants' paint be used. It proved unsatisfactory and lasted only three months.

Held
The defendants were liable on a collateral warranty.

McNair J:

'I am satisfied that, if a direct contract of purchase and sale of the (paint) had then been made between the plaintiffs and the defendants, the correct conclusion on the facts would have been that the defendants gave to the plaintiffs the warranties substantially in the form alleged in the statement of claim
...
Counsel for the defendants submitted that in law a warranty could give rise to no enforceable cause of action except between

the same parties as the parties to the main contract in relation to which the warranty was given. In principle, this submission seems to me unsound. If, as is elementary, the consideration for the warranty in the usual case is the entering into of the main contract in relation to which the warranty is given, I see no reason why there may not be an enforceable warranty between A and B supported by the consideration that B should cause C to enter into a contract with A or that B should do some other act for the benefit of A.'

Comment
Applied in *Andrews* v *Hopkinson* [1956] 3 WLR 732.

Southern and District Finance plc v *Barnes and Another; J & J Securities Ltd* v *Ewart and Another; Equity Home Loans Ltd* v *Lewis* [1995] TLR 225 Court of Appeal (Leggatt, Roch and Aldous LJJ)

• *Consumer credit regulated agreements – power to alter interest rates*

Facts
In each of the above cases, application had been made to the county court for a time order under ss129 and 136 Consumer Credit Act 1974. Problems of interpretation arose, both as to the meaning of the term 'sum owed' and as to the scope of the court's powers to allow more time to pay and the extent to which the court might amend existing agreements.

Held
A county court had power to make an order giving a debtor time to pay. If possession proceedings had been brought then the amount 'owed' would normally be the total indebtedness plus interest. If the sum owed was the whole of the outstanding balance, the court could order the rate of interest to be altered; or alter the amount of the instalments.

4 Default by the Debtor

Bentinck Ltd v *Cromwell Engineering Co* [1971] 1 QB 324 Court of Appeal (Lord Denning MR, Fenton Atkinson and Cairns LJJ)

- *Car recovered 'from the hirer'?*

Facts

Mr Faulkner wished to buy a car from his employers, the defendants. The plaintiff finance company bought the car and let it out on a hire purchase to Mr Faulkner, the defendants agreeing to indemnify the plaintiffs against any default. Mr Faulkner paid the initial instalment and the next three or four and then fell into arrear. The car was severely damaged in an accident. Mr Faulkner took it to a garage but did not give an order for the repairs to be carried out. The plaintiffs traced Mr Faulkner but, after giving a false telephone number, he disappeared. Six months later they found the car and, with the garage owner's consent, took possession of it. When they sued to recover the balance outstanding on the hire purchase agreement, the defendants maintained that, in the terms of the relevant statute, the car was 'potential goods' and, as the plaintiffs had recovered the car 'from the hirer ... otherwise than by action', they had no claim which could be enforced.

Held

The plaintiffs' action would be successful.

Lord Denning MR:

'Let me say at once that in the ordinary way, once goods are "protected goods", ie more than one-third has been paid, the finance company cannot recover possession – except by action – from the hirer, nor from any garage or repairer with whom the hirer

may have left it. The words "from the hirer" include all those to whom the hirer has bailed it. That is quite clear from *FC Finance Ltd* v *Francis* (1970) 114 SJ 568. But that does not touch the question of abandonment ...

It seems to me that if a hirer has in fact abandoned the goods, he no longer has possession of them, either by himself or his agent. If the owner retakes them, he does not recover possession "from the hirer". He does nothing illegal. But the abandonment, to entitle the finance company to retake possession, must be abandonment of all rights in the car so as to evince quite clearly that the hirer no longer has any interest in it. The judge has so found in this case ... Here was a car with all the costs running up. Mr Faulkner would not want to shoulder the liability. He disappeared altogether. The judge was quite entitled to find that he had abandoned it in the real legal sense as abandoning all rights whatever which he had in the car.

I think that the finance company acted quite lawfully in retaking the car which had been thus abandoned. The defence therefore fails.'

Capital Finance Co Ltd v *Bray* [1964] 1 WLR 323 Court of Appeal (Lord Denning MR, Harman and Salmon LJJ)

- *Car – possession taken without court order*

Facts

The hirer of a car under a hire purchase agreement had paid £113, more than one-third of the hire purchase price. Having fallen two months in arrears with his instalments, the owners took possession of the vehicle without, as required by statute, obtaining a court order. As a result, again in accordance with the statute, the agreement was determined and the hirer became entitled to the return of his £113. Realising their mistake, the owners left the car outside the hirer's house: as it was causing an obstruction, the hirer moved it to a piece of ground near his business. Seven months later, believing that there was evidence that the car was being used, the owners wrote to the hirer claiming the return of the car and the outstanding instalments and, as the hirer had not complied, and on the footing that the agreement had subsisted throughout, the owners commenced proceedings, adding shortly before the trial a claim for damages in detinue.

Held

By virtue of the statute, the hirer was able to recover his £113: the agreement had not been revived by the conduct of the parties. The owners' claim in detinue failed.

Lord Denning MR:

'There is no obligation on a person who has another person's goods to return them to him, except by contract. The rule is accurately stated in Salmond on the Law of Torts (13th Edn) at p264:

"No one is bound, save by contract, to take a chattel to the owner of it; his only obligation is not to prevent the owner from getting it when he comes for it."

In order that there should be a wrongful detention of goods, the defendant must withhold the goods and prevent the plaintiff from having possession of them. He is not bound to be active and send the goods back unless there is an obligation by contract to do so. It seems to me, therefore, that this letter of demand ... was not a good demand such as to found a claim in detinue. It did not merely demand delivery up. It demanded the hirer should take the car back to one of ... three addresses. He was under no obligation to do so.

The only way in which a claim in detinue might be made here was the way in which

counsel for the owners put it. He said that, if a man uses a car in defiance of the owner's rights, that may give a claim in detinue. I agree. It may. No doubt, after receiving the letter ... the hirer had no right to use the car. The owners had withdrawn their consent to it, and if he did use it after the letter there might be a claim in detinue. But what evidence of that is there here? There is no evidence of any user by the hirer after the letter. It was argued that the judge inferred user from that time; but I am not at all sure that he did. In any event, if he did, there was no evidence of it, and I do not think that it should be inferred; so that there is no claim on that score.'

Forward Trust Ltd v *Whymark*
[1989] 3 WLR 1229 Court of Appeal
(Lord Donaldson of Lymington MR,
Stuart-Smith and Farquharson LJJ)

• *Default – amount of judgment*

Facts

The defendant obtained from the plaintiff finance company a personal loan repayable over ten years. The agreement was a regulated consumer credit agreement to which the provisions of the Consumer Credit Act 1974 and the Consumer Credit (Rebate on Early Settlement) Regulations 1983 applied. Within two years the defendant had defaulted. The plaintiffs claimed and entered judgment for the full amount outstanding. The defendant applied to pay the amount in instalments; the registrar set aside the judgment on the grounds of the defendant's entitlement to a rebate under ss94–95 of the Consumer Credit Act for early settlement; the county court judge upheld his decision; the plaintiffs appealed.

Held

The appeal would be allowed and the matter remitted to the county court to consider the defendant's application to be allowed to discharge the judgment debt by instalments.

Lord Donaldson of Lymington MR:

'It is quite clear from ss94 and 95 of the 1974 Act that Parliament has intended that a debtor should be free to discharge his indebtedness before the expiration of the term fixed under the regulated consumer credit agreement and that, should he do so, he should be entitled to a rebate reflecting the unearned interest element. It is also clear that Parliament intended that a rebate might also be required on refinancing or where, as a result of breach of the agreement or for any other reason, the indebtedness of the debtor became payable before the time fixed by the agreement. In principle one would have expected that the rebate would have reflected the advantage to the creditor of expedited payment and would only have been available if there was such payment, since an expedited liability, unaccompanied by payment, is of no benefit to the creditor who is called on to allow the rebate. However, whether or not this expectation is realised depends not on the Act, but on the 1983 rebate regulations made under s95.

Regulation 2 of the rebate regulations, headed "Entitlement to rebate", might have been expected to provide the answer, but does not in fact do so. It merely reflects s95 without answering the question. The answer is to be found in the formulae for calculating the rebate, all of which require a determination of "the settlement date", and in reg 6, which defines that date by reference to the date of payment by the debtor.

That being so, the debtor's position at the date when judgment is entered is that he owes the full outstanding amount and there is no reason why judgment should not be entered for that amount. The effect of his potential entitlement to a rebate is not to reduce his indebtedness, but to enable him, in some circumstances, to discharge that indebtedness by a payment which may be less than 100p in the pound, depending on when he discharges it. For completeness, I should add that the effect of entering judgment is not to extinguish the debtor's consumer credit agreement indebtedness. It is to leave him with the same indebtedness, including that for "charges for credit to the debtor under a regulated consumer credit agreement" (s95), the cause of action for which has become merged in the judgment.

The underlying assumption which has bedevilled the recovery through the courts of debts due under consumer credit agreements has been that a judgment for £100 can only be satisfied by the payment of £100. This is the normal rule … In my judgment the Consumer Credit Act 1974 and the Consumer Credit (Rebate on Early Settlement) Regulations 1983 produce [an] … exception. When the debtor decides, or is forced, to discharge the judgment debt, he can do so by payment of the amount stated in the judgment less any rebate which is applicable in respect of such discharge at that date.'

Goulston Discount Co Ltd v *Clark*
[1967] 2 QB 493 Court of Appeal (Lord Denning MR, Danckwerts and Diplock LJJ)

• *Recourse agreement – recover of whole loss*

Facts
The defendant dealer sold a car to the plaintiff finance company and gave a 'Specific Indemnity and Repurchase Undertaking' that he would 'indemnify [the finance company] against any loss that [they] may suffer by reason of the fact that the hirer … does not pay the amounts which he would if he completed his agreement by exercising the option to purchase'. The hirer defaulted: the finance company terminated the hiring and re-took the car and sold it. The finance company sought to recover from the dealer the loss they had suffered as a result of the hirer's default.

Held
Their action would be successful.

Lord Denning MR:

'Owing to the decision of this court in *Financings Ltd* v *Baldock* [1963] 2 QB 104 the plaintiffs could only sue the hirer for the arrears of the instalments. They could not get anything more from him. So they came down on the defendant. He had signed a specific recourse agreement, ie, a recourse agreement in respect of this very car. The question in the case is whether that is an agreement of guarantee or of indemnity. If it is a guarantee, the defendant is under no more liability than the hirer, ie, to pay the arrears; but if it is an indemnity, he will be liable to pay the whole of the hire purchase price ...

The only difficulty is the decision of the court in *Unity Finance Ltd* v *Woodcock* [1963] 1 WLR 455. The judge felt that on that case he was bound to hold that this agreement here was a guarantee. I can well understand the judge taking that view, seeing what was said in that case; but on reading the case again, I think that the decision should be based on illegality. The finance company there had acted quite illegally. They had repossessed the car in breach of the statute when more than one-third had been paid. On so doing the hire-purchase agreement came to an end altogether. There was no hire purchase price and no sums payable under the agreement. Yet by the action they were seeking to be paid the full amount which by the statute they had forfeited. They were seeking indemnity from the consequences of their own illegal act. That they could not be allowed to do. That is the ground on which the decision should rest. The case should not be taken as establishing that all these recourse agreements are contracts of guarantee and not indemnity. Quite the contrary. A simple specific recourse agreement, such as that before us here, is clearly a contract of indemnity and not a guarantee.'

Helby v *Matthews*

See SALE OF GOODS, Chapter 1, above.

Western Credit Ltd v *Alberry* [1964] 1 WLR 945 Court of Appeal (Sellers, Davies and Russell LJJ)

• *Hire purchase agreement – indemnity or guarantee?*

Facts

A young adult entered into a hire purchase agreement in respect of a Jaguar car after his father had signed a 'guarantee' which provided, inter alia, that he would 'indemnify' the finance company 'against any loss or damage' sustained as a result of his son's 'act default or negligence'. The hire purchase agreement made provision (in cl 9) for its early termination by the son: the son exercised this right and, in consequence, the finance company received £93 less than it would have received had the agreement run its full course. The finance company sued to recover this sum from the father.

Held

The claim could not succeed.

Sellers LJ:

'The son is now admittedly under no outstanding liability to the plaintiffs and it would ... require a very clear and unambiguous contract to impose a further liability on a signatory to what might well be thought by anyone signing such a document as this, to be a guarantee and nothing more.

The word "indemnity" is used but the sentence is descriptive in its context of the kind of non-performance or non-observance which might arise under the guarantee, following as it does the guarantee of the performance and observance by the hirer under the agreement. I cannot read it as an indemnity against any loss or damage as a result of the termination of the contract by the hirer when the contract of hire has been fully performed by him according to its tenor. It would be a remarkable contract. It would release the hirer completely and leave the "surety" liable for the best possible performance of it in favour of the finance company without any redress against the hirer. If there were said to be redress against the hirer then cl 9 would be a snare, for the hirer's liability would, in effect, not terminate but would continue to his surety who had paid it. Further, in the context "act default or negligence" the word "act" does not include a termination of the contract in accordance with the hirer's rights under the contract and a contract so terminated creates no "loss" in the sense of the clause. A salesman does not make a loss merely because he sells at a price less than he seeks to get. The contract he makes is a less advantageous one than he desired.

It would seem that the judge would have taken the view of no liability, but for *Yeoman Credit Ltd* v *Latter* [1961] 2 All ER 294 and some of the observations in the judgments there. In my view that case in no way bound the learned judge and its reasoning is not properly to be applied to the circumstances of the present case. It concerned the hire of a car to an infant, and, because of that fact and the unenforceability of the infant's liability and probably of a guarantee of the bargain, it was stipulated that an adult must sign a special form of indemnity. The second defendant, an adult, signed the special form which was described "Hire purchase indemnity and undertaking" and the liability for loss and the basis thereof was specifically set out. The circumstances and the defined liability are so different that the case in no way bears on the solution of the present provisions on which the plaintiffs relied.'

5 Termination

Capital Finance Co Ltd v *Bray*

See CONSUMER CREDIT, Chapter 4, above.

Forward Trust Ltd v *Whymark*

See CONSUMER CREDIT, Chapter 4, above.

6 Judicial Control

Avon Finance Co Ltd v *Bridger*
[1985] 2 All ER 281 Court of Appeal
(Lord Denning MR, Brandon and
Brightman LJJ)

- *Non est factum – reasonable care*

Facts
The defendants, an elderly couple, had purchased a house. Part of the purchase price was
made up of a mortgage to a building society.
The defendants' son had obtained a loan from
the plaintiff finance company and, as security
for the loan, had undertaken to obtain the execution by the defendants of a legal charge on
their property. The son procured the defendants' signatures to the legal charge by telling
them that the documents they were signing
were in connection with the mortgage to the
building society. When the son defaulted in
his payments to the plaintiffs, they sought
recovery of the loan by bringing an action for
possession of their property against the defendants.

Held
The defendants were not entitled to rely on the
defence of non est factum. This doctrine was
of limited application and could only be relied
on if a defendant had exercised reasonable
care in the transaction and it was not possible,
in the circumstances of this case, to find that
the defendants had exercised the appropriate
reasonable care. However, the transaction was
voidable in equity on the grounds of undue
influence.

Comment
It should be noted that this decision was made
in October 1979. Applied: *Saunders* v *Anglia
Building Society* [1970] 3 WLR 1078.

Distinguished: *Lloyds Bank Ltd* v *Bundy*
[1974] 3 WLR 501. Distinguished in
Coldunell Ltd v *Gallon* [1986] 2 WLR 466.

Davies v *Directloans Ltd* [1986] 1
WLR 823 High Court (Edward
Nugee QC)

- *Loan – extortionate credit bargain?*

Facts
The plaintiffs took out a loan, from the defendants, secured by a legal charge over the house
which was to be bought using the loan. They
were unable to maintain the payments, and
eventually sold the house and repaid the loan
from the proceeds of sale. In this action they
challenged the contract by which the legal
charge was granted on the ground that it was
an extortionate credit bargain.

Held
Whether a contract was an extortionate credit
bargain was to be determined by reference to
the matters stated in s138 of the Consumer
Credit Act 1974 and it did not depend on the
finance company acting in a morally reprehensible way. Mr Nugee was of the opinion
that morally reprehensible conduct by a creditor would make the bargain extortionate, but
that it was also possible for a bargain to be
extortionate even if the creditor had acted
fairly in the conduct of negotiations, if the rate
of interest was excessively high. The opinion
of Professor Goode that 'extortionate' means
'harsh and unconscionable' was rejected. The
creditors here had acted quite fairly, explain-
ing all relevant matters to the plaintiffs in clear
terms, and the plaintiffs obtained independent
legal advice. The only substantial ground of
challenge was because of the rate of interest

charged, but that rate was reasonable and did not require the plaintiffs to make 'grossly exorbitant' payments.

First National Bank plc v *Syed* [1991] 2 All ER 250 Court of Appeal (Dillon and Ralph Gibson LJJ)

• *Order for payment by instalments – exercise of discretion*

Facts
The defendants appealed against a refusal to stay or suspend a warrant of possession. Previously they had proceeded on the footing that the only relevant statutory provision was s36 of the Administration of Justice Act 1970, as amended; now they introduced s129 of the Consumer Credit Act 1974.

Held
The appeal would be dismissed.

Under s129 of the 1974 Act the court may order payment by instalments which are reasonable having regard to the means of the debtor, but the court can only exercise the power if it appears, or is considered, just to do so. When considering what was 'just' the creditor's position, as well as the debtor's position should be looked at. In the circumstances (long history of default, merely sporadic payments, no realistic prospect of improvement in the defendants' finances) it was not just to require the plaintiff to accept the instalments the defendants can afford. The instalments would be too small even to keep down the accruing interest of the defendants' account.

Further, a time order would have the effect of rescheduling the whole of the indebtedness. Because of default, the principal as well as the arrears and current interest had become payable but the court could see no prospect of the defendants being able to repay any principal without a sale of the property.

National Westminster Bank plc v *Morgan* [1985] 2 WLR 588 House of Lords (Lords Scarman, Keith of Kinkel, Roskill, Bridge of Harwich and Brandon of Oakbrook)

• *Undue influence – banker and customer*

Facts
Mrs Morgan and her husband owned a house. It was mortgaged to the building society, who threatened to seek possession for unpaid debts. The defendant bank offered to 'refinance' the couple and to relieve the pressure put on them by the society. This was to be done by way of a loan, secured by a further mortgage, this time in favour of the bank. Mr Morgan readily agreed, but when the bank manager visited Mrs Morgan to obtain her signature to the mortgage deed, she wanted reassurance that the loan to be made would not be used by her husband for the purpose of his business, but would go to pay off the society. The manager reassured her and she signed the deed. The loan was not repaid and the bank, in turn, sued for possession of the house. Mrs Morgan argued that the bank manager exercised undue influence over her and that a special relationship existed between her and the bank which required it to ensure that she receive independent legal advice before entering into a further mortgage. She also sought to rely upon the remarks of Lord Denning in *Lloyds Bank* v *Bundy*.

Held
The bank was entitled to possession.

Lord Scarman:

'... the relationships which may develop a dominating influence of one over another are infinitely various. There is no substitute in this branch of the law for a "meticulous examination of the facts".

A meticulous examination of the facts of the present case reveals that [the bank] never "crossed the line". Nor was the transaction unfair to the wife. The bank was, therefore, under no duty to ensure that she had independent advice. It was an ordinary banking transaction whereby the wife sought to save her home; and she obtained an honest and truthful explanation of the bank's intention which, notwithstanding the terms of the mortgage deed which in the circumstances the trial judge was right to dismiss as "essentially theoretical", was correct; for no one has suggested that ... the bank sought to make the wife liable, or to make her home the security, for any debt of her husband other than the loan and interest necessary to save the house from being taken away from them in discharge of their indebtedness to the building society.

For these reasons, I would allow the appeal. In doing so, I would wish to give a warning. There is no precisely defined law setting limits to the equitable jurisdiction of a court to relieve against undue influence. This is the world of doctrine, not of neat and tidy rules. The courts of equity have developed a body of learning enabling relief to be granted where the law has to treat the transaction as unimpeachable unless it can be held to have been procured by undue influence. It is the unimpeachability at law of a disadvantageous transaction which is the starting point from which the court advances to consider whether the transaction is the product merely of one's own folly or of the undue influence exercised by another. A court in the exercise of this equitable jurisdiction is a court of conscience. Definition is a poor instrument when used to determine whether a transaction is or is not unconscionable: this is a question which depends on the particular facts of the case.'

Comment
Followed in *Cornish* v *Midland Bank plc* [1985] 3 All ER 513. See also *Midland Bank plc* v *Shephard* [1988] 3 All ER 17 and *Bank of Credit and Commerce International SA* v *Aboody* [1989] 2 WLR 759.

Photo Production Ltd v *Securicor Transport Ltd*

See SALE OF GOODS, Chapter 7, above.

7   Credit Cards

Charge Card Services Ltd, Re [1988]
3 WLR 764 Court of Appeal (Sir
Nicolas Browne-Wilkinson V-C,
Nourse and Stuart Smith LJJ)

- *Charge card scheme – to whom were
debts due?*

Facts

A company operated a charge card scheme,
financing its business by factoring its debts to
a finance company. By agreement between the
two companies, cardholders' debts were
assigned to the finance company which paid to
the charge card company the amount of the
debts less a discounting charge. The charge
card company went into liquidation owing
almost £2m to unsecured creditors: substantial
sums were owed to garages which had supplied fuel on customers' charge cards and a
substantial sum was owed by customers for
products purchased by them. Were the receiv-
ables due from cardholders' debts due to the
finance company or did they belong to the
garages? The judge decided in favour of the
finance company: the garages appealed.

Held

The appeal would be dismissed.

Sir Nicolas Browne-Wilkinson V-C:

'A sale using the Fuel Card for payment did
not, in my judgment, differ in any material
respect from an ordinary credit card sale.
The one peculiarity of the transaction (viz
that the contract for sale of the petrol took
place when the tank was filled and not, as
in a supermarket, at the till) does not make
any relevant difference. The question
remains on what terms did the supplier
accept the card in payment?...

To my mind ... quite apart from any
special features of the Fuel Card Scheme,
the transaction was one in which the garage
was accepting payment by card in substitution for payment in cash, ie as an unconditional discharge of the price. The garage was
accepting the company's obligation to pay
instead of cash from a purchaser of whose
address he was totally unaware. One way of
looking at the matter is to say that there was
a quasi-novation of the purchaser's liability. By the underlying scheme, the company
had bound the garage to accept the card and
had authorised the cardholder to pledge the
company's credit. By the signature of the
voucher all parties became bound: the
garage was bound to accept the card in
payment; the company was bound to pay the
garage; and the cardholder was bound to pay
the company and knowing that it was entitled to payment from the company which
the garage itself had elected to do business
with, must in my judgment be taken to have
accepted the company's obligation to pay
in place of any liability on the customer to
pay the garage direct ...

The question therefore is whether, under
the subscriber agreement, the cardholder
could be required to pay the company even
though the company had not paid the
garage...

In my judgment ... the cardholder is liable
to pay the company whether or not the
company has paid the garage. It follows
that, on the garages' argument, the cardholder might be liable to pay twice, once to
the company and again to the garage. That is
a result which no one could have intended in
the context of a credit card transaction.
Accordingly, apart from any guidance to be
obtained by analogy with the authorities on
cheques and letters of credit, I would reach
the conclusion that payment by credit card is

normally to be taken as an absolute, not a conditional, discharge of the buyer's liability and that the particular features of the present case support this conclusion.

I do not find the analogy with cheques at all close or helpful. Payments by cheque involve the unilateral act of the buyer and his agent, the bank on which the cheque is drawn. The buyer's basic obligation to pay the price is sought to be discharged through a third party, the bank, which is in no contractual relationship with the seller. Moreover, the seller has had no say in the selection of the bank. It is very far from the position in a credit card sale where the seller has agreed to rely on the credit of the credit card company and there is a pre-existing contractual obligation on the credit card company to pay the supplier quite separate from any obligation of the buyer.

The analogy with letters of credit is much closer. In both, there are three parties to the arrangement and, once the letter of credit is issued, the bank is contractually bound to pay on the presentation of the documents. But the whole commercial context of the two types of transaction is totally different. The letter of credit is primarily an instrument of international trade issued pursuant to an individually negotiated contract of considerable substance made in writing; the credit card is used for small, over-the-counter transactions between strangers, there being, at best, an oral agreement and more often an agreement by conduct. In the case of credit card sales, the seller does not even know the address of the purchaser, which makes it hard to infer an intention that he will have a right of recourse against the purchaser. It is normally the buyer, not the seller, who selects the bank issuing the letter of credit; if unusually, the seller does

select the bank, this factor may rebut the presumption of conditional payment by letter of credit … In contrast, in a credit card transaction the seller has decided long before the specific supply contract is made whether or not to accept the cards of the credit card company and has entered into an overall contract with it, under which the seller is obliged to accept the card and the credit company is bound to pay him. With letters of credit, the issuing bank is the agent of the buyer and not the seller and it is the buyer who pays for the facility; in credit card transactions the credit card company is in a contractual relationship with both but it is the seller who pays for the facility by allowing the deduction of the commission. These differences are, in my judgment, so fundamental that the law affecting letters of credit is not of great assistance in deciding what law should apply to credit card transactions.

Accordingly, I agree with the judge, and broadly for the same reasons, that the cardholder's obligations to the garages were absolutely, not conditionally, discharged by the garage accepting the voucher signed by the cardholder and that accordingly the appeal should be dismissed. I reach this conclusion with satisfaction since I think it reflects the popular perception of the role of credit cards in modern retail trade as "plastic money".

The judge expressed certain views as to the effect of payment by use of a cheque supported by the production of a bank card (see [1987] Ch 150 at 166). As the point is not directly material in the present case and there may well be features of such transactions of which I am ignorant, I prefer to express no view on that point.'

Agency

1   Introduction

AMB Imballaggi Plastici SRL v
Pacflex Ltd [1999] 2 All ER (Comm)
249 Court of Appeal (Peter Gibson,
Judge and Waller LJJ)

• *Commercial agent – definition of commercial agent under the Commercial Agent (Council Directive) Regulations 1993*

Facts

This was an appeal by Pacflex from a judgment of His Honour Judge Jack QC, which related to a counterclaim by the appellants.

At first instance AMB had brought an action against Pacflex for the price of goods and materials supplied. The claim had been successful but Pacflex had made a counterclaim against AMB for compensation under reg 17 of the commercial agent (Council Directive) Regulations 1993. Pacflex claimed they acted as a commercial agent under a contract with AMB which entitled them to compensation when that relationship was terminated. Regulation 17 provides the right to either an indemnity or for compensation, the former is based upon German law and the latter on French law. The court of first instance dismissed the counterclaim on the finding that AMB did not act as a commercial agent.

Held

The first issue for the Court of Appeal was whether or not Pacflex acted as a commercial agent within the definition of the Regulations and the Directive. The appeal would only succeed if Pacflex could bring themselves within this definition, as the Regulations only apply to commercial agents, which is defined by reg 2(1):

'A self-employed intermediary who has continuing authority to negotiate the sale or purchase of goods on behalf of another person (the 'principal'), or to negotiate and conclude the sale or purchase of goods on behalf of an in the name of that principal ...'

The Regulations also exclude those agents whose commercial agency activity is 'secondary'. Thus, the activity carried on should be the main activity by the commercial agent. Regulation 2(3) and the provisions of the Schedule to the Regulations define what is meant by secondary.

Their Lordships examined the facts and found that all trading between AMB and Pacflex was carried out by a sale of goods from AMB to Pacflex, and a resale by Pacflex to the end-users. AMB wrote to Pacflex on the 31 January 1992 giving them the option to either arrange contracts between AMB and end-users (creating an agency relationship) and Pacflex would then receive commission, or, alternatively, Pacflex could purchase from AMB and then resell to end-users at a mark-up-price. Pacflex chose the latter option, which gave them a better mark-up than taking commission. Pacflex, acting on this basis, were in substance independent contractors with the end-user. Thus, the resale contracts were being made between Pacflex and the end-user and not between AMB and the end-user, as no commercial agency relationship existed. The Regulations are prescriptive – 'to negotiate the sale or purchase of goods on behalf of another person' – which is consistent with the true construction of an agency agreement. The Court of Appeal found that such an agreement did not exist between AMB and Pacflex and dismissed the appeal.

153

Comment

The 1993 Regulations give commercial agents greater rights than they would have previously enjoyed under the common law. However, there must be this tripartite agreement, a principal, a third party and the agent who acts as the negotiator, bringing about a contract between the principal and third party. This case clearly demonstrates if this three-way relationship is not present there will be no agency agreement.

2   The Creation of Authority

Armagas Ltd v Mundogas SA, The Ocean Frost [1986] 2 WLR 1063
House of Lords (Lords Keith of Kinkel, Brandon of Oakbrook, Templeman, Griffiths and Oliver of Aylmerton)

• *Authority to make charterparty contract?*

Facts
Mundogas sold their ship, the Ocean Frost, to Armagas. Armagas were only prepared to buy if Mundogas chartered the ship for three years at a minimum hire of $US 350,000 per month. The purpose of this was to ensure that Armagas would receive enough money to finance the purchase of the vessel. Magelssen, who was a senior executive in Mundogas, and Johannesen, a broker, arranged the sale in negotiations with Mr Jensen and Mr Dannesboe who acted for Armagas, and set up a serious fraud. Johannesen bribed Magelssen to negotiate a three year charter of the ship to Mundogas, which Mundogas would not be told about and also to negotiate a separate one year charter of the same ship to Mundogas to run during the first year of the three year charter. The purpose of these transactions was to make Armagas believe that the ship was chartered for three years, so that they would be content to receive $US 350,000 per month for all three years; in fact the vessel would be free after one year and could be hired to another charterer for the next two years. This would mean that if the rates of hire for such vessels went up after the first year, Magelssen and Johannesen could charter the ship to another charterer at a higher rate while Armagas would be content with $US 350,000

per month, and the two men could pocket the difference. In fact the market fell and the whole fraud was exposed.

Held
Mundogas were not bound by the three year charter because Magelssen had no actual or apparent authority to make such a charterparty contract.

Lord Keith of Kinkel:

'Ostensible authority comes about where the principal, by words or conduct, has represented that the agent has the requisite actual authority, and the party dealing with the agent has entered into a contract with him in reliance on that representation. The principal in these circumstances is estopped from denying that actual authority existed. In the commonly encountered case, the ostensible authority is general in character, arising when the principal has placed the agent in a position which in the outside world is generally regarded as carrying authority to enter into transactions of the kind in question. Ostensible general authority may also arise where the agent has had a course of dealing with a particular contractor and the principal has acquiesced in this course of dealing and honoured transactions arising out of it. Ostensible general authority can, however, never arise where the contractor knows that the agent's authority is limited so as to exclude entering into transactions of the type in question, and so cannot have relied on any contrary representation by the principal.

It is possible to envisage circumstances which might give rise to a case of ostensible specific authority to enter into a particular transaction, but such cases must be very rare and unusual. Ex hypothesi the contractor knows that the agent has no general authority to enter into the transaction, as was the position here. The principal might conceivably inform the contractor that, in relation to a transaction which to the contractor's knowledge required the specific approval of the principal, he could rely on the agent to enter into the transaction only if such approval had been given. In such a situation, if the agent entered into the transaction without approval, the principal might be estopped from denying that it had been given. But it is very difficult to envisage circumstances in which the estoppel could arise from conduct only in relation to a one-off transaction such as this one was.'

Comment

See *British Bank of the Middle East* v *Sun Life Assurance Co of Canada (UK) Ltd* [1983] 2 Lloyd's Rep 9 which compares actual and ostensible authority.

Couturier v *Hastie*

See SALE OF GOODS, Chapter 9, above.

Hely-Hutchinson v *Brayhead Ltd*
[1968] 1 QB 573 Court of Appeal
(Lord Denning MR, Lords
Wilberforce and Pearson)

• *Chairman's implied authority*

Facts

The second defendant, R, was the chairman and chief executive of Brayhead Ltd and acted as de facto managing director with the acquiescence of the board. The plaintiff was the managing director of P Ltd and sold a large number of shares in that firm to the first defendant, Brayhead Ltd. In May 1965 immediately following a board meeting R and the plaintiff, now a director of Brayhead Ltd, discussed the possibility of the plaintiff providing money for P Ltd. The plaintiff did supply money on R signing documents on behalf of Brayhead Ltd, guaranteeing to indemnify the plaintiff. This transaction was never reported to the board of

Brayhead Ltd. The plaintiff sued on the guarantee.

Held
1. He could succeed as R had implied authority from the board to enter into the contracts of indemnity and guarantee. The failure to disclose his interest to the board rendered the contract voidable but it was too late now to rescind.
2. If the plaintiff's claim against Brayhead had failed, R would have been liable for breach of warranty of authority.

Lord Denning MR:

'It is plain that Mr. Richards had no express authority to enter into these two contrcts on behalf of the company; nor had he any such authority implied from the nature of his office. He had been duly appointed chairman of the company but that office in itself did not carry with it authority to enter into these contracts without the sanction of the board; but I think that he had authority implied from the conduct of the parties and the circumstances of the case. The judge did not rest his decision on implied authority, but I think that his findings necessarily carry that consequence. The judge finds that Mr. Richards acted as de facto managing director of Brayhead. He was the chief executive who made the final decision on any matter concerning finance. He often committed Brayhead to contracts without the knowledge of the board and reported the matter afterwards. The judge said:

"... I have no doubt that Mr Richards was, by virtue of his position as de facto managing director of Brayhead, or, as perhaps one might compendiously put it, as Brayhead's chief executive, the man who had, if I may use the words of Diplock LJ, 'actual authority to manage', and he was acting as such when he signed those two documents."

Later the judge said:

"... The board of Brayhead knew of and acquiesced in Mr Richards acting as de facto managing director of Brayhead."

The judge held that Mr Richards had ostensible or apparent authority to make the contract, but I think that his findings carry with them the necessary inference that he had also actual authority, such authority being implied from the circumstances that the board by their conduct over many months had acquiesced in his acting as their chief executive and committing Brayhead to contracts without the necessity of sanction from the board.'

Lord Wilberforce:

'I consider first the question of Mr Richards' authority. I agree, of course (and there is no dispute about this), that Mr Richards had no actual express authority to enter into the two agreements of May 19, 1965, on which this action is brought. But the question remains whether he had implied authority to do so. Now, when one is considering whether he had implied authority, one asks first: from what is the implication to be drawn? The suggestion was made that his authority might be implied from the mere fact of his holding the office of director and chairman of Brayhead Ltd., at the relevant time. The learned judge dealt with that and held that, merely by virtue of his position as chairman, he would not have the necessary authority to enter into these agreements I agree with that; but the question as to implication does not stop there. I quote some words in this connection from Diplock LJ's judgment in *Freeman & Lockyer v Buckhurst Park Properties (Mangal) Ltd* to which my lord has referred. He says:

> "An 'actual' authority is a legal relationship between principal and agent created by a consensual agreement to which they alone are parties. Its scope is to be ascertained by applying ordinary principles of construction of contracts, including any proper implications from the express words used, the usages of the trade, or the course of the business between the parties."

I think, therefore, that it is legitimate to go on and consider, over and above the powers that he had as chairman, what the actual circumstances of the relationship between him and the board of directors may show. Looked at in that way, it seems to me clear from the findings of the judge that Mr Richards in fact impliedly had authority to do what he did by these two agreements.'

Keighley, Maxsted & Co v Durant
[1901] AC 240 House of Lords (Earl of Halsbury LC, Lords Macnaghten, Shand, Davey, James of Hereford, Brampton, Robertson and Lindley)

• *Contract – ratification by third party*

Facts
Authorised to buy wheat at a certain price on a joint account for himself and the appellants, a corn merchant purchased wheat from the respondents at a higher price in his own name. Next day the appellants ratified the transaction but subsequently failed to take delivery of the wheat. The respondents sought damages for breach of contract.

Held
Their action could not succeed.

Lord Shand:

'The question which arises ... is whether, where a person has avowedly made a contract for himself – first, without a suggestion that he is acting to any extent for another (an undisclosed principal), and, secondly, without any authority to act for another, he can effectually bind a third party as principal, or as a joint obligant with himself, to the person with whom he contracted, by the fact that in his own mind merely he made a contract in the hope and expectation that his contract would be ratified or shared by the person as to whom he entertained that hope and expectation. I am clearly of opinion ... that he cannot. The only contract actually made is by the person himself and for himself; and it seems to me to be conclusive against the argument for the respondent, that if his reasoning were sound it would be in his power, on an averment of what was passing in his own mind, to make the contract afterwards, either one for himself only, as in fact it was, or one affecting or binding on another as a contracting party, even although he had no authority for this. The result would be to give one of two contracting parties in his option, merely from what was passing in his own mind, and not disclosed, the power of saying that the contract was his alone, or a contract in which others were bound to him. That I think he certainly cannot do in any case where he had no authority when he made the contract to bind anyone but himself.'

Kelner v *Baxter* (1866) LR 2 CP 174 Court of Common Pleas (Erle CJ, Willes and Byles JJ)

• *Principal and agent – no existing principal*

Facts

It was proposed that a company yet to be formed, would purchase the plaintiff's hotel and stock and the promoters of the company signed an agreement to purchase the plaintiff's 'extra stock' of wines. This agreement the promoters signed 'on behalf of the proposed ... company'. Subsequently the company received a certificate of incorporation, but it collapsed before payment was made for the wine.

Held

The promoters were personally liable.

Erle CJ:

'It was once ... thought that an inchoate liability might be incurred on behalf of a proposed company, which would become binding on it when subsequently formed: but that notion was manifestly contrary to the principles upon which the law of contract is founded. There must be two parties to a contract; and the rights and obligations which it creates cannot be transferred by one of them to a third person who was not in a condition to be bound by it at the time it was made.'

Comment

Distinguished in *Newborne* v *Sensolid (Great Britain) Ltd* [1954] 1 QB 45.

Panorama Developments (Guildford) Ltd v *Fidelis Furnishing Fabrics Ltd* [1971] 2 QB 711 Court of Appeal (Lord Denning MR, Salmon and Megaw LJJ)

• *Company secretary – ostensible authority to hire cars*

Facts

The defendants' company secretary, a Mr Bayne, fraudulently hired cars from the plaintiffs in the defendants' name. The defendants refused to settle the accounts.

Held

The defendants were liable for the hire charges.

Lord Denning MR:

'... counsel for Fidelis ... says that the company is not bound by the letters which were signed by Mr Bayne as "Company Secretary". He says that, on the authorities, a company secretary fulfils a very humble role; and that he has no authority to make any contracts or representations on behalf of the company. He refers to *Barnett Hoares & Co* v *South London Tramways Co* (1887) 18 QBD 815 where Lord Esher MR said:

"A secretary is a mere servant; his position is that he is to do what he is told, and no person can assume that he has any authority to represent anything at all ..."

... But times have changed. A company secretary is a much more important person nowadays than he was in 1887. He is an officer of the company with extensive duties and responsibilities. This appears not only in the modern Companies Acts, but also by the role which he plays in the day-to-day business of companies. He is no longer a mere clerk. He regularly makes representations on behalf of the company and enters into contracts on its behalf which come within the day-to-day running of the company's business. So much so that he may be regarded as held out as having authority to do such things on behalf of the company. He is certainly to sign contracts connnected with the administrative side of the company's affairs, such as employing staff, and ordering cars, and so forth. All such matters now come within the ostensible authority of a company's secretary. Accordingly I agree with the judge that Mr R L Bayne, as company secretary, had ostensible authority to enter into contracts for the hire of these cars and, therefore, the company must pay for them. Mr Bayne was a fraud. But it was the company which put him in the position in which he, as company secretary, was able to commit the frauds. So the defendants are liable.'

Comment

See also *Freeman & Lockyer* v *Buckhurst Park Properties (Mangal) Ltd* [1964] 2 QB 480 which discusses apparent authority through the acquiescence of a board of directors and their de facto managing director.

Springer v *Great Western Railway Co* [1921] 1 KB 257 Court of Appeal (Bankes, Warrington and Scrutton LJJ)

• *Sale of goods in emergency*

Facts

The defendants had undertaken to carry tomatoes from Jersey to the plaintiffs in Covent Garden. Due to bad weather, the journey to Weymouth took three days: on arrival there, there was a strike on the railway. The tomatoes began to go off and, without communicating with the plaintiffs, the defendants sold them all locally. The plaintiffs were awarded damages for breach of duty: the defendants appealed.

Held

The appeal would be dismissed.

Scrutton LJ:

'The railway company sold somebody else's goods, and they have not the right to sell other people's goods unless they can establish certain conditions. They are agents to carry the goods, and not to sell them. To sell them, circumstances must exist which put them in the position of agents of necessity for the owners, to take the action which is necessary in the interests of the owners. Those conditions do not arise if the railway company can communicate with the owners and get their instructions. If the railway company can ask the owner what is to be done in the circumstances with any reasonable chance of getting an answer, they have no business to take upon themselves the sale of the property. They must give the owner a chance of deciding the way in which he will deal with the property, and very often he knows very much better than the railway company what is the best thing to do ... The first thing which the railway company must show to justify their selling the goods is that it was impossible commercially to communicate with the owner and receive instructions from him. If they show that, they must then justify the sale by showing that it was the only reasonable business course to take in the circumstances ... Was it commercially impossible ... to communicate with the consignee at Covent Garden? The question answers itself. Of course, it was not commercially impossible. The reason why [the defendants seem] to have not communicated is that [they] did not then know the exact state of the tomatoes, and consequently could not give the fullest information to the consignee. That was not a reason which justified [them] in not communicating. [They] should, in my view, have communicated with the consignee, stating the probable delay, anything [they] knew about the condition of the goods, and asking for instructions as to what [they] should do.'

Comment

Approved: *Sims & Co* v *Midland Railway Co* [1913] 1 KB 103.

See also *Prager* v *Blastspiel, Stamp and Heacock Ltd* [1924] 1 KB 566 which discusses commercial necessity and acting in good faith.

Watteau v *Fenwick* [1893] 1 QB 346 High Court (Lord Coleridge CJ and Wills J)

• *Undisclosed principal – liability*

Facts

One Humble sold his public house to the defendants, but remained there as their manager. His name remained over the door and the licence continued to be in his name. Although he was forbidden by the defendants to buy cigars on credit, he bought some from the plaintiff who gave credit to him alone for them, not knowing of the defendants.

Held

The defendants were liable.

Lord Coleridge CJ:

'... once it is established that the defendant was the real principal, the ordinary doctrine as to principal and agent applies – that the principal is liable for all the acts of the agent which are within the authority usually confided to an agent of that character, notwithstanding limitations, as between the principal and the agent, put upon that authority. It is said that it is only so where there has been a holding out of authority, which cannot be said of a case where the person supplying the goods knew nothing of the existence of a principal. But I do not think so; otherwise in every case of undisclosed principal, or at least in every case where the fact of there being a principal was undisclosed, the secret limitation of authority would prevail, and defeat the action of the person dealing with the agent and then discovering that he was an agent and had a principal. But in the case of a dormant partner it is clear law that no limitation of authority as between the dormant partner and active partner will avail the dormant partner as to things within the ordinary authority of a partner. The law of partnership is, in such a question, nothing but a branch of the general law of principal and agent, and it appears to me to be undisputed and conclusive on the point now under discussion.'

Comment

Distinguished in *Jerome* v *Bentley & Co* [1952] 2 All ER 114.

3 Powers of Attorney

R (Enduring Power of Attorney), Re
[1990] 2 WLR 1219 High Court
(Vinelott J)

• Enduring power of attorney – restriction on gifts

Facts
In 1988 Mrs R, now in her eighties, gave an enduring power of attorney to a nephew, conferring on him a general authority to act on her behalf, subject to the restriction, inter alia, that he was not to make gifts to friends or relatives. Since 1967 Miss K had lived with Mrs R, first as cook and housekeeper and, she said, more recently as a companion. Miss K maintained that, in recent times, her wages had been less than she would normally have expected to receive, partly because of her close relationship with Mrs R but also because Mrs R had encouraged her to believe that she would look after her and accommodate her for the whole of her life. Shortly after giving the power of attorney Mrs R was found by the Court of Protection to be incapable of managing her affairs. Miss K applied under the Enduring Powers of Attorney Act 1985 for an order that the attorney make provision out of Mrs R's estate for her maintenance and accommodation.

Held
Her application could not succeed.

Vinelott J:

'I think counsel for the attorney was right when he said that the purpose and effect of the 1985 Act is to enable somebody to give a power of attorney, which will endure despite a supervening incapacity, to a person of his choice, and to empower that person to deal with his property in the way that he thinks fit. It should be approached on the footing that the court's powers are primarily directed to the proper supervision of the attorney, and to giving consents or authorisations which are necessary to supplement the powers but which are not inconsistent with restrictions imposed by the donor of the power.'

Walia v Michael Naughton Ltd
[1985] 1 WLR 1115 High Court
(Judge John Finlay QC)

• A general power of attorney sufficient?

Facts
The vendor acquired freehold registered property from three joint proprietors, two of whom executed the transfer personally and one also acted on behalf of the third as donee of a power of attorney made under s10 of the Powers of Attorney Act 1971. Before he had been registered as proprietor, the vendor contracted to sell the land as beneficial owner: the purchasers contended that the original joint proprietor's power of attorney should have been made under s25 of the Trustee Act 1925, as amended by s9 of the 1971 Act.

Held
This was the case.

Judge John Finlay QC:

'... the question which arises here [is] whether where three trustees purport to transfer as beneficial owners a general power of attorney is sufficient to enable the person deriving title under them to claim that he can show title.

As proprietors of the freehold property are, I think, trustees it may or may not be that they are between them the only persons who are beneficially interested at the date of the transfer. It seems to me incontrovertible that they are not at the present time the only persons beneficially interested because whatever the effect of the transfer ... may have been, it appears to have vested some interest in the transferee, ie the vendor.

In my judgment the power of attorney in the s10 form is not appropriate to entitle the donee to execute on behalf of the donor a transfer in which the transferor, whether or not he is purporting to transfer as beneficial owner, is inevitably exercising the function of trustee. He is exercising the function of a trustee because it is as trustee that he is registered as one of the three joint proprietors. The trusts of course do not come on the title, but the very fact that there is more than one proprietor must ... mean that the proprietors (and each one of them) are trustees of the land. That they may also be beneficial owners appears to me to be neither here nor there. The matter, I think, can be tested thus: unless the transfer relied on by the vendor ... transferred the freehold interest of which the transferors were registered as proprietors, it did not confer a good title on the vendor. If it merely transferred the beneficial interest of the transferors, then that transfer could not be completed by registration of the transferee. Only, in my judgment, if it affected the registered property, that is the property of which the registered proprietors were the trustees, could it vest that property in the transferee entitling him to be registered as proprietor of the freehold. Accordingly, on that ground I come to the conclusion that the view taken by the purchasers' solicitors, and in the first place accepted by those of the vendor's, that the power of attorney is in the wrong form, is well founded. It should have been a power of attorney under s9, and not under s10.'

4 Contracts Made by Agents

Benton v Campbell, Parker & Co Ltd [1925] 2 KB 410 High Court (Salter and Swift JJ)

• *Sale of car – agency alone disclosed*

Facts

Auctioneers, the defendants, sold a Ford car to the plaintiff. They disclosed the fact of agency, but not the name of their principals who, it subsequently appeared, had no right to sell.

Held

The defendants were not liable to the plaintiff.

Salter J:

'When an agent purports to make a contract for a principal, disclosing the fact that he is acting as an agent but not naming his principal, the rule is that, unless a contrary intention appears, he makes himself personally liable on the authorised contract. It is presumed that the other party is unwilling to contract solely with an unknown man. He is willing to contract with an unknown man and does so, but only if the agent will make himself personally liable, if called on, to perform the contract which he arranges for his principal. The agent is presumed to agree. The liability of the agent is not joint, nor is it contingent on default by the principal. Two contracts are made in identical terms, one with the principal and the other with the agent, and the opposite party, unless prevented by some election, can enforce either, but not both.

The first question is whether this general rule applies in this case, or the circumstances are such as to rebut the presumption. Where the agency is to buy goods, whether ascertained or not, so that the liability imposed on the principal by the contract is a liability to accept and pay, there is nothing in the circumstances inconsistent with a presumption that the seller requires that the agent shall make himself personally liable to take and pay for the goods in accordance with the contract of sale, if called on, or with a presumption that the agent agrees to do so.

So, again, if the agency is to sell unascertained goods, there is nothing inconsistent with a presumption that the buyer stipulates, and the agent agrees, that the agent will himself deliver goods in accordance with the contract of sale if called on. If he has not the necessary goods, he can procure them and make delivery. But when the agency, as in this case, is an agency for the sale of a specific chattel, which the buyer knows is not the property of the agent, it seems to me impossible to presume that the buyer, who contracts to buy that chattel from the principal, would stipulate that the agent, if called on, shall himself sell the chattel to the buyer, and shall warrant his own title to a thing which the buyer knows is not his. It is impossible to presume that the agent would agree to undertake such a liability. The only way in which he could discharge it would be by acquiring the chattel from his principal, a thing he has no right to demand and a thing inconsistent with the contract he has been instructed to make, by which the principal sells that chattel to the buyer. For this reason, I think that the presumption above mentioned is rebutted in the case of a sale of a specific chattel by a known agent for an undisclosed principal.

This applies to an auctioneer as to any other selling agent. An auctioneer has a special property in the chattel delivered to him for sale. He has a lien on it and on the price of it; he has rights against the buyer, and liabilities to him which do not accrue to other selling agents. These rights and liabilities do not arise from the contract of sale, which binds only the buyer and the principal; they arise from the contract which the auctioneer makes on his own account with the buyer. Every agent to contract, when he makes the authorised contract between his principal and the other party, makes also a contract on his own account with the other party – he warrants his authority. If he is an agent for sale, he also warrants that he knows of no defect in his principal's title. If he is an auctioneer to whom a chattel has been delivered for sale, he gives both these warranties, he undertakes to give possession against the price paid into his hands, and he undertakes that such possession will not be disturbed by his principal or himself. There may, of course, be other terms in this contract, arising on the facts of the case. The warranties are implied terms; the duty to deliver and the right to receive the price are usually expressed in the conditions of sale. But whatever its terms may be, the contract is entirely independent of the contract of sale. To that contract the auctioneer who sells a specific chattel as an agent is, in my opinion, no party; he has no right to enforce it and is not bound by it.'

Boyter v *Thomson* [1995] 3 WLR 36 House of Lords (Lords Jauncey of Tullichettle, Lloyd, Nolan, Nicholls of Birkenhead and Hoffmann)

- *Sale of goods by agent for undisclosed principal – breach of implied terms – whether any action available against undisclosed principal*

Facts
The defender instructed a firm to sell his cabin cruiser under a brokerage and agency agreement. The boat was bought by the purchaser who thought that the boat belonged to the firm. He was not told the name of the owner, nor that the owner was not selling by way of business, nor that the firm were acting as

agents only. Defects were discovered in the boat that rendered it unseaworthy. The purchaser brought an action for breach of s14(2), (3) and (5) Sale of Goods Act 1979.

Held
Any action for breach of the implied terms in s14(2) and (3) might under s14(5) SGA 1979 be brought against the principal himself and not only against the agent acting on his behalf. Subsection (5) was applicable to any sale by an agent, whether for an undisclosed principal or otherwise. Since it had not been brought to the purchaser's attention that the seller was not selling in the ordinary way of business he was entitled to succeed in his action.

Lord Jauncey of Tullichettle (after considering in detail the construction of s14 Sale of Goods Act 1979):

'Subsection (5) of s14 was first introduced into the Sale of Goods Act 1893 (56 & 57 Vict c71) by the Supply of Goods (Implied Terms) Act 1973 (s3) following upon reccommendations of the Law Commissions of England and Scotland. The Report of the Law Commissions (Exemption Clauses in Contracts First Report: Amendments to the Sale of Goods Act 1893 (1969) (Law Com No 24) (Scot Law Com No 12)) drew attention to the fact that no sale of goods by private individuals was subject to any implied condition of fitness even where such individuals sold through auctioneers or agents, a situation which could cause hardship where buyers relied on the agent's reputation. Subsection (5) was drafted by the Law Commissions to meet this situation.

The Dean argued that if the subsection extended beyond the liability of agents acting for undisclosed principles, as the Extra Division held, there would be a measure of overlap inasmuch as an individual selling in the course of business through an agent would already be within the ambit of subss (2) and (3). Such duplication, it was said, could not have been the intention of Parliament. It is correct and was recognised by the Extra Division in their judgment, at p1319c, that there would be an overlap.

However, there are more weighty considerations to be taken into account.

If the Dean's argument were correct it would follow that the second part of the subsection starting with the word "except" would be wholly superfluous. Where an agent is acting for an undisclosed principal, that is to say a principal of whose very existence the buyer is unaware, the latter could not possibly know of the business of the unknown principal. However, the second part of the subsection clearly presupposes that there will be a principal of whose existence the buyer will be aware prior to the contract of sale. The restricted construction advanced by the Dean would involve not only giving no effect to these words but also creating statutory alterations to the normal common law rules, (a) that where an agent contracts on behalf of a disclosed principal the latter alone is liable on the contract (*Bowstead on Agency*, 15th ed (1985), pp281 and 424) and (b) that an undisclosed principal may be sued on any contract made on his behalf (*Siu Yin Kwan* v *Eastern Insurance Co Ltd* [1994] 2 AC 199, 207; *Bowstead on Agency,* 15th ed, p312). Such restricted construction would also mean that the Law Commissions had very substantially failed to achieve the results which they intended.

My Lords, I cannot accept that a construction which produces such results can be correct. In my view subs (5) is applicable to any sale by an agent on behalf of a principal whether disclosed or undisclosed, where circumstances giving rise to the exception do not exist. Where the subsection applies the normal common law rules of principal and agent also apply. There having been, in this case, no attempt to bring to the notice of the pursuer the fact that the defender was not selling in the course of the business it follows that the pursuer was entitled to claim damages from the defender in reliance on the provisions of ss14(2), (3) and (5). For these reasons I would affirm the judgment of the Extra Divison and dismiss the appeal.'

Braymist Ltd v *Wise Finance Co Ltd*
[2002] 3 WLR 322 Court of Appeal (Judge, Latham and Arden LJJ)

• *Agency – authority – pre-incorporation contracts and the Companies Act 1985*

Facts

The appeal involved the appellants, the Wise Finance Company Ltd (WFC), and the respondents, William Sturges & Co (a firm) (WS). WFC agreed to purchase a piece of land from the first claimant, Braymist Ltd (the vendor), which was owned by the second claimant, Plumtree Ltd. The third claimant was Colin Anthony Pool who owned 75 per cent of the shareholding in Pique Holding plc, which also owned the second claimant, Plumtree Ltd.

The fourth claimant, WS, signed the agreement for the sale of the piece of land as solicitors and agents for the first claimant, Braymist Ltd, who had not, at the time, been incorporated. This was primarily a pre-incorporation contract and s36C(1) Companies Act (CA) 1985 applied. This section states:

'A contract which purports to be made by or on behalf of a company at a time when the company has not been formed has effect, subject to any agreement to the contrary, as one made with the person purporting to act for the company or as agent for it, and he is personally liable on the contract accordingly.'

When the appellants found out that Braymist Ltd had not been incorporated they refused to complete. However, as the respondents were to be personally liable they also believed they should be able to enforce the contract against the appellants, WFC. Therefore, as a result of the appellants' actions the respondents issued a notice to complete the purchase, pursuant to condition 22 of the National Conditions of Sale (20th ed) which had been incorporated into the contract. When the notice expired and WFC failed to complete WS informed WFC's solicitor that Braymist Ltd had rescinded the agreement, forfeited the deposit and brought an action for breach of contract against the appellants. At first instance the court found in favour of the fourth claimant and ordered that the £5,000 deposit paid by appellants be forfeited to the fourth claimant and also ordered the payment of £67,700.58p, representing damages for breach of contract and interest.

The WFC appealed and the appeal was based upon the interpretation of s36C(1) CA 1985 and whether section merely granted rights of action against the agent in favour of the purporting contracting party (WFC) or also conferred a benefit (the right to enforce the contract) upon the agent of the non-existent purported principal.

Held

The Court of Appeal examined the judgment of Etherton J, at first instance, which dealt with WS's right to enforce the agreement under s36C(1). Etherton J considered the enactment of this piece of legislation: it emanated from s9(2) of the European Communities Act 1972, which has attempted to give force to art 7 of the First Council Directive on Harmonisation of Company Law (68/151/EEC). The Court of Appeal also noted (at p325) that Etherton J made reference to the text of art 7, which states:

'If, before a company being formed has acquired legal personality, action has been carried out in its name and the company does not assume the obligation arising from such action, the persons who acted shall, without limit, be jointly and severally liable therefore, unless otherwise agreed.'

Based upon this Etherton J, at first instance, held that s36C(1) would give the agent of an unformed company the right to enforce the contract and supported this finding using *Phonogram Ltd* v *Lane* [1982] QB 938, which was the first case to come before the Court of Appeal dealing with the construction of s9(2) of the 1972 Act.

On appeal Mark Blackett-Ord, who acted for WFC, believed it would be a bizarre result to allow an agent to be able to enforce a contract in such circumstances. He argued that:

'... no agent has succeeded on this basis and that there is no reported case in which the point has been taken. If the judge is right, agents for non-existent companies will get an advantage. They can take advantage of their own carelessness in making the contracts on behalf of unformed companies ... A further bizarre result is that the third party becomes liable to a party with whom he did not intend to contract ... The effect may be to impose a contract on a party who particularly wished to contract with the company which was in course of incorporation ... There is no reason why Parliament should want to confer the benefit on agents.'

However, Arden J pointed out: 'In this case the identity of the vendor was of no particular concern to Wise'. Also, Arden J noted the argument put forward by Barbara Rich, who acted for the fourth claimant, that:

'... s36C states that the contract takes effect as a contract to which the agent is a party. The court must give effect to this wording ... where identity is relevant, the counterparty can rescind the contract, but that is not the case here.'

Arden J examined the evidence and various authorities and concluded that:

'... the general law is not that an agent can in all circumstances come in and claim to be principal on a contract which he made as agent ... In my judgment, it should not be assumed that Parliament intended in that situation that the agent should be able to enforce the contract to the same extent as if he had been the company itself. As to what the rules should be in a situation which I have postulated, that matter will have to await another case. It is clear in that in this particular instance it is of no moment to the defendant whether the party selling the property is Braymist or Sturges ... I conclude that Sturges are entitled to enforce the agreement.'

Comment

This case demonstrates that in certain circumstances (for example, when the identity of the principal is not important), an agent who has the burden imposed by s36C(1) may also take the benefit under the contract. However, this was an exception to the rule and the dictum of Judge, Latham and Arden LJJ suggest it will remain at the discretion of the court unless Parliament intervenes and amends s36C(1).

Clarkson, Booker Ltd v *Andjel* [1964] 2 QB 775 Court of Appeal (Willmer, Davies and Russell LJJ)

• *Agent's liability – election*

Facts
The defendant, acting as agent for undisclosed principals called Peters and Milner Ltd, purchased airline tickets from the plaintiffs on credit. The plaintiffs later discovered that he was acting as an agent and wrote both to him and to Peters and Milner Ltd demanding payment. They issued a writ against Peters and Milner Ltd, but found they were insolvent and sued the defendant. He contended that the plaintiffs had made a binding election to pursue their remedy against his principals.

Held
The plaintiffs' action would be successful as, on the facts, they had not finally elected to rely on the liability of Peters and Milner Ltd in exoneration of the defendant.

Willmer LJ:

'The whole case for the defendant rests on the fact that ... having taken instructions, the plaintiffs' solicitors wrote to Peters and Milner Ltd, announcing their intention "to obtain judgment" against them. It is true that they did not at that time write any similar letter to the defendant, but they did not then or at any other time ever withdraw their threat to take proceedings against him. There is not (and could not be) any suggestion that the defendant was in any way prejudiced by the course which the plaintiffs took, or that he was in any sense lulled into

a false sense of security. Had the plaintiffs carried out their threat to obtain judgment against Peters and Milner Ltd, they would, of course, have been precluded from subsequently taking proceedings against the defendant, for their cause of action would then have been merged in the judgment obtained against Peters and Milner Ltd; but in fact the plaintiffs took no step against Peters and Milner Ltd, beyond the issue and service of the writ. On being informed of the proposal to put the company into liquidation they took no further action whatsoever against that company. They did not, for instance (as in *Scarf* v *Jardine* (1882) 7 App Cas 345 seek to prove in the liquidation; instead they proceeded to give effect forthwith to their already announced, and never withdrawn, threat to sue the defendant.

On the whole, though I regard the case as being very near the borderline, I ... do not think that the plaintiffs, by the mere institution of proceedings against Peters and Milner Ltd, made such an unequivocal election as to debar them from taking the present proceedings against the defendants.'

Dyster v *Randall & Sons* [1926] Ch 932 High Court (Lawrence J)

• *Land purchased for undisclosed principal – specific performance*

Facts
The plaintiff procured one Crossley to enter into an agreement with the defendants to purchase some of their land. Crossley did not disclose that he was acting as agent for the plaintiff, a former employee of the defendants who knew that the defendants would not sell the land to him. The defendants resisted the plaintiff's claims for specific performance on the ground, inter alia, that the plaintiff had deceived them as to the purchaser's identity and, therefore, that there was no contract.

Held
The plaintiff's action would be successful.

Lawrence J:

'In considering the first ground it is essential to bear in mind that the agreement which the plaintiff seeks to enforce is not one in which any personal qualifications possessed by Crossley formed a material ingredient, but is a simple agreement for sale of land in consideration of a lump sum to be paid on completion. It is an agreement which the defendants would have entered into with any other person. It is well settled that the benefit of such an agreement is assignable and that the assignee can enforce specific performance of it. If Crossley had entered into the agreement on his own behalf (as the defendants believed he had) he could immediately have assigned it to the plaintiff and the defendants would have been bound to convey the plots to the plaintiff. Moreover, as Crossley had not before signing the agreement disclosed the fact that he was acting as agent, he was liable under it as principal and the defendants could have compelled him to complete the purchase. Further, it is to be noted that, in this case, there was no direct misrepresentation such as there was in *Archer* v *Stone* (1898) 78 LT 34. Crossley was not asked by the defendants whether he was buying for the plaintiff and he made no statement to the defendants on the subject. The real question, therefore, is whether Crossley's silence in the circumstances amounted to a misrepresentation which renders the agreement unenforceable in this court. In my judgment, mere non-disclosure as to the person actually entitled to the benefit of a contract for the sale of real estate does not amount to misrepresentation, even though the contracting party knows that, if the disclosure were made, the other party would not enter into the contract, secus if the contract were one in which some personal consideration formed a material ingredient: see *Nash* v *Dix* (1898) 78 LT 443 and *Said* v *Butt* [1920] 3 KB 497. In *Nash* v *Dix* North J held that the ostensible purchaser was acting on his own account and not as agent, but it appears to me that the learned judge

would have arrived at the same conclusion if the alleged agency had been established. In *Said* v *Butt* McCardie J relied entirely on the personal consideration which entered into the contract and would obviously have decided otherwise if the personal element had been absent. I, therefore, hold that the first ground relied upon by the defendants does not afford a good defence to the plaintiff's claim for specific performance.'

Kelner v *Baxter*

See AGENCY, Chapter 2, above.

Newborne v *Sensolid (Great Britain) Ltd* [1954] 1 QB 45 Court of Appeal (Lord Goddard CJ, Morris and Romer LJJ)

• *Contract signed on behalf of unregistered company*

Facts

The plaintiff contracted to sell tinned ham to the defendants in the name of a company – Leopold Newborne (London) Ltd – which he had formed but not yet registered. The plaintiff – Leopold Newborne – had signed the contract in his own name, below the name of the company. The market fell and the defendants refused to take delivery of the ham. The plaintiff sued for damages for breach of contract.

Held

His action could not succeed.

Lord Goddard CJ:

'Counsel for the plaintiff has contended that the case is governed by a well-known series of cases of which *Kelner (Kelmer)* v *Baxter* (1866) LR 2 CP 174 is one. The plaintiff in that case intended to sell wine to a company which was to be formed, but under the contract he agreed to sell it to the proposed directors of the company. The proposed directors intended to buy the wine on behalf of the company, but, as it was not in existence when the contract was made or the goods were delivered, they personally took delivery. It was held that, as they had contracted on behalf of a principal who did not exist, they, having received the wine, must pay for it. It seems to me a very long way from saying that every time a prospective company, not yet in existence, purports to contract everybody who signs for the company makes himself personally liable. Counsel also relied strongly on *Schmalz (Schmaltz)* v *Avery* (1851) 16 QB 655, which lays down the principle, acted on in subsequent cases and notably *Harper & Co* v *Vigers Brothers* [1909] 2 KB 549, that where a person purports to contract as agent he may nevertheless disclose himself as being in truth a principal and bring an action in his own name. Those cases are well established and we are not departing in any way from the principle they lay down, but we cannot find that the plaintiff purported to contract as agent or as principal. He was making the contract for the company, and, although counsel has argued that, in signing

as he did, he must have signed as agent, for a company can only contract through an agent, that is not the true position. A company makes a contract. No doubt, it must do its physical acts through the directors, but their relationship is not the ordinary one of principal and agent. The company contracts and its contract is authenticated by the signature of one or more of the directors. This contract purports to be made by the company, not by Mr Newborne. He purports to be selling, not his goods, but the company's goods. The only person who has any contract here is the company, and Mr Newborne's signature is merely confirming the company's signature. The document is signed "Yours faithfully, Leopold Newborne (London) Ltd", and the signature underneath is that of the person authorised to sign on behalf of the company.

In my opinion, as the company were not in existence when the contract was signed, there never was a contract, and the plaintiff cannot come forward and say: "It was my contract".'

5 Torts Committed by Agents

Armagas Ltd v Mundogas SA, The Ocean Frost

See AGENCY, Chapter 2, above.

Lloyd v Grace, Smith & Co [1912] AC 716 House of Lords (Earl Loreburn LC, Earl of Halsbury, Lords Macnaghten, Atkinson, Shaw and Robson)

• *Fraudulent solicitor's clerk – solicitor's liability*

Facts

The plaintiff, a widow, sought advice from the defendants, a firm of solicitors of high repute, and in fact saw one Sandles, a managing clerk who conducted their conveyancing work without supervision. Sandles advised the plaintiff to sell two cottages and induced her to sign two documents which he said would enable the properties to be sold. The documents were in fact conveyances to Sandles and he dishonestly proceeded to dispose of the cottages to his advantage.

Held

Although the fraud was not committed for the benefit of the defendants, they were liable as Sandles had acted in the course of his employment.

Earl Loreburn LC:

'It is clear, to my mind, upon [the] simple facts that the jury ought to have been directed, if they believed them, to find for the plaintiff. The managing clerk was authorised to receive deeds and carry through sales and conveyances and to give notices on the defendants' behalf. He was instructed by the plaintiff, as the representative of the defendants' firm – and she so treated him throughout – to realise her property. He took advantage of the opportunity so afforded him as the defendants' representative to get her to sign away all that she possessed and put the proceeds into his own pocket. In my opinion, there is an end of the case. It was a breach by the defendants' agent of a contract made by him as defendants' agent to apply diligence and honesty in carrying through a business within his delegated powers and intrusted to him in that capacity. It was also a tortious act committed by the clerk in conducting business which he had a right to conduct honestly, and was instructed to conduct, on behalf of his principal. At the hearing the learned judge ... appears to have been prevailed upon to put no less than six questions, with sub-divisions making in all ten questions, to the jury. Some of them were quite immaterial. Others were framed in order to raise a point of law supposed to be affirmed by Willes J in *Barwick v English Joint Stock Bank* (1867) LR 2 Exch 259 and admittedly of more than one meaning. The meaning of the answers depends upon how the jury understood the questions, and we were not told how they were explained to the jury. That Sandles committed this fraud in order to steal the money for himself is obvious, and any jury must so find. That he did it in the sense in which Willes J means the word "benefit" is not true upon the admitted facts. Willes J cannot have meant that the principal is absolved whenever his agent intended to appropriate for himself the proceeds of his fraud. Nearly every rogue intends to do that. As to *Barwick v English Joint Stock Bank*, I entirely concur [that if] the agent commits the fraud purporting to act in the course of business such as he was authorised, or held out as authorised, to transact on account of his principal, then the latter may be held liable for it, and if the whole judgment of Willes J be looked at instead of one sentence alone, he does not say otherwise.'

Comment
Applied in *United Bank of Kuwait Ltd* v *Hammond* [1988] 3 All ER 418.

McCullagh v Lane Fox and Partners Ltd [1995] EGCS 195
Court of Appeal (Sir Christopher Slade, Nourse and Hobhouse LJJ)

• *Agent's duty of care – negligent misstatement – disclaimers – Unfair Contract Terms Act 1977*

Facts
The plaintiff contracted to buy a property which the owners had instructed the defendant estate agents to sell. The particulars include a standard disclaimer that 'none of the statements contained in these particulars are to be relied on as statements of representations of fact'. The plaintiff viewed the property personally. The grounds were stated to be 'nearly an acre' but were in fact 0.48 acres. The plaintiff sought to recover damages of £450,000 from Lane Fox.

Held
An estate agent acting for the seller owed no duty of care to a purchaser in respect of negligent misstatement. The purchaser had not been reasonably entitled to believe that the estate agent, at the time of making the statement, was assuming responsibility for it, especially in view of the disclaimer of responsibility published in the particulars of sale. Moreover, estate agents under the provisions of Unfair Contract Terms Act 1977 are not precluded from relying on such a disclaimer. The plaintiff was not entitled to recover damages from Fox Lane for negligent misstatement.

Hobhouse J:

'It is clear from more recent cases that *Hedley Byrne* is still the governing authority in cases such as the present. The elements of reasonable foreseeability and reliance are fundamental, as is the element of assumption of responsibility.'

Sir Christopher Slade:

'The Property Misdescriptions Act 1991 gave protection to the public by making estate agents criminally liable for false statements as to specified matters. But Parliament has not thought it necessary to legislate to impose civil liability on them. Doubtless in some circumstances civil liability … could arise from misrepresentations …'

Ocean Frost, The
See *Armagas Ltd* v *Mundogas Ltd, The Ocean Frost* in AGENCY, Chapter 2, above.

United Bank of Kuwait Ltd v Hammond [1988] 1 WLR 1051
Court of Appeal (Lord Donaldson of Lymington MR, Glidewell and Staughton LJJ)

Facts
In order that a client might have a temporary loan, a salaried partner in a firm of solicitors, a Mr Emmanuel, signed an undertaking and guarantee in the bank's favour. The money was not repaid and the bank sought to recover the amount of the loan from, inter alia, the firm's equity partners.

Held
The bank's action would succeed.

Staughton LJ:

'It is elementary law that an agent cannot hold himself out; the holding out must come from his principal, or from some agent duly authorised by the principal. So one might think that what Mr Emmanuel himself said about the [transaction] in which he was engaged could not by itself demonstrate that [it was] part of the ordinary business of solicitors, and thus within the authority which he was held out as having. But the defendant solicitors ... do not take that point; and in my judgment they are right not to take it. The decisions in *Lloyd* v *Grace Smith & Co* [1912] AC 716 and *Uxbridge Permanent Benefit Building Society* v *Pickard* [1939] 2 KB 248 show that a third party is only concerned as to whether a transaction appears to be of a kind that is within the ordinary authority that the agent is held out as having, not whether it is in fact a transaction of that kind. To depart from that doctrine would gravely weaken the credit which is given to solicitors' undertakings; it would also do much to destroy the rule that any agent can be held out as having general ostensible authority to bind his principal. On the facts ... I agree ... that the [transaction] reasonably did appear to the [bank] to be of a kind that was within the ordinary authority of a solicitor.'

6　Obligations of Principal to Agent

Alpha Trading Ltd v *Dunnshaw-Patten Ltd* [1981] QB 290 Court of Appeal (Lawton, Brandon and Templeman LJJ)

- *Agent's commission – implied term*

Facts

The plaintiffs were appointed by the defendants to introduce a buyer for 10,000 tonnes of cement. They were to receive a commission of $1.50 per tonne and certain other payments. They introduced a buyer and a contract was entered into between the buyer and the defendants but the defendants were unable or unwilling to carry it out. The plaintiffs claimed to be entitled to their commission under the contract or alternatively claimed damages for breach of an implied term that the defendants would not break their contract with the buyer and thus deprive the plaintiffs of commission.

Held

Where a principal and agent agree that the agent will receive a commission on any contract that the principal concludes with a buyer introduced by the agent, a term will be implied that the principal will not commit a breach of contract with the buyer that would deprive the agent of his commission. Accordingly the plaintiffs were entitled to damages.

Brandon LJ:

'In reaching (his) conclusion, the learned judge evidently relied very much on certain observations made by Lord Wright in *Luxor (Eastbourne) Ltd* v *Cooper* [1941] AC 108. That was a case concerned with an estate agent. The headnote reads ([1941] AC 108):

"Where an agent is promised a commission only if he brings about the sale which he is endeavouring to effect there is no room for an implied term that the principal will not dispose of the property himself or through other channels or otherwise act so as to prevent the agent earning his commission. Dissenting judgment of Scrutton LJ in *Trollope and Sons* v *Martyn Brothers* ([1941] 2 KB 436) approved."

The actual decision, as appears from that headnote, was that, in the case of an estate agent, the law will not imply a term that the principal will not dispose of the property himself or through other channels. The House of Lords did not need to consider whether, after an agent had introduced a purchaser to someone who wanted to sell, and a concluded contract had then been made, there would be any term implied to protect the agent in that situation.

Lord Wright in his speech made an extensive examination of the situation arising in contracts of this kind, particularly in the field of estate agency. There are two passages in his speech which bear on the situation which we have in this case. He said:

"However, it is necessary to reserve certain eventualities in which an agent may be entitled to damages where there is a failure to complete even under a contract like one in this case. For instance, if the negotiations between the vendor and the purchaser have been duly concluded and a binding executory agreement has been achieved, different considerations may arise. The vendor is then no longer free to dispose of his property. Though the sale is not completed, the property in equity has passed from his to the purchaser. If he refuses to complete he would be guilty of a breach of agreement vis-a-vis the purchaser. I think, as at present advised, that it ought then to be held that

173

he is also in breach of his contract with the commission agent – that is, of some term which can properly be implied. However, that question and possibly some other questions do not arise in this case and may be reserved."

Lord Wright referred to the dissenting judgments of Scrutton LJ in *Martyn*'s case, and to the expression 'wrongful act' which had been used by Scrutton LJ in that judgment. He said:

"I take it that Scrutton LJ, meant an act which was wrongful under contract between the appellants and the respondents. There could be no wrongful act as between the employer and the prospective purchaser in breaking off the negotiations while they were going on "subject to contract", and no wrongful act thereby, in my opinion, as between the appellants and the respondents, for the reasons I have attempted to state. It may well be, as I have already stated, that, as soon as binding executory contract is effected between the employer and the purchaser, a different state of things arises. The property is transferred in equity, and the seller can be specifically ordered to complete. The agent may then fairly claim that he is entitled to his commission, or at least to substantial damages, and, as at present advised, I think that a term of that nature may be implied in the contract. It cannot have been contemplated that, when a binding contract with the purchaser has been made on the agent's mediation, the principal can, as between himself and the agent, break that contract without breaking his contract with the agent. I understand that this was the view of Scrutton LJ, and, though the question does not arise in this case, I am, as at present advised, in agreement with it. In that case, it may fairly be said that the employer prevented the fulfilment of the condition, and was in default under the commission agreement just as much as under the agreement of sale. While the matter is still in negotiation, however, it is a different matter …"

In my judgment, the reasoning underlying the observations of Lord Wright in *Luxor (Eastbourne) Ltd* v *Cooper* which I have read is sound and sensible reasoning, and is fully applicable to a case of this kind.

There is no question here of denying the defendants' freedom to deal with their own property as they choose. There is no question of denying them freedom either to continue their business or not to continue it as they wish. This was what one might call a "one-off" transaction. The defendants were introduced by the plaintiffs to a buyer of cement. It was in the contemplation of the plaintiffs that the defendants would make a contract of sale with the buyer. The defendants did make a contract of sale with that buyer on the basis that, if the contract was performed, the agent would receive substantial remuneration. The only reason the contract was not performed was that the defendants were either unwilling or unable to perform it.

It seems to me that, in a case of that kind, it is right for the court to imply a term that the defendants will not fail to perform their contract with the buyer so as to deprive the agent of the remuneration due to him under the agency contract.

Various tests have been propounded from time to time with regard to the implications of terms in a contract. The officious bystander is one of the tests which has been used. It seems to me that the officious bystander, looking over the shoulders of Mr Brodie and Mr Marchant Lane, as they made the contract which they did, and asking himself whether the defendants could make a contract with Muellers and then break it without incurring any liability to the plaintiffs, would have answered, "No, that cannot be what is intended. It must be intended that, if they make the contract, after having had the buyer introduced to them, they will perform it and enable the agent to earn his remuneration."

For the reasons that I have given, I am of the opinion that the learned judge was right in the view which he took that the plaintiffs' case based on an implied term of the contract succeeded.'

Comment

Distinguished: *French (L) & Co Ltd* v *Leeston Shipping Co Ltd* [1922] 1 AC 451.

Attorney-General for Hong Kong v *Reid* [1994] 1 All ER 1 Privy Council (Lords Templeman, Goff, Lowry and Lloyd and Sir Thomas Eichelbaum)

• *Trust – trustee – bribes – agent as trustee*

Facts

Reid was a public prosecutor in Hong Kong and had been convicted for accepting bribes to obstruct prosecution of certain criminals. He was sentenced to a term of imprisonment and his assets (of 12.4 million Hong Kong dollars) were seized, on the basis that such funds could only have come from bribes. Subsequently, three properties in New Zealand were traced, against which the Attorney-General laid claims, alleging that the properties had been bought with bribes received by Reid, and were held in trust for the Crown.

Held

When a person in a position of public trust accepts a bribe to betray that trust, the bribe and all proceeds from it are held in trust for the person to whom the duty is owed. The party taking the bribe is not allowed, should the proceeds of the bribe increase in value, to retain any surplus in excess of the initial sum. If this was the case the party would be receiving a benefit from taking a bribe, even if the amount of the original bribe was returned. The properties were thus held on trust for the Crown and the Attorney-General for Hong Kong was entitled to have a caveat entered against the title of all three.

Lord Templeman:

'This (judgment of Jessel MR in *Re Caerphilly Colliery Co, Pearson's Case* (1877) 5 Ch D 366) is an emphatic pronouncement by the most distinguished equity judge of his generation that the recip-

ient of a bribe holds the bribe and the property representing the bribe in trust for the injured person.'

Comment

Although this case is concerned with a public servant rather than a commercial agent, the same rule will apply to a situation where an agent takes a bribe. Any increase in the value of the bribe or property purchased with the bribe will be the property of the principal and recoverable by him.

Burney v *The London Mews Company Limited* [2003] EWCA Civ 766 Court of Appeal (Civil Division) (Waller and Kay LJJ, Lindsay J)

• *Rights of an agent against his principal – remuneration*

Facts

This was an appeal from the decision of Richardson J who dismissed an appeal from a decision of Sherratte J. At first instance the judge had refused to set aside a default judgment, which the claimant had obtained, for commission earned by an estate agent, the claimant (respondent) London Mews (LM).

The appellant, Stephen Burney (SB), appointed LM as a sole agent to sell his property and a term of the agreement allowed LM to claim commission. The term in question stated:

'You [Stephen Burney] will be liable to pay remuneration to us [London Mews] in addition to any other costs or charges agreed, if at any time unconditional contracts for the sale of the property are exchanged (and subsequently completed) with a purchaser introduced by us during the period of our sole agency or with whom we had negotiations about the property during that period; or with a purchaser introduced by another agent during that period.'

LM prepared the necessary documentation to market the property and advertised the property in various newspapers. Another agent, Kaye & Co (K), then approached LM. LM sent K the documentation but on the basis that they (K) would only circulate this documentation to retained clients. Retained clients are those who had retained an agent to find a particular property, as opposed to the agent being paid for selling a property. However, it appears from the evidence presented that K placed its headed notepaper on the particulars of sale supplied by LM. K then circulated the particulars to retained clients and non-retained clients.

One of the main points clarified by the Court was that K was not the sub-agent of LM and did not have authority to contact SB. Thus, K had no authority to visit the property or arrange any visits.

A Mr Cullinane obtained a copy of the particulars on K's headed notepaper and believed it was the agent for the seller, SB. Mr Cullinane outlined the order of events that took place in a letter dated the 8 August 2001 which stated:

'After receipt of the details, I spoke to Mr Bikhit of Messrs Kaye & Co and expressed interest in viewing the property. It was explained to myself and my girlfriend, Ms Suzanna Wong, that the vendors were out of the country for the weekend and were thus uncontactable but that Messrs Kaye & Co would seek to arrange an appointment for us to view the property on Monday 26 March 2001. During the course of the morning of 26 March, there were various calls between ourselves and representatives of Kaye & Co and eventually Mr Bikhit admitted to us there seemed to have been some misunderstanding between themselves and the vendor and that they were not retained to sell the property on the vendor's behalf, but "could get us into the property" if we agreed to pay them a commission equivalent to 1 per cent of the purchase price. At this point I expressed my extreme dissatisfaction with the way in which Messrs Kaye & Co conduct their business. I explained that to my mind they had misrepresented themselves as being appointed as agents to sell the property on behalf of the vendor and I did not, at this nor at any prior or subsequent stage, agree to pay the 1 per cent commission they requested on the purchase of the property nor any other property. In reply to this Mr Bikhit said that they thought that Messrs Kaye & Co had been appointed by the vendor and if I was not prepared to pay the 1 per cent commission then I could, of course, seek to gain access to the property through contacting the estate agents instructed by the vendor to sell the property or making my own private enquiries.'

Mr Cullinane informed the court that K would not tell him the name of SB's agent and as a result Mr Cullinane wrote directly to SB, using the address on the particulars of sale. In his letter he informed SB he was interested in buying the property, informed him of his dealing with K and gave a contact number. In his final paragraph he stated:

'It may not be relevant to you, but I would suspect that if you were to contact us directly there may well be an estate agent commission saving for you.'

This correspondence resulted in SB selling the property to Mr Cullinane. However, while the negotiations for the sale took place SB wrote to LM and asked them to take the property off the market while his wife was having a baby, and that he would instruct them in the near future. LM found out that SB had sold the property, wrote to him and claimed the 2 per cent commission. At first instance the judge agreed with LM's claim and awarded them their commission. SB appealed.

Held

Waller LJ examined the facts in question and identified the key issue as being whether LM had performed its task of introducing a purchaser and was now entitled to its commission. Waller LJ answered this question by finding that the particulars of sale had been prepared by LM and the mere handing of those particulars to some other person still amounts to an introduction by LM, if a sale resulted. Waller LJ believed LM should succeed in this case as they did nothing wrong. LM had introduced Mr Cullinane to the transaction by the use of their particulars of sale. Kay LJ and Lindsay LJ agreed with this decision.

Comment

One of the most important aspects of an agency relationship is remuneration. An agent has no automatic right to remuneration for services rendered to his principal: it is perfectly legal for an agency to be gratuitous. Thus, the rule is that an agent is only entitled to remuneration if there is an express or implied term within his contract. Estate agents must earn their commission before they are entitled to payment. Payment becomes available only upon the sale of the property, and not with the mere marketing of the property. Thus, not only must the agent introduce a potential purchaser but the sale must be completed. The stages of purchasing real property are not as straightforward as when dealing with personal property. In the former there will be an introduction, negotiation, exchange and completion before the transaction has been performed. Therefore, the commission agent is only paid on the sale of a property rather than an aborted sale. This was clearly explained in the case of *Howard Houlder & Partners Ltd v Manx Isles Steamship & Co* [1923] 1 KB 110 by McCardie J who stated:

> 'It is a settled rule for the construction of commission notes and the like documents which refer to the remuneration of an agent that a plaintiff cannot recover unless he shows that the conditions of the written bargain have been fulfilled. If he proves fulfilment he recovers. If not, he fails. There appears to be no halfway house, and it matters not that the plaintiff proves expenditure of time, money and skill.'

Therefore, the estate agent is placed in a position where he may spend time and money attempting to bring about a sale but not necessarily earn commission. However, the Court of Appeal appears to have been mindful of the agent's position and in this instance found the

agent was entitled to his commission. The leading case on agents' commission is *Luxor (Eastbourne) Ltd v Cooper* [1941] AC 108.

Ellis (WA) Services Ltd v Wood [1993] 31 EG 78 Chancery Division (Antony Watson QC)

- *Estate agent's contract – implied terms – common custom or usage*

Facts
The plaintiffs, a firm of estate agents, brought an action against the director of a company on whose behalf they had sold a property. The company had become insolvent since the sale. The plaintiffs argued that there was an implied term that commission would be paid out of the proceeds of the sale, or, alternatively, that the contract created an equitable charge on the proceeds of the sale.

Held
The plaintiffs' claim must fail. The implication of such a term was not necessary to achieve business efficacy, nor was there any strong evidence that it was normal custom or usage among estate agents that commission should be paid from the proceeds of the sale. If an agent desired such a term to be included in the contract, he must request it to be expressly incorporated. It would not be implied.

Harrods Ltd v Lemon [1931] 2 KB 517 Court of Appeal (Lord Hanworth MR, Lawrence and Romer LJJ)

- *Agent acting for both parties – commission*

Facts
Mrs Lemon asked Harrods Ltd in their capacity as estate agents to sell a property for her. The proposed purchaser asked Harrods Ltd in their capacity as builders and surveyors to survey the property. Harrods subsequently discovered that they were acting in two capac-

ities and disclosed this fact to Mrs Lemon suggesting that she should use an independent surveyor. Mrs Lemon refused to use an independent surveyor and completed the sale through Harrods Ltd. She then refused to pay Harrods their commission on the basis that they had acted in breach of their duty as there was a conflict.

Held

Although there had been a conflict, Harrods Ltd. were entitled to their commission because Mrs. Lemon had by her action waived the breach of duty.

Lord Hanworth MR:

> 'Have the plaintiffs, then, lost the right to commission? It is right that I should repeat on behalf of Messrs Harrods, that they make it quite plain that they regret that they acted in an equivocal position. Mr Ford, who negotiated the sale to Mrs Campbell, says this: "It would be wrong for us to act for both vendor and purchaser"; and he also says this: "I never said anything to Mrs Campbell or Mrs Lemon about the drains, and knew nothing about their condition". The manager of the estate office, Mr Robinson Steel Smith, agrees that the telegram of 12 July would tend to diminish the price and would be in the interest of the purchaser. Reliance has been placed on a decision of Lord Alverstone as justifying the view that the commission is not recoverable. In *Hippisley* v *Knee Bros* he said:

>> "If the court is satisfied that there has been no fraud or dishonesty upon the agent's part, I think that the receipt by him of a discount will not disentitle him to his commission unless the discount is in some way connected with the contract which the agent is employed to make or the duty which he is called upon to perform."

> It is said that there was a conflict, and, therefore, that the principle of *Hippisley* v *Knee Bros* does not apply. But is must be remembered that the offer was made that Harrods should drop out of it, and that was not accepted. It appears to me that after that acceptance of the situation, it is not possible for the defendant to impute to Harrods that they have lost their right to commission, when she has accepted their services with full knowledge, and rejected the opportunity to put the matter right by having an independent surveyor. If the facts were different, if the whole transaction had gone off and this was an action by Mrs Lemon for a loss of part of the price, different considerations might have applied. If the eventualities contemplated in the letter which I read, of 17 July had been carried out, again we might have had to apply a different set of rules. But all that we have to consider here is whether, in the present circumstances, after the knowledge was conveyed to Mrs Lemon and she acted as she did, it can be said that Messrs Harrods have lost their right to commission. It appears to me, re-affirming the principles which I have already laid down, and which are not in any way contested by Messrs Harrods, that they are entitled to be paid for their services.'

Merrett, Gooda Walker and Feltrim Cases [1994] 2 Lloyd's Rep 468 House of Lords (Lords Goff of Chieveley, Keith of Kinkel, Browne-Wilkinson, Nolan and Mustill)

• *Negligence – duty of care – agents under a duty to exercise reasonable skill and care – whether duty extra-contractual*

Facts

Individuals wishing to become Names at Lloyd's, who were not themselves professional Lloyd's underwriters, have always had to employ underwriting agents to act on their behalf. Until 1987 their agreements were not made in any set form, but after that date the Council of Lloyd's required the agreement to be according to terms laid out in the Agency Agreements Bye-law of 1985. In the three cases named above (and a number of others still pending) Names at Lloyd's brought proceedings against their respective underwriting agents, alleging negligence in conducting underwriting affairs. The Names alleged that agents were under a legal duty to exercise due care and skill and perform their functions as reasonably competent, diligent and efficient professional underwriters.

The agents denied that such a duty of care existed, arguing that at the most they were only obliged not to act in bad faith or in a wholly irrational way. In view of the contractual basis of their relationship with their principals it would be wrong, they argued, to impose extra-contractual duties. The whole idea of a contractual form of agency was so that exact terms could be delineated precisely.

Held

The contract required by Lloyd's Council made it very clear that the agents were to be given the widest possible discretion. They received remuneration for exercising skills with reasonable care and competence appropriate to a professional underwriter. The very existence of this professional relationship led irresistibly to the conclusion that there was a duty of reasonable skill and care and there was nothing in the express contractual terms to indicate that this duty had been in any way modified or excluded. However, it was pointed out that only the relationship between the Names and the managing agents was contractual; there was no direct relationship, contractual or otherwise, between sub-agents and the Names.

Lord Goff of Chieveley:

'I am of the opinion that this House should now, if necessary, develop the principle of assumption of responsibility as stated in *Hedley Byrne* to its logical conclusion and make it clear that a tortious duty of care may arise not only in cases where the relevant services are rendered gratuitously,but also where they are rendered under a contract … My own belief is that in the present context the common law is not antipathetic to concurrent liability and there is no sound basis for a rule which automatically restricts the claimant to either a tortious or a contractual remedy.'

Comment

The 'Lloyd's Litigation', of which these three cases are just a part, has given (and presumably will continue to give) the courts an opportunity to examine in detail the level of skill and care required of agents, and to a lesser extent, sub-agents. This is not an area that has hitherto been explored in great depth, so these cases are important illustrative material should a question on that aspect of agency law appear in the examinations.

7   Obligations of Agent to Principal

Arab Monetary Fund v *Hashim*
[1993] 1 Lloyd's Rep 543 Queen's
Bench Division (Evans J)

- *Agency – bribes and secret commission*

Facts
The plaintiffs (AMF) were an organisation
formed of 20 plus Arab States in 1977. Dr
Hashim was its first President from 1977-
1982. An English firm, Bernard Sunley
(Middle East) (BSME), successfully tendered
to build headquarters for the AMF. The building work started in January 1980 and was
completed in 1982. The plaintiffs alleged that
a payment of $1.8m was made by BSME to a
Swiss bank account in a name which was later
found to be fictitious. The plaintiffs alleged
that this payment was a bribe, destined for Dr
Hashim. They claimed the amount of the
payment and/or damages from Dr Hashim and
BSME.

Held
As agent for AMF in Dubai, Dr Hashim was
certainly under a duty not to make a secret
profit nor to take bribes. If the contract was
induced by a bribe, as the plaintiffs alleged,
then the principal (AMF) would certainly be
entitled to recover the amount of the bribe
from either the contractor or from the agent.
Whether or not damages would also be
awarded depended on the circumstances.

However, the plaintiffs were not able to
prove that the bribe was paid out of advance
payments to BSME by the plaintiffs. Dr
Hashim was not liable to make restitution for
the amount of the bribe.

Boston Deep Sea Fishing and Ice Co v *Ansell* (1888) 39 Ch D 339 Court of Appeal (Cotton, Bowen and Fry LJJ)

- *Agent's secret commissions – duty to account*

Facts
A was appointed managing director by the
plaintiff company by an agreement made
before the company was registered. The agreement was subsequently adopted by the
company. At the first meeting of directors, he
received express instructions to negotiate for
the building of four to five ships with E. A
agreed with E that E should pay A a commission of 1 per cent on the price payable by the
plaintiffs to E. A further contract was entered
into between the plaintiffs and E in which it
was said A managed to keep E's prices down.
However, for doing this, A received £50 from
E.

In addition, A was a member of two incorporated companies which did business with
the plaintiffs. He had been a member of them
before the existence of the plaintiff company.
One of these companies, the Ice Company,
supplied ice to the plaintiffs. A placed the
orders on behalf of the plaintiff company and
received a commission for so doing from the
Ice Company. Also, A belonged to a carrying
company, whose articles placed a duty upon
its members to ensure that all fish caught in
the ships of members should only be brought
to shore in this way. A had sold his ships to
the plaintiff company but nevertheless the
Carrying Company was still used to bring the
fish ashore. In respect of his, A was entitled to
and did in fact receive a bonus. After some
time the plaintiff company became suspicious

of and dissatisfied with A's conduct. An inquiry was directed and A was at first suspended and later dismissed. A claimed wrongful dismissal. The plaintiff company claimed an account of the various commissions received by A.

Held

1. In relation to the shipbuilding company, E, A had committed a fraud upon his principals while acting as their agent. Accordingly, the plaintiff company was entitled to dismiss A and recover the money which A received in consequence of his position with the company. Interest at 5 per cent was also awarded.

Fry LJ:

'Having come without hesitation to the conclusion that Mr Ansell's conduct was fraud of a gross character, the result appears to me to be very plain. In the first place, it gives the company a plain right to recover the money which Mr Ansell received, and received, according to my view, in consequence of his position for the use of the company, the fact of which receipt he never disclosed to the company with interest at 5 per cent. I take that to be the undoubted right of a principal who has been defrauded by his agent.'

Cotton LJ:

'In my opinion, if a servant or a managing director, or any person who is authorised to act, and is acting for another in the matter of any contract, receives as regards the contract any sum, whether by way of percentage or otherwise, from the person with whom he is dealing on behalf of his principal, he is committing a breach of duty. It is not an honest act, and, in my opinion, it is an act sufficient to show that he cannot be trusted to perform the duties which he has undertaken as servant or agent.

He puts himself in such a position that he has a temptation not faithfully to perform his duty to his employer. He has a temptation, especially where he is getting a percentage on expenditure, not to cut down the expenditure, but to let it be increased so that his percentage may be larger. In my opinion, where an agent entering into a contract on behalf of his principal and without the knowledge or assent of that principal receives money from the person with whom he is dealing, he is doing a wrongful act, he is misconducting himself as regards his agency, and, in my opinion, that gives to an employer, whether a company or an individual, whether he be servant or whether he be managing director, power and authority to dismiss him from his employment as a person who by that act is shown to be incompetant of faithfully discharging his duty to his principal.'

2. In relation to the Ice Company and the carrying companies, the commission/bonus received by A was repayable with interest.

Cotton LJ:

'Kekewich J [the third judge] considered that the plaintiff company were not entitled to that £50 which the defendant has received by way of bonus in respect of the ice supplied since the vessels were no longer his but were the vessels of the plaintiff company, and he so held on the ground, as I understand it, that the plaintiff company could never themselves have been entitled to receive the bonus profit, and therefore, they cannot claim it from the defendant, who was their agent, whom, however, he held accountable for the sum which he received when he was their agent from Earle's Shipbuilding Co. In my opinion, that is wrong. The question is not whether the company could directly have claimed this sum, but whether, when their agent received this profit in respect of a contract which he had entered into on behalf of the company as their agent for goods supplied to the company, the company are not entitled as against their agent to claim the money. In my opinion, they are. It is a profit arising from a contract which he on the party of the company entered into, and in consequence of the supply to the company by his order of a particular quantity of ice. It was said that he was entitled under the articles (No 68) to enter into the contracts and do business with the company. He was; but that, in my opinion, did not justify him, when contracting on behalf of the company, in putting into his own pocket a profit obtained entirely in consequence of the goods being supplied under that order to the plaintiff company. On that point, therefore, I differ from the view taken by Kekewich J, in my opinion, the plaintiffs are entitled to an account as to the sums so received by him as bonuses from the ice company.'

On the same grounds he decided that the bonus paid by the Carrying Company must be repaid.'

Chaudhry v *Prabhaker* [1988] 3 All ER 718 Court of Appeal (May, Stocker and Stuart-Smith LJJ)

• *Gratuitous agent – duty of care*

Facts
The plaintiff asked the defendant, a close friend who had some knowledge of cars, to find a suitable secondhand one for her to buy, stipulating that it should not have been involved in an accident. The defendant saw a car being offered for sale by a car sprayer and panel beater and he noticed that its bonnet had been crumpled at some stage. Nevertheless, he recommended its purchase. The plaintiff bought the car and a few months later it appeared that it had been involved in a very bad accident and that it was unroadworthy. The plaintiff sued for damages.

Held (May LJ dubitante)
Her action would be successful.

Where, as here, the relationship of principal and agent leads to a contract between the principal and the third party, this is strong evidence that the occasion is in a business connection and not purely a social one.

The plaintiff clearly relied on the defendant's skill and judgment and the defendant knew that the plaintiff was relying on him. It

was clearly in a business connection, because the defendant knew that the plaintiff was going to commit herself to buying the car for £4,500 through his agency.

The standard of care, or the nature and extent of the duty, should be the same as that required of an unpaid agent. Stuart-Smith LJ stated the duty as 'to take such care as is reasonably to be expected of him in all the circumstances'.

Whatever standard of care is required, the defendant fell below it. The plaintiff had stipulated that the car should not have been involved in an accident. The defendant never asked the vendor about this but assured the plaintiff that it had not. When asked about this in evidence he said that he said 'No' because he had no knowledge of any accident. He went on to advise her that she need not have the car examined by a mechanic. The court thought that this answer and advice could not be justified simply because the defendant thought the car looked so well that it could not have been in an accident. The trial judge had already found that the defendant was put on notice by the crumpled bonnet so the case against him was a strong one.

Harrods Ltd v *Lemon*

See AGENCY, Chapter 6, above.

Kelly v *Cooper* [1992] 3 WLR 936 Privy Council (Lords Keith of Kinkel, Ackner, Browne-Wilkinson, Mustill and Slynn of Hadley)

• *Agency – estate agents – conflict of interest*

Facts
The plaintiff instructed the defendant's firm of estate agents to sell his house, and agreed to pay a percentage of the selling price by way of commission. The estate agent showed the house to a prospective purchaser, who was particularly interested because the adjacent

property was also for sale. The agent was also acting for the adjacent owner. The purchaser first made a successful bid for the adjoining property. The estate agent did not, however, inform the plaintiff of this fact. The plaintiff agreed to sell his house at the first offered price. He sued the estate agent for damages, alleging he could have held out for much more had he known the purchaser's plans to buy both properties.

Held

Since estate agents frequently acted for numerous principals, some of whom might be in competition with each other, unless there was some special term of 'exclusivity' written into the contract, there would be no conflict of interest. An agent might have several principals and was under no duty to reveal the existence of each to the others. The plaintiff's action failed, and he could not withhold commission.

Light v *Ty Europe Ltd* [2003] Eu LR 858 Court of Appeal (Ward and Tuckey LJJ, Lightman J)

• *Agency – sub-agent's rights under the Commercial Agents (Council Directive) Regulations 1993*

Facts

This was an appeal from the decision of McGonigal J on preliminary issues, which concerned the rights of a sub-agent under the Commercial Agents (Council Directive) Regulations 1993.

Ty Incorporation designed and manufactured cuddly toys. Up until June 1997 Ty Incorporation used Ty UK Ltd, which was partly owned by a Mr Swallow, to distribute its products within the UK. Ty Incorporation were not happy with the performance of Ty UK Ltd but were not in a legal position to end their relationship. However, Ty Incorporated persuaded Ty UK Ltd to relinquish their legal rights by giving Mr Swallow sole selling

rights for Ty products within the UK for three years, commencing 1 June 1997. To this end Mr Swallow liquidated the company (Ty UK Ltd) and formed a new company called Ty Europe, which then entered into an agreement with a new Swallow company, called Swallow Corporate Sales Ltd (SCS). This contract allowed SCS to sell Ty Incorporation products for Ty Europe on commission (which was in the region of 15 per cent). This agreement also involved SCS promoting and selling Ty Incorporation products on terms and conditions and prices being set by Ty Europe, which in addition gave Ty Europe the right to decline or cancel any orders. After three years, in accordance with the contract, the selling rights agreement was not renewed and SCS appears to have ceased trading.

At least nine of the respondents worked for Ty UK Ltd as self-employed agents before 1 June 1997, and their contracts could be terminated upon notice. From 1 June 1997 the respondents entered into a new agreement with SCS. This agreement was preceded by an agreement that took effect from 1 June 1998. However, the earlier agreement provided that termination would take effect when SCS ceased to be the sole agent for Ty Europe for the sale of Ty Incorporation products, whilst the latter agreement stated termination would take effect on the 31 May 2000. The respondents argued that they were representing Ty Europe, as Ty Europe delivered the products to the retailers and all enquiries relating to sales were dealt with between the sales agents and Ty Europe. All but one of the respondents was offered employment with Ty Europe from 1 June 2000 but they declined this offer and commenced legal proceedings.

The initial issue to be dealt with, at first instance, was whether the appellant was the respondents' principal and whether the respondents were the appellant's agent within the meaning of the Regulations, which would deal with the sub-agency question. The primary focus under the Regulations was reg 8, which deals with an agent's right to the entitlement to commission on transactions concluded after the agency contract had been terminated, and reg 17, which deals with an agent's right to either an indemnity or compensation on termination of an agency contract. The latter regulation was pertinent because the parties had entered into an agreement of a fixed period, two years, which expired on the 31 May 2000 and they were seeking compensation in accordance with reg 17, where a period ends automatically through the effluxion of time. However, at first instance the appellant argued that the respondents were not its commercial agents because the agents derived their authority from SCS. Thus, under the Regulations an agent could only derive his authority from an agency contract with the principal and if there was no such contract between the respondents and appellant then there was no such authority.

McGonigal J made reference to reg 2(1):

'In these Regulations –
"commercial agent" means a self-employed intermediary who has continuing authority to negotiate the sale or purchase of goods on behalf of another person (the "principal"), or to negotiate and conclude the sale or purchase of goods on behalf of and in the name of that principal.'

Based upon this Regulation, McGonigal J found the respondents to have continuing authority derived from the appellant and were commercial agents of the appellant. The appellant appealed.

Held

Tuckey LJ considered the facts and the definition of a commercial agent under the Regulations. He found the respondents to be 'self-employed intermediaries' who negotiated 'the sale of goods on behalf of another person'. Thus, Tuckey LJ agreed with McGonigal J's finding of fact (about which there was no appeal) that the respondents acted with the appellant's authority. Therefore, the respondents were indeed commercial agents under this part of the Regulations. However, what has not been

answered and comes under the appeal is the question of whether there was a contract between the commercial agents and the principal before the substantive provisions of the Regulations were applied. The appellant had made its submission that the respondents must demonstrate there was a contract between the principal and agent, that is, the appellant (Ty Europe Ltd) and respondents (Light).

For the respondents to be entitled to commission on a transaction that was concluded during the agency contract there must have been a contract. As stated in reg 7(1):

'A commercial agent shall be entitled to commission on commercial transactions concluded during the period covered by the agency contract.'

This is supported by reg 8 which states:

'Subject to reg 9 below, a commercial agent shall be entitled to commission on commercial transactions concluded after the agency contract has terminated.'

In turn, reg 17(1) supports both sections by stating:

'This Regulation has effect for the purposes of ensuring that the commercial agent is, after termination of the agency contract, indemnified in accordance with paras (2) to (5) below or compensation for damage in accordance with paras (6) and (7) below.'

Having considered these Regulations, Tuckey LJ was of the opinion that, through the repeated reference to the wording 'the agency contract', a contract between the principal and the agent is required. Tuckey LJ found no such contract to exist between the appellant and respondents. The respondents' contract was with SCS, who appointed them as their agents. Any legal obligations within this arrangement did not affect the appellant's position. However, Mr Hand QC, who appeared on behalf of the respondents, argued that the purpose of reg 17 was to afford sub-agents, such as the respondents, protection which the Directive was designed to give commercial agents. Thus, Mr Hand believed the words 'the agency contract' should be perceived as including sub-agency contracts, which would achieve the purpose of the Regulations. Tuckey LJ was unable to find any case law involving commercial agents within the UK or Europe to support Mr Hand's contention on sub-agency contracts. Case law suggests there must be a contract between the principal and commercial agent to activate the Regulations. Only then can the respondents' claim be supported. The Regulations were intended to protect commercial agents who were in a contractual relationship with their principal. Tuckey LJ believed this was the correct interpretation of the Regulations. He believed that to acknowledge a sub-agent as having any contractual rights against the original principal would lead to chaos and confusion. To support the sub-agency argument would place the principal in a position were he would not know who his agents were and how to remunerate them under Part III of the Regulations. This observation raises the question as to whether the principal would be liable to pay commission to both his agent and his sub-agents. Thus, Tuckey LJ was of the opinion that McGonigal J's decision was wrong. Once he established the agents were commercial agents under reg 2(1) he did not need to give any detailed consideration to the substantive points to be addressed. Tuckey LJ allowed the appeal and this was supported by Lightman J and Ward LJ.

Comment
The decision has given some guidance on sub-agency and the interpretation of the Commercial Agents (Council Directive) Regulations 1993. Tuckey LJ made it clear that there was no contract between the original principal and sub-agents and it was this fact that barred any claims under the Regulations. The delegations of an agent's duties under common law are specific and an agent must act personally. This duty is usually expressed by the Latin maxim: 'delegatus non potest delegare' (a delegate must not sub-delegate). However, delegation is allowed if the principal expressly or impliedly agrees to it, or if

the task delegated is purely ministerial (requiring no skill or competence). It is interesting to note that under common law, if delegation is allowed, then privity of contract may exist between the principal and sub-agent. This was demonstrated in the case of *De Bussche* v *Alt* (1878) 8 Ch D 286.

Mortgage Express Ltd v *Bowerman and Partners (A Firm)* [1996] 2 All ER 83 Court of Appeal (Sir Thomas Bingham MR, Millett and Schiemann LJJ)

• *Solicitor (agent) acting for mortgagee and mortgagor – breach of duty*

Facts
This was a cross-appeal by a firm of solicitors, Messrs Bowerman & Partners, against the decision of Arden J on the 11 May 1994. A Mr Gilroy (G), a partner in Messrs Bowerman, had been instructed by the plaintiff Mortgage Express (ME) (the mortgagee) and Mr Hadi (H) (the mortgagor) in relation to a secured loan on the purchase of a leasehold flat by H. The purchase price was £220,000 and the secured loan was to be £180,150. When G received ME's instructions also enclosed, which was central to the appeal, was the valuation report. The valuation of the flat in its existing condition was stated to be £199,000.

The seller of the leasehold flat was a Mr Ahmed Arrach (A) and his solicitor was a Mr F G Litchfield (L). G received a fax from L on the 26 November 1990 informing him:

'I have just been instructed by a Mr Ahmed Arrach in relation to his proposed purchase of [119 Queen's Court – the leasehold flat] and its sub-sale to Mr Ali Hadi for £220,000. I have been told that you are acting for Mr Hadi and that he already has a mortgage offer. I phoned the vendor's solicitor, John Healy & Co, to ascertain the position and was advised that their client had only recently purchased the property and they expect the purchaser to register the transfer to their client ...' (p838)

G informed H, in writing, the transaction was a sub-sale, ie A was purchasing the leasehold flat and simultaneously selling it on to H at a profit but did not know (at this juncture) the original purchase price. However, further correspondence was received from L, on the 26 November, which enclosed a copy of a letter he had received from the first vendor's solicitor, John Healy & Co, which stated:

'We refer to our telephone conversation this morning and understand that you have been instructed by Mr Ahmed Arrach who has agreed, subject to contract, to purchase the leasehold interest in [119 Queen's Court] from our client at a price of £150,000. As you are aware, our client has only recently completed his purchase of the leasehold interest on 2nd November and the transfer has yet to be stamped ...' (p839)

Upon receiving this correspondence G added a postscript to his initial correspondence, to his client H, and enclosed a copy of the correspondence received from L. This would ensure H was aware the initial sale price was £150,000 compared to the price H was to pay: £220,000, a £70,000 increase. However, G had not informed ME of the sub-sale or the difference between the two purchase prices. G, in his written witness statement, discussed this issue in relation to his client H:

'Whilst I considered that I should draw the fact of the sub-sale and the obvious discrepancy between the price being paid by Mr Arrach and the price being paid by Mr Hadi to his attention in case he was not aware of it, I did not regard this as particularly unusual or as a matter giving rise to any cause for concern provided the purchasing client understood and accepted the situation. In this case I was aware that Hadi was to pay £220,000 for the property when his immediate vendor Arrach was only paying £150,000. I was of course conscious that this was a large difference and recall that I discussed this with Mr Hadi and also pointed out to him the discrepancy between the valuation of £199,000 and the price he was paying. This caused me the greatest concern since it appeared that Mr Hadi was

paying too much. I was satisfied that he understood the position (he spoke perfect English). He said that he wanted a flat in that block and was prepared to pay the price and to accept that Arrach was making a substantial profit.' (p839)

G went ahead with the purchase of the leasehold flat. Contracts were exchanged on the 10 December 1990, on the sale from Mr Rasool (the very first seller in the chain) to Mr Arrach and the purchase price was £150,000 and on the sub-sale from Mr Arrach to Mr Hadi for £220,000.

When G submitted his report on title to ME he confirmed the title was good, marketable and could be safely accepted as security. No mention was made of the contemporaneous purchase at £150,000. ME, having received a good report on title forwarded the advance for £180,150 to G for H's purchase of the leasehold property and the purchase took place on the 19 December 1990, H meeting the shortfall from his own resources. At the time contracts were exchanged and completion had taken place G was acting for both G and ME and had not disclosed the full facts to ME. H made only one payment to ME, and ME subsequently repossessed the flat, and it was sold for £96,000 – the best market price at the time of sale. When full knowledge of the facts were brought to the attention of ME they commenced proceedings against G for breach of duty in failing to inform them of the simultaneous transactions and the difference in purchase price(s). An open market price at the time of the purchase to A would have been £120,000 and had ME known of these facts they would have requested a second valuation and would have withdrawn their mortgage offer to H. Arden J, at first instance, found Bowerman & Partners (BP) liable but accepted BP's submission for damages. ME appealed against the issue of damages and BP cross-appealed on the issue of liability.

Held

On the issue of damages the appeal of ME was heard as part of one of a group of six cases, raising the issue on the measure of damages. The appeal on this issue was allowed in favour of ME. On the issue of G's liability, the cross-appeal, Sir Thomas Bingham MR discussed at length the liability placed upon G's role and whether or not he had breached his duty to ME. Sir Thomas Bingham MR acknowledged G was a solicitor and not a valuer. G was not asked to advise on the valuation but to deal with the purchase and give a report on title. However, that does not detract from the fact that G was not only acting for H but also ME and owed a duty to ME. The issue of that duty was central to liability.

Sir Thomas Bingham MR described that duty, in the given circumstance:

'The information which Mr Gilroy received concerning the sale to Mr Arrach at £150,000 and the sub-sale to Mr Hadi at £220,000 was information which Mr Gilroy received as a solicitor to each of his respective clients. It was directly relevant to the conveyancing transaction he was carrying out for Mr Hadi since it went to show how and when Mr Arrach acquired title to sell. For the same reason it was relevant to Mr Gilroy's instructions from Mortgage Express, who wanted to be sure that it's borrower was obtaining a good and marketable title which might safely be accepted as security. The present case is not, therefore, one in which a solicitor acting for two parties receives information confidential to one of them. In such a case it may be necessary for the solicitor to obtain the consent of the client whose information it is to disclose it to the other and, if consent is refused, the solicitor may be obliged to cease to act for the other party or both parties. But that is not this case. It has not been suggested that Mr Gilroy would have been in breach of any duty to Mr Hadi if he had disclosed the information in question to Mortgage Express.'

Reference was made to the December 1990 guidance on mortgage fraud in Annex 24 of the Guide to the Professional Conduct of Solicitors, which stated: 'Solicitors must not withhold information relevant to a transaction from any client and for a lender this includes not only straightforward price reductions but may also include other allowance'. Given the nature of the fiduciary relationship between all parties and the particular facts of this case Sir Thomas Bingham MR was of the opinion that:

'... if, in the course of investigating title, a solicitor discovered facts which a reasonably competent solicitor would realise might have a material bearing on the valuation of the lender's security or some other ingredient of the lending decision, then it is his duty to point this out. ...He [Gilroy] was aware that Mortgage Expres had obtained its own valuation and regarded valuation (sic) as no concern of his. Up to a point he was right. But he rightly accepted a duty to report the facts to Mortgage Express if he had reason to doubt the valuation and, on the facts here, I find it impossible to escape the conclusion that if he had applied his mind to these facts he would have appreciated that they might have caused Mortgage Express to doubt the valuation.' (p842–843)

On this basis the cross-appeal by BP was dismissed and the court of first instance's decision was upheld.

Comment

This case would have sent shock waves through those who practise in the field of conveyancing. It was interesting to note the valuation was in line with the security being offered, yet this did not release G from his liability. He owed a duty to his principal, ME, which was in breach and resulted in a consequential loss. If G had informed ME of the full facts before submitting his report on title the onus would have been on ME to decide whether or not to proceed. For a further analysis on the fiduciary duty of an agent, solicitor: see *Bristol and West Building Society* v *Fancy & Jackson (A Firm)* [1997] 4 All ER 582 and *National Home Loans Corp plc* v *Gifen Couch & Archer (A Firm)* [1997] 3 All ER 808.

8 Termination of Agency

Alpha Trading Ltd v *Dunnshaw-Patten Ltd*

See AGENCY, Chapter 6, above.

Drew v *Nunn* (1879) 4 QBD 661
Court of Appeal (Bramwell, Brett and Cotton LJJ)

- *Principal's insanity – agency terminated?*

Facts

N, when sane, empowered his wife with absolute authority to act for him. He held out to D that she had such authority. Afterwards, unknown to D, N went completely mad. The wife ordered goods from D and was supplied with them. N recovered his sanity but refused to pay for the goods on the grounds that the authority given to the wife was terminated by his insanity.

Held

D could recover the price of the goods. Where a principal is so insane as to be completely incapable of entering into a contract himself, authority previously given to an agent to contract on his behalf is thereby terminated. If, however, the principal has held out his agent to have that authority as in this case, he will be liable on the contracts made on his behalf when insane if the third party had no knowledge of the insanity.

Brett LJ:

'If it is held that such insanity as existed here did not put an end to the agent's authority, then clearly the plaintiff is entitled to recover upon that ground. It is admitted that

there are certain changes of status which do put an end to it. For instance, the bankruptcy or death of a principal puts an end to it. The reason why the authority is then put an end to is stated to be because the person who otherwise would be liable has become a different person from the giver of the authority. In bankruptcy the assignee, in death the heir or executor, would be substituted for the person who gave the authority. If the change of the person who gave the authority were the real ground upon which we had to proceed, then the lunacy of the principal would not put an end to the authority until that lunacy was established by a commission having been held, so that the committee would be liable instead of the lunatic. But I do not think that is a satisfactory principle upon which to base the rule. In bankruptcy the assignee, although he is a different person, is bound to carry out some contracts made by the bankrupt. In the case of death the executors are the representatives of the dead person for many purposes. I, therefore, think the true ground is that the agent, being a person appointed when the principal could act for himself to act for him, when the principal, according to law, cannot act for himself, the person who represents him ceases to be able to act for him. If that is so, where there is lunacy like that in the present case – lunacy is so great that the person who suffers from it has no contracting mind, and cannot contract or do any legal act for himself for want of mind – then, as the principal at law is incapable of doing the act for himself, his agent cannot do it for him. Such lunacy, therefore, puts an end to the authority of the agent, and if any agent acts for his principal after such lunacy is brought to his knowledge, that agent would be doing a wrongful act both to the principal and the person with whom he dealt, and he would be liable to any person with whom he so acted for the principal ...

Supposing there is no lunacy, but a principal holds out a person to be his agent and then of his own accord withdraws the agency. As between the principal and the agent the right to bind the principal has ceased, and then the agent does a wrongful act by acting with a third person as though the authority continued; nevertheless if the agent has been held out as having authority to the third person, and the latter acts with the agent before he has received any notice of the authority having ceased, the principal is still bound upon the ground that he made representation upon which the third party had a right to act, and cannot retract from the consequences of those representations. It is true that if the principal becomes lunatic he cannot himself give notice to the third person of the agency having ceased, and he may be an innocent sufferer from the wrongful act of the agent. But so is the other; and it is a principle of law that where it is a question which of two innocent parties shall suffer, that one must suffer who caused the state of things upon which the other has acted. Therefore, in my opinion, although the lunatic recovers his reason, he cannot, after his recovery, any more than if he had never been a lunatic, say that an innocent person who acted on representations made before lunacy had not a right to do so.'

Hannan's Empress Goldmining and Development Co Ltd, Re, ex parte Carmichael (1896) 75 LT 45 Court of Appeal (Lindley, Lopes and Rigby LJJ)

• *Agent's authority coupled with interest*

Facts

The agent was a promoter of a company and was authorised by the principal to apply for 1,000 shares for him should the public not take them up. The company was incorporated on 24 March and on 30 March the principal wrote to the agent purporting to repudiate the authority given. On 2 April the agent applied for the shares of the principal and they were allotted to him.

Held

The authority given to the agent was coupled with an interest, for its purpose was to allow the agent to obtain the purchase price for the company. Accordingly, the authority could not be revoked.

Lindley LJ:

'In this case the appellant's (ie the principal's) counsel ask us to regard this as a complex transaction, treating this document as consisting of two parts, a transaction and an authority; and they contend that there is power for the appellant to revoke that authority. But when I come to consider the document and see the purpose for which the authority was given, it appears to me that the illustration put forward is not in point at all. Now, let us look at the document. It is called an "underwriting contract"... What is the true meaning of it? It is part of the bargain that the appellant shall for valuable consideration take certain shares in the company; and in order to enable Phillips to better carry out the transaction the appellant authorises him to make any further or other application for shares on the appellant's behalf, and he agrees not to revoke the contract. Phillips, acting upon that, does apply in the appellant's name for shares in the company. Why is the appellant not to be held to be a member of the company? Can it be said that under these circumstances his name was, in the words of s35 of the Companies Act 1862, "without sufficient cause entered in the register of members of the company"? It appears to me that there was ample cause for entering his name in the register. And the contention that the appellant had power to revoke the authority appears to me to be entirely futile ... the meaning of an authority coupled with an interest ... "What is meant by an authority coupled with an interest being irrevocable is this – that where an agreement is entered into on a sufficient consideration, whereby an authority is given for the purposes of securing some benefit to the donee of the authority, such an authority is irrevocable". That is the principle on which Stirling J, decided the present case, and that is the principle on (unreported)which I think that this appeal ought to be decided. It appears to me quite obvious that the appellant's attempt to revoke the authority which he gave to Phillips fails utterly ...'

Moore v *Piretta PTA Ltd* [1999] 1 All ER 174 (John Mitting QC)

• *Termination of an agency agreement under the Commercial Agents (Council Directive) Regulations 1993 – plaintiff's right to claim an indemnity*

Facts
The plaintiff, Duncan Moore, had acted as an agent for the defendant, Piretta PTA Ltd, through a series of agency agreements since January 1988. The last contract entered into was on the 18 February 1994, which was to take effect from the 1 January 1994. This latter contract was to continue until either party gave no less than six months' written notice. On the 30 October 1994 the defendant gave the plaintiff notice to terminate the agreement, with effect from the 2 May 1995. Clause 11 of the 1994 agreement stated:

'The agent shall be entitled to indemnity on the termination of this agreement for reasons other than a breach of the terms of this agreement by the agent or termination of this agreement by the agent. The parties agree that the indemnity payable to the agent, if any, shall be assessed equitably by applying Regulations 17 and 18 of the Regulations to allow the agent the minimum indemnity as permitted by the Regulations.'

The Regulations referred to in this clause are the Commercial Agents (Council Directive) Regulations 1993 (SI 1993/3053) (which will be referred to as the Regulations) which came into force on the 1 January 1994.

Based upon cl 11 and the Regulations the plaintiff brought an action against the defendant, claiming an indemnity. The plaintiff made this claim under reg 17, which deals with termination of an agency agreement and the right to either compensation or an indemnity.

Held
In order to deal with this case John Mitting QC had to give meaning and purpose to the Regulations through a European interpretation. He made reference to the wording of the Regulations and their ambiguity and stated at p176: 'The duty of an English court in construing the regulations is to give effect to the manifest purpose of the directive under which the regulations are made.' Before attempting to apply the Regulations John Mitting QC made further reference to Lord Templeman's dictum in the House of Lords decision of *Lister* v *Forth Dry Dock and Engineering Co Ltd* [1989] 1 All ER 1134 at 1139: 'Thus the courts of the United Kingdom are under a duty to follow the practice of the European Court by giving a purposive construction to directives and to regulations issued for the purpose of complying with directives.'

Thus, the primary purpose of the Directive is to harmonise Community law, by introducing rights and duties in relation to commercial agents which are similar to those already existing in at least two other member states of the Community, for example, the Federal Republic of Germany and France. To give effect to the Directive John Mitting QC felt it was necessary to:

'... look into the law and practice of the country in which the relevant right, in this case the right to an indemnity originated, namely the Federal Republic of Germany; and to do so for the purpose of construing the English regulations and to use them as a guide to their application.' (p177)

This was further defined with reference to Part IV of the Regulations which makes provision for the parties on the termination of an agency agreement. Regulation 17 entitles an agent to claim either an indemnity, which is derived from the law of Germany, or compensation, which is derived from the law of France, on the termination of the agreement. Both these remedies differ from damages awarded under the common law system and would be payable where damages would not be awarded. To put this into context John Mitting QC outlined (at p178), a selection of the salient reg 17 provisions, which state:

'(1) This regulation has effect for the purpose of ensuring that the commercial agent is, after termination of the termination of the agency contract, indemnified in accordance with paras (3) to (5) below or compensated for damage in accordance with paras (6) and (7) below.
(2) Except where the agency contract otherwise provides, the commercial agent shall be entitled to be compensated rather than indemnified.
(3) Subject to para (9) and to reg 18 below, the commercial agent shall be entitled to an indemnity if and to the extent that –
(a) he has brought the principal new customers or has significantly increased the volume of business with existing customers and the principal continues to derive substantial benefits from the business with such customers; and
(b) the payment of this indemnity is equitable having regard to all the circumstances and, in particular, the commission lost by the commercial agent on the business transacted with such customers.
(4) The amount of the indemnity shall not exceed a figure equivalent to an indemnity for one year calculated from the commercial agent's average annual remuneration over the preceding five years and if the contract goes back less than five years the indemnity shall be calculated on the average for the period in question ...
(9) The commercial agent shall lose his entitlement to the indemnity or compensation for damage in the instances provided for in paras (2) to (8) above if within one year following termination of his agency contract he has not notified his principal that he intends pursuing his entitlement.'

In light of the wording and interpretation of the Regulations it was found, based upon the evidence presented, that the plaintiff had been retained through a series of unbroken contracts, the last one originating on the 18 February 1994. The construction of the Regulations and their interpretation through the German and French systems meant that the plaintiff was entitled to be indemnified in relation to the unbroken chain of contracts that spanned from January 1988 to May 1995. This was based upon the finding that the plaintiff, as agent, had been instrumental in obtaining new customers and increasing the value of the business between the above dates outlined. The calculation of the indemnity, in the words of John Mitting QC (at p184), 'emerged at the 59th minute of the 11th hour of the case.' The figure, which was eventually assessed, having applied reg 17(4), was £64,526.33.

Comment
This case clearly demonstrates the implementations of the Commercial Agents (Council Directive) Regulations 1993, reg 17. It illustrates the relationship between principal and agent and termination by either party before the expiry of the agency agreement. In such cases termination may be treated as a repudiatory breach of contract resulting in either compensation, under the French system, or an indemnity under the German system.

Page v Combined Shipping and Trading Co Ltd [1997] 3 All ER 656 Court of Appeal (Staughton, Millett and Otton LJJ)

• *Termination of agency agreement under the Commercial Agents (Council Directive) Regulations 1993*

Facts
The plaintiff, a sole trader who traded as Graham Page Trading (GPT) in essential oils, had acted as agent for the defendant, Combined Shipping and Trading Co Ltd

(CST), for six years. GPT entered into an agency agreement with CST on the 3 January 1995 to buy and sell commodities for CST. CST agreed to finance the transactions conducted by GPT and the net profits were to be divided in equal shares over a four-year period.

On the 6 June 1995 CST informed GPT that their (CST) parent company, called Tiger Oats Ltd, had decided to close down its trading activities. GPT believed this to be a repudiation of their agreement. GPT wrote to CST on the 2 February 1996 informing them he would treat their actions as a wrongful repudiation of their agreement. GPT then commenced proceedings against CST, having been deprived of the commission he would have earned had he been allowed to perform the agency contract and that he had suffered damages under reg 17(7) of the Commercial Agents (Council Directive) Regulations 1993. GPT also applied for a Mareva injunction on the basis that he believed there was a real risk that the combined assets of CST would not be available when the case came to trial. At first instance Wright J refused GPT an injunction on the basis that GPT did not have an arguable case to recover a significant sum of compensation. GPT appealed.

Held
On appeal Staughton LJ examined the facts and was of the opinion that:

'... there is a right to recover substantial compensation, not under domestic law of this country but by virtue of the regulations of the European Community. Those are the Commercial Agents (Council Directive) Regulations 1993, SI 1993/3053, as enacted in this country. They deal with contracts between commercial agents and their principals.' (p659)

He then went on to identify the specific right to damages under reg 17(7) which states:

'For the purpose of these Regulations such damage shall be deemed to occur particularly when the termination takes place in either or both of the following circumstances, namely circumstances which –
(a) deprive the commercial agent of the commission which proper performance of the agency contract would have procured for him whilst providing his principal with substantial benefits linked to the activities of the commercial agent; or
(b) have not enabled the commercial agent to amortize the cost and expenses that he had incurred in the performance of the agency contract on the advice of his principal.' (pp659–660)

Staughton LJ examined the preamble of the Council Directive (EEC) 86/653 and found the purpose of the Directive was to harmonise the law of member states of the Community so that people could compete at equal levels there was a 'a motive of social policy, that commercial agents are a down-trodden race, and need and should be afforded protection against their principals ... These are regulations to protect and improve the position of commercial agents (p660).' On the nature and circumstances of the facts Staughton LJ found GPT had an arguable case and would be able to make a claim for substantial damages. He allowed the appeal and granted the restraint injunction.

Comment
There is a small, but significant, body of case law applying the Regulations and once again it is the interpretation of European legislation that appears to cause many of the problems and appeals. However, the protection being offered to commercial agents is evident when applying the provisions of the Directive. For a further discussion on the Regulations and termination: see *Moore* v *Piretta PTA Ltd* [1999] 1 All ER 174.

Law Update 2005– due March 2005

An annual review of the most recent developments in specific legal subject areas, useful for law students at degree and professional levels, others with law elements in their courses and also practitioners seeking a quick update.

Published around March every year, the Law Update summarises the major legal developments during the course of the previous year. In conjunction with Old Bailey Press textbooks it gives the student a significant advantage when revising for examinations.

Contents

Administrative Law • Commercial Law • Company Law • Conflict of Laws • Constitutional Law • Contract Law • Conveyancing • Criminal Law • Criminology • Employment Law • English and European Legal Systems • Equity and Trusts • European Union Law • Evidence • Family Law • Jurisprudence • Land Law • Law of International Trade • Public International Law • Revenue Law • Tort

For further information on contents or to place an order, please contact:

Mail Order
Old Bailey Press
at Holborn College
Woolwich Road
Charlton
London
SE7 8LN

Telephone: 020 8317 6039
Fax: 020 8317 6004
Website: www.oldbaileypress.co.uk
E-Mail: mailorder@oldbaileypress.co.uk

ISBN 1 85836 571 6
Soft cover 246 x 175 mm
400 pages approx
£10.95
Due March 2005

Revision Aids

Designed for the undergraduate, the 101 Questions & Answers series and the Suggested Solutions series are for all those who have a positive commitment to passing their law examinations. Each series covers a different examinable topic and comprises a selection of answers to examination questions and, in the case of the 101 Questions and Answers, interrograms. The majority of questions represent examination 'bankers' and are supported by full-length essay solutions. These titles will undoubtedly assist you with your research and further your understanding of the subject in question.

101 Questions & Answers Series

Only £7.95 Published December 2003

Constitutional Law
ISBN: 1 85836 522 8

Criminal Law
ISBN: 1 85836 432 9

Land Law
ISBN: 1 85836 515 5

Law of Contract
ISBN: 1 85836 517 1

Law of Tort
ISBN: 1 85836 516 3

Suggested Solutions to Past Examination Questions 2001–2002 Series

Only £6.95 Published December 2003

Company Law
ISBN: 1 85836 519 8

Employment Law
ISBN: 1 85836 520 1

European Union Law
ISBN: 1 85836 524 4

Evidence
ISBN: 1 85836 521 X

Family Law
ISBN: 1 85836 525 2

For further information or to place an order, please contact:

Mail Order
Old Bailey Press at Holborn College
Woolwich Road
Charlton
London
SE7 8LN

Telephone: 020 8317 6039
Fax: 020 8317 6004
Website: www.oldbaileypress.co.uk
E-Mail: mailorder@oldbaileypress.co.uk

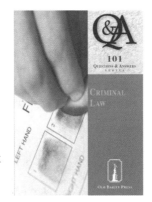

Unannotated Cracknell's Statutes for Use in Examinations

New Editions of Cracknell's Statutes

Only £11.95 Due 2004

Cracknell's Statutes provide a comprehensive series of essential statutory provisions for each subject. Amendments are consolidated, avoiding the need to cross-refer to amending legislation. Unannotated, they are suitable for use in examinations, and provide the precise wording of vital Acts of Parliament for the diligent student.

Commercial Law
ISBN: 1 85836 562 7

Family Law
ISBN: 1 85836 566 X

Company Law
ISBN: 1 85836 563 5

Medical Law
ISBN: 1 85836 567 8

Conflict of Laws
ISBN: 1 85836 564 3

Public International Law
ISBN: 1 85836 568 6

Evidence
ISBN: 1 85836 565 1

Revenue Law
ISBN: 1 85836 569 4

Succession
ISBN: 1 85836 570 8

For further information or to place an order, please contact:

Mail Order
Old Bailey Press at Holborn College
Woolwich Road
Charlton
London
SE7 8LN

Telephone: 020 8317 6039
Fax: 020 8317 6004
Website: www.oldbaileypress.co.uk
E-Mail: mailorder@oldbaileypress.co.uk

Old Bailey Press

The Old Bailey Press Integrated Student Law Library is tailor-made to help you at every stage of your studies, from the preliminaries of each subject through to the final examination. The series of Textbooks, Revision WorkBooks, 150 Leading Cases and Cracknell's Statutes are interrelated to provide you with a comprehensive set of study materials.

You can buy Old Bailey Press books from your University Bookshop, your local Bookshop, directly using this form, or you can order a free catalogue of our titles from the address shown overleaf.

The following subjects each have a Textbook, 150 Leading Cases, Revision WorkBook and Cracknell's Statutes unless otherwise stated.

Administrative Law
Commercial Law
Company Law
Conflict of Laws
Constitutional Law
Conveyancing (Textbook and 150 Leading Cases)
Criminal Law
Criminology (Textbook and Sourcebook)
Employment Law (Textbook and Cracknell's Statutes)
English and European Legal Systems
Equity and Trusts
Evidence
Family Law
Jurisprudence: The Philosophy of Law (Textbook, Sourcebook and Revision WorkBook)
Land: The Law of Real Property
Law of International Trade
Law of the European Union
Legal Skills and System (Textbook)
Obligations: Contract Law
Obligations: The Law of Tort
Public International Law
Revenue Law (Textbook, Revision WorkBook and Cracknell's Statutes)
Succession (Textbook, Revision WorkBook and Cracknell's Statutes)

Mail order prices:	
Textbook	£15.95
150 Leading Cases	£12.95
Revision WorkBook	£10.95
Cracknell's Statutes	£11.95
Suggested Solutions 1999–2000	£6.95
Suggested Solutions 2000–2001	£6.95
Suggested Solutions 2001–2002	£6.95
101 Questions and Answers	£7.95
Law Update 2004	£10.95

Please note details and prices are subject to alteration.

To complete your order, please fill in the form below:

Module	Books required	Quantity	Price	Cost
		Postage		
		TOTAL		

For the UK and Europe, add £4.95 for the first book ordered, then add £1.00 for each subsequent book ordered for postage and packing.
For the rest of the world, add 50% for airmail.

ORDERING

By telephone to Mail Order at 020 8317 6039, with your credit card to hand.

By fax to 020 8317 6004 (giving your credit card details).

Website: www.oldbaileypress.co.uk
E-Mail: mailorder@oldbaileypress.co.uk

By post to: Mail Order, Old Bailey Press at Holborn College, Woolwich Road, Charlton, London, SE7 8LN.

When ordering by post, please enclose full payment by cheque or banker's draft, or complete the credit card details below. You may also order a free catalogue of our complete range of titles from this address.

We aim to despatch your books within 3 working days of receiving your order. All parts of the form must be completed.

Name

Address

Postcode

E-Mail

Telephone

Total value of order, including postage: £

I enclose a cheque/banker's draft for the above sum, or

charge my ☐ Access/Mastercard ☐ Visa ☐ American Express

Cardholder: ....

Card number

☐☐☐☐ ☐☐☐☐ ☐☐☐☐ ☐☐☐☐

Expiry date ☐☐☐☐

Signature: ....Date: ....